O9-BHJ-613

THE DAILY STUDY BIBLE
(OLD TESTAMENT)
General Editor: John C. L. Gibson

I & II KINGS

I & II KINGS

A. GRAEME AULD

THE WESTMINSTER PRESS
PHILADELPHIA

Published by
The Saint Andrew Press
Edinburgh, Scotland
and
The Westminster Press®
Philadelphia, Pennsylvania

PRINTED IN THE UNITED STATES OF AMERICA
2 4 6 8 9 7 5 3 1

Library of Congress Cataloging-in-Publication Data

Auld, A. Graeme.
  I & II Kings.

  (The Daily study Bible series)
  Bibliography: p.
  1. Bible. O.T. Kings—Commentaries. I. Title.
II. Title: I and II Kings. III. Title: First &
Second Kings. IV. Series: Daily study
Bible series (Westminster Press)
BS1335.3.A95 1986   222'.5077   86-15658
ISBN 0-664-21836-9
ISBN 0-664-24585-4 (pbk.)

GENERAL PREFACE

This series of commentaries on the Old Testament, to which the present volume on Kings belongs, has been planned as a companion series to the much-acclaimed New Testament series of the late Professor William Barclay. As with that series, each volume is arranged in successive headed portions suitable for daily study. The Biblical text followed is that of the Revised Standard Version or Common Bible. Eleven contributors share the work, each being responsible for from one to three volumes. The series is issued in the hope that it will do for the Old Testament what Professor Barclay's series succeeded so splendidly in doing for the New Testament—make it come alive for the Christian believer in the twentieth century.

Its two-fold aim is the same as his. Firstly, it is intended to introduce the reader to some of the more important results and fascinating insights of modern Old Testament scholarship. Most of the contributors are already established experts in the field with many publications to their credit. Some are younger scholars who have yet to make their names but who in my judgment as General Editor are now ready to be tested. I can assure those who use these commentaries that they are in the hands of competent teachers who know what is of real consequence in their subject and are able to present it in a form that will appeal to the general public.

The primary purpose of the series, however, is *not* an academic one. Professor Barclay summed it up for his New Testament series in the words of Richard of Chichester's prayer—to enable men and women "to know Jesus Christ more clearly, to love Him more dearly, and to follow Him more nearly." In the case of the Old Testament we have to be a little more circumspect than that. The Old Testament was completed long before the time of Our Lord, and it was (as it still is) the sole Bible of the Jews, God's first people, before it became part of the Christian Bible. We must take this fact seriously.

Yet in its strangely compelling way, sometimes dimly and sometimes directly, sometimes charmingly and sometimes embarrassingly, it holds up before us the things of Christ. It should not be forgotten that Jesus Himself was raised on this Book, that He based His whole ministry on what it says, and that He approached His death with its words on His lips. Christian men and women have in this ancient collection of Jewish writings a uniquely illuminating avenue not only into the will and purposes of God the Father, but into the mind and heart of Him who is named God's Son, who was Himself born a Jew but went on through the Cross and Resurrection to become the Saviour of the world. Read reverently and imaginatively the Old Testament can become a living and relevant force in their everyday lives.

It is the prayer of myself and my colleagues that this series may be used by its readers and blessed by God to that end.

New College   JOHN C.L. GIBSON
Edinburgh   General Editor

CONTENTS

2 KINGS

INTRODUCTION

(i)

The Biblical narrative handled in this commentary covers a period of almost four centuries in the history of Israel and Judah: from the death of King David and the accession of Solomon some time before the middle of the tenth century B.C., to the final collapse of Jerusalem and the monarchy of Judah in face of forces from Babylon in 587 or 586 B.C.. The familiar division of the story into two 'Books' of Kings is not original, but represents the same sort of convenient splitting of a longer account as we find in Samuel and Chronicles.

More appropriate might be a three-way division into almost equal parts, with sections ending at 1 Kings 16 and 2 Kings 10: that is, treating the long Elijah/Elisha saga, beginning in 1 Kings 17, as a middle section on its own. Alternatively, a three-way division can be effected from a political point of view: the story of the united monarchy ends in 1 Kings 12 with Israel's defection from Rehoboam; Israel and Judah are handled separately until 2 Kings 17; and in the last eight chapters (2 Kings 18-25) Judah is the sole nominally independent survivor of the people of Yahweh.

(ii)

There is a wealth of material in these pages; and yet also very many gaps, as must be the case when 400 years are despatched in 47 short chapters. The Judaean Kings, Hezekiah, Josiah and even Rehoboam, are quite fully depicted. The treatment of Solomon, builder and proverbially wise man, is even more extended. Yet of most kings of northern Israel we learn hardly the barest minimum. And quite the most generous portraits (I mean in size as well as approval) from that kingdom are those of Elijah and Elisha. Indeed, to borrow the title of one of the best-

1

loved books of one of my great New College forebears, Adam Welch, I would find *Kings and Prophets of Israel* a better title than the familiar shorter one.

The unevenness in treatment may say something about the sources which were and were not available to historians after Judah's collapse and exile. But it probably tells us even more about their interests, their aims—and their prejudices. For the main narrative of the book, the secession of Israel under Jeroboam I from both the leadership of the house of David and worship in the house of God built by Solomon was simply a bad thing. (It is noteworthy that the tellers of the tales of Elijah and Elisha at the centre of the work were free of this fixation.)

Yet, even granted these critical remarks, the Books of Kings (and Chronicles) remain our vital source for most of what we profess to know about the history of classical Israel and Judah. Our information has been augmented, occasionally corrected, and often set in new perspective by the decipherment of inscriptions and the evaluation of excavated material remains. However these biblical books remain our point of departure, and our point of return.

(iii)

A more serious question of literary structure must be asked about the beginning of Kings. Why is the account of David's end separated from the long story of his rise and reign in 1 and 2 Samuel? It may again be a simple matter of size and convenience; for, as we noted at rather greater length in the Introduction to our volume on Joshua, Judges and Ruth, the present 'Books' of Joshua, Judges, Samuel and Kings are all parts of one connected narrative. Since Martin Noth's pioneering work in the 1940s, this story has been widely known as the Deuteronomistic History. It may in fact have once begun with that part of the Moses story which we find in Deuteronomy. Is the division between Samuel and Kings just as casual as that between 1 Kings and 2 Kings? In favour of this view is the fact that the ancient tradition preserved in Greek and Latin Bibles deals, not with two books of Samuel and two of Kings, but rather with four books of 'Reigns' or 'Kingdoms', as they are called.

Many scholars invite us, therefore, to read the beginning of Kings in the larger perspective of the whole Deuteronomistic work; as simply the end of the story of David. In fact they undergird this by suggesting that 1 Kings 1–2 contains the climax of the 'Court History of David' or the 'Succession Narrative': two common titles for that strikingly frank and intimate and brilliantly-told story we read in 2 Samuel 9–20—a tail now separated from its body by miscellaneous materials in 2 Samuel 21–24. I find this widespread view hard to accept; and will attempt to explain this when we turn to the text. Just one hint at this stage:

Samuel and Kings are not our only biblical witnesses to the monarchical period. To our good fortune we have also a parallel narrative in Chronicles. This is both closely related and strikingly different. It is very widely supposed that the later Chronicler knew and used the Books of Samuel and Kings in much the form we know them; *ie* that where he tells more or less, he either added to or subtracted from his source which is also in our hands for comparison.

The freedom the writer of Chronicles exercised over his sources must certainly be reckoned with. However, I suspect the matter is more complex; and that the Chronicler worked with a substantially earlier 'edition' of the Books of Samuel and Kings than we now possess. As we discuss several portions of Kings we must be open to a second possibility too: that both Samuel/Kings and Chronicles (as we know them) have developed in their separate directions the traditions common to them both.

This brings our Introduction to a close just where our main business begins, for the Chronicler does not report most of the material in the opening two chapters of Kings. Were they in his source, but suppressed for some reason? Or are they a new and developed preface to the story told in Kings?

DAVID IN DECLINE I—TEXT

1 Kings 1:1–53

[1]Now King David was old and advanced in years; and although they covered him with clothes, he could not get warm. [2]Therefore his servants said to him, "Let a young maiden be sought for my lord the king, and let her wait upon the king, and be his nurse; let her lie in your bosom, that my lord the king may be warm." [3]So they sought for a beautiful maiden throughout all the territory of Israel, and found Abishag the Shunammite, and brought her to the king. [4]The maiden was very beautiful; and she became the king's nurse and ministered to him; but the king knew her not.

[5]Now Adonijah the son of Haggith exalted himself, saying, "I will be king"; and he prepared for himself chariots and horsemen, and fifty men to run before him. [6]His father had never at any time displeased him by asking, "Why have you done thus and so?" He was also a very handsome man; and he was born next after Absalom. [7]He conferred with Joab the son of Zeruiah and with Abiathar the priest; and they followed Adonijah and helped him. [8]But Zadok the priest, and Benaiah the son of Jehoiada, and Nathan the prophet, and Shime-i, and Rei, and David's mighty men were not with Adonijah.

[9]Adonijah sacrificed sheep, oxen, and fatlings by the Serpent's Stone, which is beside En-rogel, and he invited all his brothers, the king's sons, and all the royal officials of Judah, [10]but he did not invite Nathan the prophet or Benaiah or the mighty men or Solomon his brother.

[11]Then Nathan said to Bathsheba the mother of Solomon, "Have you not heard that Adonijah the son of Haggith has become king and David our lord does not know it? [12]Now therefore come, let me give you counsel, that you may save your own life and the life of your son Solomon. [13]Go in at once to King David, and say to him, 'Did you not, my lord the king, swear to your maidservant, saying, "Solomon your son shall reign after me, and he shall sit upon my throne"? Why then is Adonijah king?' [14]Then while you are still speaking with the king, I also will come in after you and confirm your words."

5

¹⁵So Bathsheba went to the king into his chamber (now the king was very old, and Abishag the Shunammite was ministering to the king). ¹⁶Bathsheba bowed and did obeisance to the king, and the king said, "What do you desire?" ¹⁷She said to him, "My lord, you swore to your maidservant by the Lord your God, saying, 'Solomon your son shall reign after me, and he shall sit upon my throne.' ¹⁸And now, behold, Adonijah is king, although you, my lord the king, do not know it. ¹⁹He has sacrificed oxen, fatlings, and sheep in abundance, and has invited all the sons of the king, Abiathar the priest, and Joab the commander of the army; but Solomon your servant he has not invited. ²⁰And now, my lord the king, the eyes of all Israel are upon you, to tell them who shall sit on the throne of my lord the king after him. ²¹Otherwise it will come to pass, when my lord the king sleeps with his fathers, that I and my son Solomon will be counted offenders."

²²While she was still speaking with the king, Nathan the prophet came in. ²³And they told the king, "Here is Nathan the prophet." And when he came in before the king, he bowed before the king, with his face to the ground. ²⁴And Nathan said, "My lord the king, have you said, 'Adonijah shall reign after me, and he shall sit upon my throne'? ²⁵For he has gone down this day, and has sacrificed oxen, fatlings, and sheep in abundance, and has invited all the king's sons, Joab the commander of the army, and Abiathar the priest; and behold, they are eating and drinking before him, and saying, 'Long live King Adonijah!' ²⁶But me, your servant, and Zadok the priest, and Benaiah the son of Jehoiada, and your servant Solomon, he has not invited. ²⁷Has this thing been brought about by my lord the king and you have not told your servants who should sit on the throne of my lord the king after him?"

²⁸Then King David answered, "Call Bathsheba to me." So she came into the king's presence, and stood before the king. ²⁹And the king swore, saying, "As the Lord lives, who has redeemed my soul out of every adversity, ³⁰as I swore to you by the Lord, the God of Israel, saying, 'Solomon your son shall reign after me, and he shall sit upon my throne in my stead'; even so will I do this day." ³¹Then Bathsheba bowed with her face to the ground, and did obeisance to the king, and said, "May my lord King David live for ever!"

³²King David said, "Call to me Zadok the priest, Nathan the prophet, and Benaiah the son of Jehoiada." So they came before the king. ³³And the king said to them, "Take with you the servants of your lord, and cause Solomon my son to ride on my own mule,

and bring him down to Gihon; ³⁴and let Zadok the priest and Nathan the prophet there anoint him king over Israel; then blow the trumpet, and say, 'Long live King Solomon!' ³⁵You shall then come up after him, and he shall come and sit upon my throne; for he shall be king in my stead; and I have appointed him to be ruler over Israel and over Judah." ³⁶And Benaiah the son of Jehoiada answered the king, "Amen! May the Lord, the God of my lord the king, say so. ³⁷As the Lord has been with my lord the king, even so may he be with Solomon, and make his throne greater than the throne of my lord King David."

³⁸So Zadok the priest, Nathan the prophet, and Benaiah the son of Jehoiada, and the Cherethites and the Pelethites, went down and caused Solomon to ride on King David's mule, and brought him to Gihon. ³⁹There Zadok the priest took the horn of oil from the tent, and anointed Solomon. Then they blew the trumpet; and all the people said, "Long live King Solomon!" ⁴⁰And all the people went up after him, playing on pipes, and rejoicing with great joy, so that the earth was split by their noise.

⁴¹Adonijah and all the guests who were with him heard it as they finished feasting. And when Joab heard the sound of the trumpet, he said, "What does this uproar in the city mean?" ⁴²While he was still speaking, behold, Jonathan the son of Abiathar the priest came; and Adonijah said, "Come in, for you are a worthy man and bring good news." ⁴³Jonathan answered Adonijah, "No, for our lord King David has made Solomon king; ⁴⁴and the king has sent with him Zadok the priest, Nathan the prophet, and Benaiah the son of Jehoiada, and the Cherethites and the Pelethites; and they have caused him to ride on the king's mule; ⁴⁵and Zadok the priest and Nathan the prophet have anointed him king at Gihon; and they have gone up from there rejoicing, so that the city is in an uproar. This is the noise that you have heard. ⁴⁶Solomon sits upon the royal throne. ⁴⁷Moreover the king's servants came to congratulate our lord King David, saying, 'Your God make the name of Solomon more famous than yours, and make his throne greater than your throne.' And the king bowed himself upon the bed. ⁴⁸And the king also said, 'Blessed be the Lord, the God of Israel, who has granted one of my offspring to sit on my throne this day, my own eyes seeing it.'"

⁴⁹Then all the guests of Adonijah trembled, and rose, and each went his own way. ⁵⁰And Adonijah feared Solomon; and he arose, and went, and caught hold of the horns of the altar. ⁵¹And it was

told Solomon, "Behold, Adonijah fears King Solomon; for, lo, he has laid hold of the horns of the altar, saying, 'Let King Solomon swear to me first that he will not slay his servant with the sword.'" 52And Solomon said, "If he prove to be a worthy man, not one of his hairs shall fall to the earth; but if wickedness is found in him, he shall die." 53So King Solomon sent, and they brought him down from the altar. And he came and did obeisance to King Solomon; and Solomon said to him, "Go to your house."

DAVID IN DECLINE II—COMMENTARY

1 Kings 1:1–53 (*cont'd*)

(i)

The end of the valiant leader is tellingly depicted in the opening four verses. "King David was old and advanced in years": this first phrase is very rare. Its terms were used of Joshua too (Josh. 13:1; 23:1), David's great predecessor as commander of Israel, and so it perhaps marks the passing of a whole era. Death's cold fingers are now touching the king, and no heap of bedding is any use. For the once-great lover, who has had many women, his staff turn to the most beautiful lass in the land to warm him and coax him back to life. (Because of the similarity of the names Shunammite and Shulammite—in Song of Solomon (6:13)—tradition has often associated Abishag with the heroine of these poems.) But in artful ambiguity over the meaning of the Hebrew verb, we are told that "the king knew her not" (v.4): did he not even register her presence, or could he no longer make love with a lovely bedmate? And this question should perhaps remind us that the only other people the Bible calls "old and advanced in years" are childless Abraham and Sarah (Gen. 18:11).

(ii)

Adonijah was David's eldest surviving son. His response to his father's situation was to begin feeling his way publicly into his intended role; saying that it was he who would be king, and organizing a suitably important retinue. It is difficult to know

whether verse 6 intends us to think of the prince as a spoiled
fellow, or simply as a candidate who has been well prepared for
the freedom of oriental royalty. With David as low as he
obviously was, there must have been something of a power
vacuum; and the first in line of succession takes counsel from
Joab (David's long-time military commander) and Abiathar
(one of the two leading priests) but not from all members of the
'establishment' (v.8). Their consultations lead to a solemn
ceremony including sacrifice and involving many formal invita-
tions. But the guest list has some notable gaps. These do not
prove that Adonijah was involved in intrigue; but at the very
least they show us that he knew just which individuals would
not enjoy the spectacle of his elevation.

(iii)

One of the ways in which much Biblical story-telling most
closely mirrors our own experience of life is its dependence on
the spoken word, on oral reports and questions. As we read the
next scenes in David's bedchamber, we have to make up our
own minds whether Nathan and Bathsheba are reminding the
king of a promise once made concerning Solomon, or whether
they are 'pulling a fast one' over an old man with neither the wit
to spot their strategy nor the energy to do anything about it.

Nathan does not actually say to Solomon's mother (v.11)
that Adonijah has become king; he just asks whether she has
heard such a report. And all we have been told by the storyteller
himself is that Adonijah had played host at a solemn celebration whose character is not further specified. Nathan advises
Bathsheba to put a question to David, and promises to endorse
the suggestion she makes. But are they putting words in David's
mouth that he had never uttered? This has been argued and is
possible but far from certain.

Bathsheba and Nathan point out to David (vv.15–27) that
important events are taking place right at hand in Jerusalem of
which he has no knowledge, and which accordingly he has not
authorized. Even when we are incompetent, we do not like to
have it pointed out to us! Roused by their words the king

reasserts his proper role, and begins to give instructions.

Bathsheba had come to him first, and she is the first to be summoned back to his presence (vv.28–31). The solemn oath once made to her would be given effect to that very day. Is it out of her love and gratitude, or sheer cynicism, or plain court etiquette, that she replies to the frail old man: "May my lord King David live for ever!'"?

Then the leaders of the rival establishment are summoned to receive their practical instructions (vv.32–37): not only Nathan, but also Zadok the other leading priest, and Benaiah one of David's chief strongmen. David tells them that he has appointed Solomon to be ruler over Israel and Judah. Benaiah (whose very name means 'Yahweh has built') discreetly adds the prayer that God will confirm David's choice! And there follows the scene immortalized in Handel's *Coronation Anthem*.

What a dramatic turn of the tables! Those celebrating with Adonijah had once seemed a comfortably large representation of Jerusalem's establishment, secure in the proper order of things. Yet they are undone by the last of many bold surprises associated with David. They learn from the son of one of their leaders (vv.41–49) not only that the old king has other plans, but that they are already carried out. David has even saluted his chosen son from his couch. The guests who find that they have been at the wrong party melt away.

And our chapter ends (vv.50–53) with Solomon's elder brother seeking sanctuary in fear of his life. Solomon's message is hopeful enough to tempt him from the altar. Yet when Adonijah bows at his feet, he is simply dismissed to his house; and we know that we will hear more of this matter.

(iv)

What is the Book of Kings drawing attention to in this opening chapter? And why does the Chronicler content himself with a simple summary in a single verse: "When David was old and full of days, he made Solomon his son king over Israel" (1 Chron. 23:1; cf. 29:28)? Chapter 1 of 1 Kings leaves us in no doubt over the essential humanity of the monarchy and its workings.

Solomon was no saint; and we are left to ponder over his right
to his father's throne.

A FATHER'S ADVICE

1 Kings 2:1-9

¹When David's time to die drew near, he charged Solomon his son,
saying, ²"I am about to go the way of all the earth. Be strong, and
show yourself a man, ³and keep the charge of the Lord your God,
walking in his ways and keeping his statutes, his commandments,
his ordinances, and his testimonies, as it is written in the law of
Moses, that you may prosper in all that you do and wherever you
turn; ⁴that the Lord may establish his word which he spoke
concerning me, saying, 'If your sons take heed to their way, to walk
before me in faithfulness with all their heart and with all their soul,
there shall not fail you a man on the throne of Israel.'

⁵"Moreover you know also what Joab the son of Zeruiah did to
me, how he dealt with the two commanders of the armies of Israel,
Abner the son of Ner, and Amasa the son of Jether, whom he
murdered, avenging in time of peace blood which had been shed in
war, and putting innocent blood upon the girdle about my loins,
and upon the sandals on my feet. ⁶Act therefore according to your
wisdom, but do not let his grey head go down to Sheol in peace.
⁷But deal loyally with the sons of Barzillai the Gileadite, and let
them be among those who eat at your table; for with such loyalty
they met me when I fled from Absalom your brother. ⁸And there is
also with you Shime-i the son of Gera, the Benjaminite from
Bahurim, who cursed me with a grievous curse on the day when I
went to Mahanaim; but when he came down to meet me at the
Jordan, I swore to him by the Lord, saying, 'I will not put you to
death with the sword.' ⁹Now therefore hold him not guiltless, for
you are a wise man; you will know what you ought to do to him, and
you shall bring his grey head down with blood to Sheol."

(i)

The opening of this chapter also (vv.1-4) takes us back to the
language of the Book of Joshua, not only in the hero's farewell
speech (Josh. 23:14) but also in the divine exhortation to him
(1:1-9). Being 'a man' means following God's ways—and that

means close attention to the written legacy of Moses. However, after this impeccably orthodox and religious beginning, David's counsel becomes very worldly-wise (vv.5–9)! Three pieces of death-bed advice are very crisply proferred: two men should die; and, for good balance, the family of a third deserves to enjoy the hospitality of the new king.

Joab had apparently served David well in many situations. He was the conqueror of Jerusalem (2 Sam. 5), and of Rabbah, capital of Ammon, modern Amman (2 Sam. 12). He was David's agent in the manipulation of Uriah and the seduction of his wife Bathsheba (2 Sam. 11); he protected David at the beginning of Absalom's revolt (2 Sam. 14); and he roughly rebuked him for too much public grief at the latter's death (2 Sam. 19). The fact that he had been at Adonijah's party (1:7) is passed over in silence; and the real clue to his fate is given much earlier, in 2 Samuel chapters 2–3. As one of David's southern entourage, Joab had wanted revenge on Abner, commander of Saul's (northern) Israelite forces, who had reluctantly killed Joab's foolhardy brother in a duel. Joab took amiss a report that David had entertained his rival in Hebron and dismissed him "in peace", apparently unaware that Abner was negotiating how David might become king of Israel as well as Judah. Joab summoned Abner back to Hebron and privately killed him. His master, David, publicly—and politically—disowned the assassination. His lament is followed by an explanation to his staff (2 Sam. 3:38–39):

> Do you not know that a prince and a great man has fallen this day in Israel? And I am this day weak, though anointed king; these men the sons of Zeruiah are too hard for me. The Lord requite the evildoer according to his wickedness!

Solomon should no longer have to face the problem David has had to live with.

Israelite susceptibilities, this time in Transjordan, are soothed again in David's next recommendation. Barzillai from Gilead had been one of those who entertained him generously when he crossed the river in flight from Absalom (2 Sam.

17:27–29). On his return westwards David had in turn offered his host hospitality in Jerusalem (2 Sam. 19:31–40), but the old man had refused it on account of his age. Loyal mutuality should continue into the next generation.

The two tales just told here are interestingly twined in the third. As David retreated before Absalom he was roundly abused by Shimei, not only a Benjaminite like Saul but also a member of Saul's household. One of Joab's brothers, Abishai, had wanted to remove his head on the spot, but David interposed: "Behold, my own son seeks my life; how much more now may this Benjaminite! Let him alone, and let him curse; for the Lord has bidden him. It may be that the Lord will look upon my affliction, and that the Lord will repay me with good for this cursing of me today" (2 Sam. 16:11–12). The same Shimei came to meet the returning David at the Jordan with a substantial force from Benjamin, acknowledging his mistake and protesting his loyalty. Again the same Abishai wanted him done to death for having cursed "the Lord's anointed". But David is celebrating his resumption of rule over Israel, and wants no-one put to death that day. He gives Shimei his oath to that effect. Unhappily for Shimei, David's oath was a personal one and a formal one, and was to die with him (see 1 Kings 2:36ff.). The sentiment of verses 3–4 of Psalm 146 is rather apt:

> Put not your trust in princes,
>   in a son of man, in whom there is no help.
> When his breath departs he returns to his earth;
>   on that very day his plans perish.

(ii)

Wisdom (v.6) is one of Solomon's famed attributes; and it is instructive to ponder what that key word means in this passage. David does not leave to wise Solomon (v.9) the *decision* over what to do with Joab and Shimei—but only the *means* by which the aim is to be realized. 'Wisdom' here means political craft, diplomatic guile; those qualities of leadership which present use

of a 'dirty tricks' department as being in the best interests of
good government.

It is interesting that 'wisdom' is used as an opposite of
'loyalty' (v. 7)—or at least to qualify it. It is by wisdom that
Joab and Shimei will be struck down, while loyalty is appropriate to the family of Barzillai. To a good administrator, loyalty
must be a selective commodity. To say all this is not to sneer,
but simply to recognize the widely acknowledged 'facts of life'.
And yet it is not clear to me that this chapter of Kings does
simply recognize these as the facts. The juxtaposition of the two
opening paragraphs (vv.1–4/5–9) is somewhat ambiguous. The
former ends with David quoting a divine promise:

> If your sons take heed to their way, to walk before me in faithful-
> ness with all their heart and with all their soul, there shall not fail
> you a man on the throne of Israel.

His own detailed advice to his son is certainly designed to
enhance the security of his throne. And yet is it in the spirit of
the Mosaic Torah? Or is it a rather wilful endorsement of the
couthy principle that 'The Lord helps them as helps themselves'?

My own suspicion is that these two paragraphs want to
suggest quite discreetly that a style of autonomous statecraft
that paid more attention to God's promises than to his demands
began with Jerusalem's first great king—that it was David in
fact who sowed the seeds of that city's distant collapse to
Babylon.

THE KINGDOM ESTABLISHED I—TEXT

1 Kings 2:10–46

¹⁰Then David slept with his fathers, and was buried in the city of
David. ¹¹And the time that David reigned over Israel was forty
years; he reigned seven years in Hebron, and thirty-three years in
Jerusalem. ¹²So Solomon sat upon the throne of David his father;
and his kingdom was firmly established.

¹³Then Adonijah the son of Haggith came to Bathsheba the

mother of Solomon. And she said, "Do you come peaceably?" He said, "Peaceably." ¹⁴Then he said, "I have something to say to you." She said, "Say on." ¹⁵He said, "You know that the kingdom was mine, and that all Israel fully expected me to reign; however the kingdom has turned about and become my brother's, for it was his from the Lord. ¹⁶And now I have one request to make of you; do not refuse me." She said to him, "Say on." ¹⁷And he said, "Pray ask King Solomon—he will not refuse you—to give me Abishag the Shunammite as my wife." ¹⁸Bathsheba said, "Very well; I will speak for you to the king."

¹⁹So Bathsheba went to King Solomon, to speak to him on behalf of Adonijah. And the king rose to meet her, and bowed down to her; then he sat on his throne, and had a seat brought for the king's mother; and she sat on his right. ²⁰Then she said, "I have one small request to make of you; do not refuse me." And the king said to her, "Make your request, my mother; for I will not refuse you." ²¹She said, "Let Abishag the Shunammite be given to Adonijah your brother as his wife." ²²King Solomon answered his mother, "And why do you ask Abishag the Shunammite for Adonijah? Ask for him the kingdom also; for he is my elder brother, and on his side are Abiathar the priest and Joab the son of Zeruiah." ²³Then King Solomon swore by the Lord, saying, "God do so to me and more also if this word does not cost Adonijah his life! ²⁴Now therefore as the Lord lives, who has established me, and placed me on the throne of David my father, and who has made me a house, as he promised, Adonijah shall be put to death this day." ²⁵So King Solomon sent Benaiah the son of Jehoiada; and he struck him down, and he died.

²⁶And to Abiathar the priest the king said, "Go to Anathoth, to your estate; for you deserve death. But I will not at this time put you to death, because you bore the ark of the Lord God before David my father, and because you shared in all the affliction of my father." ²⁷So Solomon expelled Abiathar from being priest to the Lord, thus fulfilling the word of the Lord which he had spoken concerning the house of Eli in Shiloh.

²⁸When the news came to Joab—for Joab had supported Adonijah although he had not supported Absalom—Joab fled to the tent of the Lord and caught hold of the horns of the altar. ²⁹And when it was told King Solomon, "Joab has fled to the tent of the Lord, and behold, he is beside the altar," Solomon sent Benaiah the son of Jehoiada, saying, "Go, strike him down." ³⁰So Benaiah came to the

tent of the Lord, and said to him, "The king commands, 'Come forth,'" But he said, "No, I will die here." Then Benaiah brought the king word again, saying, "Thus said Joab, and thus he answered me." ³¹The king replied to him, "Do as he has said, strike him down and bury him; and thus take away from me and from my father's house the guilt for the blood which Joab shed without cause. ³²The Lord will bring back his bloody deeds upon his own head, because, without the knowledge of my father David, he attacked and slew with the sword two men more righteous and better than himself, Abner the son of Ner, commander of the army of Israel, and Amasa the son of Jether, commander of the army of Judah. ³³So shall their blood come back upon the head of Joab and upon the head of his descendants for ever; but to David, and to his descendants, and to his house, and to his throne, there shall be peace from the Lord for evermore." ³⁴Then Benaiah the son of Jehoiada went up, and struck him down and killed him; and he was buried in his own house in the wilderness. ³⁵The king put Benaiah the son of Jehoiada over the army in place of Joab, and the king put Zadok the priest in the place of Abiathar.

³⁶Then the king sent and summoned Shime-i, and said to him, "Build yourself a house in Jerusalem, and dwell there, and do not go forth from there to any place whatever. ³⁷For on the day you go forth, and cross the brook Kidron, know for certain that you shall die; your blood shall be upon your own head." ³⁸And Shime-i said to the king, "What you say is good; as my lord the king has said, so will your servant do." So Shime-i dwelt in Jerusalem many days.

³⁹But it happened at the end of three years that two of Shime-i's slaves ran away to Achish, son of Maacah, king of Gath. And when it was told Shime-i, "Behold, your slaves are in Gath," ⁴⁰Shime-i arose and saddled an ass, and went to Gath to Achish, to seek his slaves; Shime-i went and brought his slaves from Gath. ⁴¹And when Solomon was told that Shime-i had gone from Jerusalem to Gath and returned, ⁴²the king sent and summoned Shime-i, and said to him, "Did I not make you swear by the Lord, and solemnly admonish you, saying, 'Know for certain that on the day you go forth and go to any place whatever, you shall die'? And you said to me, 'What you say is good; I obey.' ⁴³Why then have you not kept your oath to the Lord and the commandment with which I charged you?" ⁴⁴The king also said to Shime-i, "You know in your own heart all the evil that you did to David my father; so the Lord will bring back your evil upon your own head. ⁴⁵But King Solomon shall be

blessed, and the throne of David shall be established before the Lord for ever." ⁴⁶Then the king commanded Benaiah the son of Jehoiada; and he went out and struck him down, and he died.
So the kingdom was established in the hand of Solomon.

THE KINGDOM ESTABLISHED II—COMMENTARY

1 Kings 2:10–46 (*cont'd*)

(i)

So David went the way of all flesh. We read for the first time in verse 10 an expression for death that will recur almost regularly in Kings and Chronicles: *ie* "slept with his fathers", in the case of the son of Jesse from Bethleham. The Pentateuch prefers the alternative "was gathered to his people". Although there was a preference for burial in a family tomb, it is plain that "the city of David" means Jerusalem; and so in the case of the son of Jesse from Bethlehem we cannot press a literal sense out of "slept with his fathers". The Chronicler for some reason passes over David's burial in silence.

The main part of our portion is sandwiched between a repeated note (vv. 12,46) that the kingdom was "firmly established" in Solomon's hands. This same note opens. 2 Chronicles; but that book lacks the narrative relating the machinations. Such duplication of a notice is often the sign that in between we are dealing with a later supplement to the original composition.

(ii)

If the sort of wisdom which David saw and admired in Solomon is necessary for a successful king, then it was well for Adonijah not to succeed to his father's throne. For it is an artless proposal he makes to a woman (vv.13–18) who knows well the ways of the world; who has cheated on her first warrior husband, and helped to establish her son's dominance despite much of the Jerusalem establishment! Why begin by reminding her of his own claim to the throne, and (even more) of all Israel's expectations? Admittedly, true to his name ('Yahweh is my

Lord'), Adonijah concedes that the change of fortune was
Yahweh's doing.

How could Adonijah not know that he was tying the noose
for his own neck when he asked for Abishag? The women of the
palace were the king's prerogative. Revolting Absalom and his
counsellors had known this full well when he agreed to make a
public spectacle of 'going in' to his father's concubines (2 Sam.
16:20–23). The opening paragraph of Kings may not call
Abishag either wife or concubine; and David may not have
"known" her— but how else could this fair lass be considered?

Solomon is outraged—and relieved? And how appropriate
that it is Benaiah ('Yahweh has built') who sees to the execution
of this feckless royal pretender! For we remember the divine
promise to David that the Lord would establish his dynasty or,
in the words of 2 Samuel 7:27, would "build [him] a house".

(iii)

Abiathar the priest suffers the lesser fate of rustication. He is
banished to his estate in Anathoth (v.26). Even before the bus
and the motorcar, this was no great distance—three miles from
Jerusalem! It was later to be Jeremiah's home, and was one of
the list of priestly cities detailed in Joshua chapter 21. We may
suppose that when he was told to return to his own property,
something like house-arrest or a 'banning order' was added to
his removal from office before Yahweh. (Interestingly he is still
named, with Zadok, as priest in 4:4.)

Again it is fair to assume that Abiathar is paying for having
backed the wrong man. This is not actually stated, but his fate is
noted immediately after the reported demise of his candidate.
David certainly had had good cause to be grateful to the man
whose father and family had been massacred by Saul on his
account (1 Sam. 22). When David was expelled by Absalom,
Abiathar and Zadok had wanted to accompany him with the
ark of the covenant—at his request they stayed in Jerusalem as
his agents for intelligence and communication. His only reported offence was to have advised Solomon's elder brother. In
Solomon's book that was worthy of death!

However there is a wider dimension as well. Abiathar's fate is linked to that of his forefather Eli. We should pause over what is actually said (v.27); for the language is much rarer in the Hebrew Bible than we might expect. "Fulfilment" of the divine word is a common enough idea in the New Testament; but in only two other passages in the Old Testament do we read of someone's 'word' being 'filled'. The RSV is less than helpful in this matter.

In 1 Kings 1:14, Nathan counsels Bathsheba to go first to David to make Solomon's case; he will follow and "confirm" (RSV) her words. I suspect a better paraphrase of "fill" in this instance might be 'amplify' or 'set in a wider context' or even 'explain further'. The other occurrence is in 2 Chronicles 36:21 in connection with Jeremiah's words about the 70 year fate of Jerusalem. What is 'amplified' in Abiathar's dismissal (2:27) is the rejection of Eli already described in 1 Samuel chapters 2–3.

In none of these cases was the first word spoken inadequate. "Fulfilment" in these Old Testament passages does not therefore mean 'completion'. Yet in each case what was complete in itself could also have new light thrown on it. This is a perfect paradigm for the Old Testament: Hebrew Scriptures complete in themselves, but also understandable in the fresh light of Jesus the Christ.

(iv)

The chapter ends with the elimination of Joab and Shimei, further to David's death-bed advice. As the whole narrative proceeds, it is increasingly hard to avoid the impression that it is not favourable to Solomon or the Davidic house. Apparently even hatchetman Benaiah has scruples over cutting Joab down at the altar, and seeks a second explicit mandate from his master. Did Solomon deliberately misunderstand Joab's wish (v.30) to see out his natural days within the sacred precinct? Or did Joab want to bring down opprobrium on the head of Solomon and his own successor as commander-in-chief? Finally Shimei played into the king's hands by 'jumping' the terms of his restriction order. Yet even Solomon is candid enough to voice the real cause of death (vv. 44-45) after mention of the convenient excuse.

The political moral of it all is a teasing conundrum. Solomon's rivals fall into his hands so easily that they are not credible alternative leaders. Yet he himself is a remarkably cynical manipulator.

A DREAM AND A 'CAUSE CÉLÈBRE'

1 Kings 3:1–28

¹Solomon made a marriage alliance with Pharaoh king of Egypt; he took Pharaoh's daughter, and brought her into the city of David, until he had finished building his own house and the house of the Lord and the wall around Jerusalem. ²The people were sacrificing at the high places, however, because no house had yet been built for the name of the Lord. ³Solomon loved the Lord, walking in the statutes of David his father; only, he sacrificed and burnt incense at the high places. ⁴And the king went to Gibeon to sacrifice there, for that was the great high place; Solomon used to offer a thousand burnt offerings upon that altar. ⁵At Gibeon the Lord appeared to Solomon in a dream by night; and God said, "Ask what I shall give you." ⁶And Solomon said, "Thou hast shown great and steadfast love to thy servant David my father, because he walked before thee in faithfulness, in righteousness, and in uprightness of heart toward thee; and thou hast kept for him this great and steadfast love, and hast given him a son to sit on his throne this day. ⁷And now, O Lord my God, thou hast made thy servant king in place of David my father, although I am but a little child; I do not know how to go out or come in. ⁸And thy servant is in the midst of thy people whom thou hast chosen, a great people, that cannot be numbered or counted for multitude. ⁹Give thy servant therefore an understanding mind to govern thy people, that I may discern between good and evil; for who is able to govern this thy great people?"

¹⁰It pleased the Lord that Solomon had asked this. ¹¹And God said to him, "Because you have asked this, and have not asked for yourself long life or riches or the life of your enemies, but have asked for yourself understanding to discern what is right, ¹²behold, I now do according to your word. Behold, I give you a wise and discerning mind, so that none like you has been before you and

none like you shall arise after you. [13]I give you also what you have not asked, both riches and honour, so that no other king shall compare with you, all your days. [14]And if you will walk in my ways, keeping my statutes and my commandments, as your father David walked, then I will lengthen your days."

[15]And Solomon awoke, and behold, it was a dream. Then he came to Jerusalem, and stood before the ark of the covenant of the Lord, and offered up burnt offerings and peace offerings, and made a feast for all his servants.

[16]Then two harlots came to the king, and stood before him. [17]The one woman said, "Oh, my lord, this woman and I dwell in the same house; and I gave birth to a child while she was in the house. [18]Then on the third day after I was delivered, this woman also gave birth; and we were alone; there was no one else with us in the house, only we two were in the house. [19]And this woman's son died in the night, because she lay on it. [20]And she arose at midnight, and took my son from beside me, while your maidservant slept, and laid it in her bosom, and laid her dead son in my bosom. [21]When I rose in the morning to nurse my child, behold, it was dead; but when I looked at it closely in the morning, behold, it was not the child that I had borne." [22]But the other woman said, "No, the living child is mine, and the dead child is yours." The first said, "No, the dead child is yours, and the living child is mine." Thus they spoke before the king.

[23]Then the king said, "The one says, 'This is my son that is alive, and your son is dead'; and the other says, 'No; but your son is dead, and my son is the living one.'" [24]And the king said, "Bring me a sword." So a sword was brought before the king. [25]And the king said, "Divide the living child in two, and give half to the one, and half to the other." [26]Then the woman whose son was alive said to the king, because her heart yearned for her son, "Oh, my lord, give her the living child, and by no means slay it." But the other said, "It shall be neither mine nor yours; divide it." [27]Then the king answered and said, "Give the living child to the first woman, and by no means slay it; she is its mother." [28]And all Israel heard of the judgment which the king had rendered; and they stood in awe of the king, because they perceived that the wisdom of God was in him, to render justice.

(i)

It is not easy to decide why it is exactly here that we are told in

all brevity (v.1) of Solomon's marriage to Pharaoh's daughter.
Is it a token of the establishment of his kingship (2:12,46)? Or is
it a whispered anticipation of the theme of chapter 11; that love
of many foreign women seduced Solomon from proper love for
Yahweh his God? Does it hint at Solomon's international
prestige; or was the marriage a means by which Pharaoh
retained some leverage on the politics of the southern Levant?

This chapter does go on to affirm that Solomon did love the
Lord (v.3); yet it immediately qualifies this with talk of worship
at sanctuaries other than Jerusalem. The tension seems unre-
solved between blame for this, and matter-of-fact acknowledgment that nothing other was possible before the construction of
that Jerusalem place of worship. Gibeon "was the great high
place" (v.4); and some of its story was told when discussing
Joshua chapter 9 in my earlier volume (*Joshua, Judges and
Ruth*).

(ii)

This Gibeon is also the scene of an important divine vision
(vv.4-15), as other sanctuaries had been in the stories of
Solomon's great biblical predecessors. It must have been
rivalled in popular memory only by Jacob's ladder at Bethel
and the night-time call of the young Samuel at Shiloh. And it is
with this vision that the story of Solomon's reign begins in the
parallel version of the Chronicler (2 Chron. 1:3-13). When we
read them quickly, the two reports seem very similar; yet the
differences are quite striking.

It is common to both that the divine appearance to Solomon
followed large-scale sacrifice at Gibeon, happened at night, and
involved a dialogue following the divine offer to the king. In
essentials, the discussion follows the same lines: Solomon
requests discernment, and is praised for not asking for long life,
or material or military success, all of which are offered as a
bonus.

Most of the differences between the two Hebrew texts are
trivial; however the Kings version is rather more wordy and
appears to me to be expanded from the other. Solomon is more

self-deprecating in 1 Kings 3—regularly calling himself "thy servant", referring to himself as "but a little child", and praising his father in rather fulsome terms (v.6).

Another point made more fully in Kings is that the revelation comes "in a dream" (vv.5,15). In Chronicles God simply appears and speaks. Sometimes in the Bible we are warned against the "dreamer of dreams" (Deut. 13; Jer. 23). In other texts, the dream is considered the normal and proper mode of divine communication: both Joseph and Daniel themselves dream and are prized for their ability to interpret the dreams of others. Then Numbers 12:6-8 even implies grades of honour: God communicates with a prophet by "vision" or "dream", but with Moses directly "mouth to mouth".

(iii)

The hardest terms to translate in the whole passage are the related Hebrew verb and noun rendered "govern" (1 Kings 3:9) and "right" (v.11). The Hebrew word *shaphat* has overtones of both ruling and judging. We have already explored this in connection with the so-called "Judges" of Israel who followed Joshua (see *Joshua, Judges and Ruth*, pp. 190ff.).

The king was the supreme judge and final arbiter. Within his domain, the ideal king sought to achieve what was right, to vindicate the just, to protect the rights of the weak. And this was achieved in practice by a series of shrewd and just decisions or verdicts or judgments (*mishpatim* in the plural) all of which are examples of what our text calls "right" (*mishpat* in the singular).

(iv)

All this is perfectly illustrated in the famous tale that follows (vv.16-28): Solomon's verdict on the one baby claimed by two colleagues in harlotry. The complaint of the wronged mother is finely presented to the king. Stripped to the bare essentials, her tale invites our imagination to flesh out the bones; to sympathize with a bereaved mother so soon after the excitement and anguish of birth, crazed into cheating on a mate with her own new baby; and to hear the bitter catalogue of claim and counter-claim that is glossed over in the words, "Thus they spoke before the king" (v.22).

Solomon's dramatic proposal is almost a trial by ordeal in reverse. The woman who can tolerate the pain is guilty, the one who cannot is innocent. His insight provokes instant respect from "all Israel" who detect a more than human wisdom, and accordingly stand "in awe of the king".

Although it is camouflaged a little in the RSV rendering, verse 28 takes us back to the Hebrew wording of the end of verse 11. More literally translated that verse had asked for "understanding to hear [a] *mishpat*" or "discernment in hearing [a] *mishpat*". Solomon's *mishpat* is what all Israel hear of at the opening of verse 28: but is it a *mishpat, ie* his 'verdict' or simply *mishpat, ie* his 'justice'? In English we have to decide which better fits the context; the Hebrew word comprehends both the abstract principle and the concrete decisions which give it practical expression. It is the very same word which is appropriately translated "justice" at the close of the last verse.

This divine wisdom with which this son of David is endowed reminds us of the idealized offspring of Jesse in Isaiah 11, on whom the Lord's spirit will rest—a spirit made more precise as follows (v.2):

> the spirit of wisdom and understanding,
> the spirit of counsel and might,
> the spirit of knowledge and the fear of the Lord.

And of course these words are immediately followed (Isa. 11:3*b*–5) by a portrait of the perfect judge:

> He shall not judge by what his eyes see,
>   or decide by what his ears hear;
> but with righteousness shall he judge the poor,
>   and decide with equity for the meek of the earth;
> and he shall smite the earth with the rod of his mouth,
>   and with the breath of his lips he shall slay the wicked.
> Righteousness shall be the girdle of his waist,
>   and faithfulness the girdle of his loins.

SOLOMON'S MANAGEMENT

1 Kings 4:1–28

¹King Solomon was king over all Israel, ²and these were his high officials: Azariah the son of Zadok was the priest; ³Elihoreph and Ahijah the sons of Shisha were secretaries; Jehoshaphat the son of Ahilud was recorder; ⁴Benaiah the son of Jehoiada was in command of the army; Zadok and Abiathar were priests; ⁵Azariah the son of Nathan was over the officers; Zabud the son of Nathan was priest and king's friend; ⁶Ahishar was in charge of the palace; and Adoniram the son of Abda was in charge of the forced labour.

⁷Solomon had twelve officers over all Israel, who provided food for the king and his household; each man had to make provision for one month in the year. ⁸These were their names: Ben-hur, in the hill country of Ephraim; ⁹Ben-deker, in Makaz, Sha-albim, Beth-shemesh, and Elon-beth-hanan; ¹⁰Ben-hesed, in Arubboth (to him belonged Socoh and all the land of Hepher); ¹¹Ben-abinadab, in all Naphath-dor (he had Taphath the daughter of Solomon as his wife); ¹²Baana the son of Ahilud, in Taanach, Megiddo, and all Beth-shean which is beside Zarethan below Jezreel, and from Beth-shean to Abel-meholah, as far as the other side of Jokmeam; ¹³Ben-geber, in Ramoth-gilead (he had the villages of Jair the son of Manasseh, which are in Gilead, and he had the region of Argob, which is in Bashan, sixty great cities with walls and bronze bars); ¹⁴Ahinadab the son of Iddo, in Mahanaim; ¹⁵Ahima-az, in Naphtali (he had taken Basemath the daughter of Solomon as his wife); ¹⁶Baana the son of Hushai, in Asher and Bealoth; ¹⁷Jehoshaphat the son of Paruah, in Issachar; ¹⁸Shime-i the son of Ela, in Benjamin; ¹⁹Geber the son of Uri, in the land of Gilead, the country of Sihon king of the Amorites and of Og king of Bashan. And there was one officer in the land of Judah.

²⁰Judah and Israel were as many as the sand by the sea; they ate and drank and were happy. ²¹Solomon ruled over all the kingdoms from the Eu-phrates to the land of the Philistines and to the border of Egypt; they brought tribute and served Solomon all the days of his life.

²²Solomon's provision for one day was thirty cors of fine flour, and sixty cors of meal, ²³ten fat oxen, and twenty pasture-fed cattle, a hundred sheep, besides harts, gazelles, roebucks, and fatted fowl. ²⁴For he had dominion over all the region west of the Eu-phrates

from Tiphsah to Gaza, over all the kings west of the Eu-phrates;
and he had peace on all sides round about him. ²⁵And Judah and
Israel dwelt in safety, from Dan even to Beer-sheba, every man
under his vine and under his fig tree, all the days of Solomon.
²⁶Solomon also had forty thousand stalls of horses for his chariots,
and twelve thousand horsemen. ²⁷And those officers supplied
provisions for King Solomon, and for all who came to King
Solomon's table, each one in his month; they let nothing be lacking.
²⁸Barley also and straw for the horses and swift steeds they brought
to the place where it was required, each according to his charge.

(i)

Verses 2–19 are a delight and a puzzle to all historians of early
monarchy in the Bible. They are a pleasure because they look as
if they have been simply transcribed from a list of officials in a
palace archive, and so represent a prime authentic source for
understanding how things were organized. And yet on closer
inspection, not everything is so straightforward.

The list of Solomon's "high officials" (vv.2–6) is very similar
to a list of his father's right-hand men that we find first in 2
Samuel 8:16–18, then repeated in 2 Samuel 20:23–26. Naturally
several of the names are the same or almost the same in both
lists. Some of the differences are simply slips of the pen; some
will be due to later editorial addition and adjustment. The same
is true of variations between the ancient versions of the list in
hand. The best manuscripts of the Greek Bible make no
mention of Azariah (v.2) and Zabud (v.5) being priests: the one
is listed as one of the secretaries, and the other is simply the
"king's friend".

The lists need some checking, but they are a valuable record.
They remind us just how little royal courts and their titles vary
over the centuries and between even widely different peoples.
And they make us recall that religion in Jerusalem of the
monarchic period was established state religion: the (high)
priests were officials of the king—just as still today the bishops
of the Church of England are appointed by the Sovereign on the
advice of the Prime Minister.

Then verses 7–19 provide our main information about a twelve-fold structure within Israel, distinct from the tribal system familiar especially in the preceding books of the Bible. Solomon had twelve local officials responsible for a form of taxation; each had to supply the provisions for the whole court for a month in the year. It is not in fact very hard to draw a map of the areas each was appointed over. Much more interesting for the specialist is to probe the links between this division of the kingdom and the tribal geography presented in such detail in Joshua chapters 13–19. Do names like Ephraim (v.8) or Naphtali, Asher, Issachar and Benjamin (vv.15–18) refer to tribal groupings or geographical areas? How much of a clue is verse 8 and its talk of "the hill country of Ephraim"? However these considerations are not our business here. We may simply note in passing that two of these officials (vv.11,15) were or became sons-in-law to the king.

(ii)

However, one detail of political geography is too important to ignore, and that is the relationship between Judah and Israel. In fact the meaning of "Israel" has to be considered anew almost each time it is read. The previous chapter ends with "all Israel" rapt in fearful admiration—and that means everyone within Solomon's realm(s) who had heard the king's verdict. Our chapter begins with the note that "Solomon was king over all Israel" (although not all ancient versions of this text include the word "all"). So far we might suppose that "all Israel" included Solomon's homeland of Judah.

However "all Israel" in verses 7–19 demands a different explanation. The twelve appointees listed there are responsible for an area that excludes Judah. And this is explicitly under-scored, albeit in a puzzling note at the end of verse 19. This records a separate "officer" for Judah, although it does not name him, and although he can hardly have been annually responsible for a month's royal supplies.

The next verse (v.20), like the rather similar verse 25, empha sizes the separate togetherness of the two entities; sharing the same good fortune and nestling together within the outer limits of northern Dan and southern Beer-sheba. It is likely that "Judah and Israel" reflects the constitutional proprieties of Solomon's own time; and that, when "Israel" is used more comprehensively in the texts, we should suspect the hands of later writers.

Some other biblical passages resonate in an interesting way with these two verses. In earlier struggles, it was generally Israel's fearsome opponents who were called "as many as the sand by the sea" (Josh. 11:4; Judg. 7:12; 1 Sam. 13:5). Perhaps when Hushai counsels Absalom (2 Sam. 17:11) "that all Israel be gathered to you, from Dan to Beer-sheba, as the sand by the sea for multitude", we should already suspect the disaster that follows; for God seems to prefer the resources of the apparently weaker side. Then we should remember that Abner, whose fatal embassy to David at Hebron we have already recalled in our first chapter, vowed (2 Sam. 3:10) when he had fallen out with Saul's son to "set up the throne of David over Israel and over Judah, from Dan to Beer-sheba".

Finally, verse 25 uses the proverbial expression for individual plenty and contentment (found also in 2 Kings 18:31, Mic. 4:4 and Zech. 3:10) which parallels the more prosaic "ate and drank and were happy" of verse 20—a phrase which is (to my surprise!) unique in the Hebrew Bible.

(iii)

Yet Judah and Israel were only the heart of Solomon's claimed domain (v.21). That extended from the upper Euphrates river in the north-east to the territory of the Philistines and their border with Egypt in the south-west (more or less where the current Egypt/Israel frontier runs). It is hard to tell if that is accurate historical memory. We are hampered in our evaluation by the odd fact that, despite the international contacts for which David and Solomon are famed in the Bible, they do not appear in any of the records that have come down to us from their neighbours. There is in fact one strong clue to our historical riddle in the Hebrew wording of verse 24 which talks of all the territory *"across* the river" (RSV "west of the Eu-phrates"). That is the official *Persian* term for Syria/Palestine, the land across—from their vantage-point, to the southwest of—the Euphrates. If Solomon's fame is early, this record of it is certainly late.

WEALTHY AND WISE

1 Kings 4:21–34

21Solomon ruled over all the kingdoms from the Eu-phrates to the land of the Philistines and to the border of Egypt; they brought tribute and served Solomon all the days of his life.

22Solomon's provision for one day was thirty cors of fine flour, and sixty cors of meal, 23ten fat oxen, and twenty pasture-fed cattle, a hundred sheep, besides harts, gazelles, roebucks, and fatted fowl. 24For he had dominion over all the region west of the Eu-phrates from Tiphsah to Gaza, over all the kings west of the Eu-phrates; and he had peace on all sides round about him. 25And Judah and Israel dwelt in safety, from Dan even to Beer-sheba, every man under his vine and under his fig tree, all the days of Solomon. 26Solomon also had forty thousand stalls of horses for his chariots, and twelve thousand horsemen. 27And those officers supplied provisions for King Solomon, and for all who came to King Solomon's table, each one in his month; they let nothing be lacking. 28Barley also and straw for the horses and swift steeds they brought to the place where it was required, each according to his charge.

29And God gave Solomon wisdom and understanding beyond measure, and largeness of mind like the sand on the seashore, 30so that Solomon's wisdom surpassed the wisdom of all the people of the east, and all the wisdom of Egypt. 31For he was wiser than all other men, wiser than Ethan the Ezrahite, and Heman, Calcol, and Darda, the sons of Mahol; and his fame was in all the nations round about. 32He also uttered three thousand proverbs; and his songs were a thousand and five. 33He spoke of trees, from the cedar that is in Lebanon to the hyssop that grows out of the wall; he spoke also of beasts, and of birds, and of reptiles, and of fish. 34And men came from all peoples to hear the wisdom of Solomon, and from all the kings of the earth, who had heard of his wisdom.

(i)

The fourth chapter of 1 Kings is not easy to divide and analyze. In this portion we overlap with the end of the previous one, and present what in the Hebrew Bible tradition is the first 14 verses of chapter 5.

Solomon's power and prestige are presented in different ways. We read an odd amalgam of attitudes towards Solomon: they range from subservience to respect. Part of the oddity seems to have been caused by strange editing. The rather different version in the ancient Greek translation of the Bible is shorter, more clearly organized, and almost certainly more original. It does not contain verses 20-21 or 25-26. It moves directly from the end of the list of officers in verse 19 to the report of their monthly provisions in verses 27-28. Only then does it offer what we read in verses 22-24, after which it proceeds to the paragraph beginning with verse 29.

This shorter Greek version gives the impression that Solomon's 12 Israelite officers catered for the sumptuous provisioning of his court. The longer account in the Hebrew Bible, from which the RSV above is translated, suggests rather that the royal court was enriched by tribute and service from all the lands round about, while Solomon's own people in their multitude "ate, drank and were happy" (v.20) and each citizen of Judah and Israel enjoyed security "under his vine and under his fig tree" (v.25)—matters of which the Greek Bible does not tell us. When we come to discuss the aftermath of Solomon's reign as described in 1 Kings 12, we shall appreciate better the importance of knowing whether Israel was content under his rule or not.

It follows from what we said above that the shorter, more original version of this information comes to talk of Solomon's external relations (RSV v.24) only after the internal structure of his realms. Read from this angle, and in a text which does not contain verse 21, verse 24 appears in a new light. Influence over his neighbours *was* of financial benefit, yet not because of tribute from outside but rather because the resulting "peace on all sides" allowed continuing prosperity at home.

(ii)

And so after this detailed report on the organization of his kingdom, we return in verses 29–34 to the theme of chapter 3: Solomon's fabled wisdom. In a manner which reminds us of the way Job is introduced—"this man was the greatest of all the people of the east" (Job 1:3)—Solomon is compared favourably with the best in the civilizations of the east and west (*ie* Egypt).

We should note *first* the terms in which the theme is introduced. "Wisdom" and "understanding" are no mere conventional pair. They describe the special endowment required by those who would spy out the promised land for Israel (Deut. 1:13). And we find them used elsewhere to distinguish a biblical hero from the rest of the world: Joseph's skills in Genesis 41:33, 39; or Israel as a whole in comparison with the other nations (Deut. 4:6).

But even more interesting is the climax which the RSV translates "largeness of mind" (v.29), of which a more literal rendering would be "breadth of heart". In no sense am I objecting to this freedom of RSV: it is quite correct to observe that in ancient Hebrew, people thought with their heart not their head, and that the bowels, not the heart, were the seat of the emotions. More remarkable is this: that elsewhere in the Bible this and similar expressions are used in a bad sense. Psalm 101:5 makes the point clearly:

Him who slanders his neighbour secretly I will destroy.
The man of haughty looks and *arrogant heart* I will not endure.

And, although the rendering is different, the same sense is plain in Proverb 21:4:

Haughty eyes and *a proud heart*,
the lamp of the wicked, are sin.

Similarly the Hebrew "largeness of heart" is translated "arrogance of heart" in Isaiah 9:9 and "arrogant boasting" in Isaiah 10:12.

Yet it is manifest that RSV is correct to translate the phrase positively in our verse here. I am reminded that it is true in English that we are properly proud of some things, yet at the same time pride is one of the seven deadly sins. I am reminded also of Paul's advice to "every one among you not to think of himself more highly than he ought to think, but to think with sober judgment" (Rom. 12:3). There is a God-given ability to seize opportunities, as well as a culpable distortion of it.

The *second* thing we note is that Solomon is put in the company of those with a special reputation for their sagacity—this is clear enough from the text although they are shadowy figures to us. They appear together again only in the Chronicler's genealogies of Judah (1 Chron. 2:6), although Heman the Ezrahite and Ethan the Ezrahite appear individually in the titles of Psalms 88 and 89 respectively. And this musical connection suggests that Hebrew *mahol*, which means "dance", may not be a proper name at all but might, in conjunction with "sons of" (v.31), designate an office (cf. Jesusalem Bible, "the cantors").

Our *third* note (v.32) has musical associations as well, in its listing of Solomon's "proverbs" and "songs". In later tradition it is only for the former that he is remembered, while his father David is patron of song and psalmody. Here, however, both are ascribed to Solomon, although it is only the first of them that is more fully developed in verse 33.

Proverbs about plants and animals encapsulated the fruits of the scientific observation of the ancient world. Several animals are well observed and thriftily summed up in the second half of chapter 30 in the biblical Book of Proverbs. Yet in that chapter too it is also plain that what has been well observed in nature is applied to the understanding of the human condition. We have clear biblical evidence that fables involving trees were used in political discussion—briefly in 2 Kings 14:9 and in a more extended way in Judges 9:8-15 (see *Joshua, Judges and Ruth*, p.183). Solomon's proverbs will have been no less 'political'.

Fourth and finally, and in a word, these verses like the previous ones set Solomon at the centre of his world, with people and rulers coming to pay him court, and test for themselves his astonishing reputation.

RELATIONS WITH HIRAM

1 Kings 5:1-18

¹Now Hiram king of Tyre sent his servants to Solomon, when he heard that they had anointed him king in place of his father; for Hiram always loved David. ²And Solomon sent word to Hiram, ³"You know that David my father could not build a house for the name of the Lord his God because of the warfare with which his enemies surrounded him, until the Lord put them under the soles of his feet. ⁴But now the Lord my God has given me rest on every side; there is neither adversary nor misfortune. ⁵And so I purpose to build a house for the name of the Lord my God, as the Lord said to David my father, 'Your son, whom I will set upon your throne in your place, shall build the house for my name.' ⁶Now therefore command that cedars of Lebanon be cut for me; and my servants will join your servants, and I will pay you for your servants such wages as you set; for you know that there is no one among us who knows how to cut timber like the Sidonians."

⁷When Hiram heard the words of Solomon, he rejoiced greatly, and said, "Blessed be the Lord this day, who has given to David a wise son to be over this great people." ⁸And Hiram sent to Solomon, saying, "I have heard the message which you have sent to me; I am ready to do all you desire in the matter of cedar and cypress timber. ⁹My servants shall bring it down to the sea from Lebanon; and I will make it into rafts to go by sea to the place you direct, and I will have them broken up there, and you shall receive it; and you shall meet my wishes by providing food for my household." ¹⁰So Hiram supplied Solomon with all the timber of cedar and cypress that he desired, ¹¹while Solomon gave Hiram twenty thousand cors of wheat as food for his household, and twenty thousand cors of beaten oil. Solomon gave this to Hiram year by year. ¹²And the Lord gave Solomon wisdom, as he promised him; and there was peace between Hiram and Solomon; and the two of them made a treaty.

¹³King Solomon raised a levy of forced labour out of all Israel;

and the levy numbered thirty thousand men. ¹⁴And he sent them to
Lebanon, ten thousand a month in relays; they would be a month in
Lebanon and two months at home; Adoniram was in charge of the
levy. ¹⁵Solomon also had seventy thousand burden-bearers and
eighty thousand hewers of stone in the hill country, ¹⁶besides
Solomon's three thousand three hundred chief officers who were
over the work, who had charge of the people who carried on the
work. ¹⁷At the king's command, they quarried out great, costly
stones in order to lay the foundation of the house with dressed
stones. ¹⁸So Solomon's builders and Hiram's builders and the men
of Gebal did the hewing and prepared the timber and the stone to
build the house.

(i)

Each new chapter of this part of Kings marks a fresh start, with
little relation to what has gone before. Here we have Hiram of
Tyre, on the southern coast of modern Lebanon, responding by
means of a formal embassy to the news of Solomon's succession
to David. This Phoenician ruler had had relations with David
too; and it would help our discussion of other biblical passages
if we knew just what to make of the end of verse 1: "for Hiram
always loved David". All that 2 Samuel tells us, immediately
after its report of David's capture of Jerusalem, is simply that
"Hiram king of Tyre sent messengers to David, and cedar trees,
also carpenters and masons who built David a house" (5:11).
And there is no further word of him until this embassy to
David's son.

There are some scholars who warn us that "love" is simply a
conventional term of ancient diplomacy, denoting acceptable
or correct relations, and especially the proper behaviour of a
lesser ruler to the great king. They go on to say that when we
read of "love" for God commended in Deuteronomy, that is
simply part and parcel of the international treaty language they
detect in that book. I am not convinced of this. In our own
culture "love" is often (mis-)used in a formal, empty way; and
'friendly relations' between states can denote little more than
absence of open hostility. Yet it is altogether too cynical not to

be open to richer use of this language even between monarchs and statesmen.

(ii)

Solomon's first message to Hiram develops another and very important theme of 2 Samuel—see the rich and complex chapter 7 with its intertwined topics of royal house and divine house. The son puts in a nutshell what Nathan had expressed more obliquely to his father; that David should not build a temple for God because of the military struggles in which he was embroiled. Only once peace was fully achieved could that Lord who had happily tented with his people all the way from Egypt, consent to dwell in a house.

The description of the totality of the 'pax Solomonica' is summed up (v.4) in an interesting phrase: "there is neither adversary nor misfortune". "Adversary" translates the Hebrew *satan*. On the two occasions it is used in the David story it refers to trouble from within: David himself is described as a potential *satan* within the Philistine army (1 Sam. 29:4); and Abishai's advice is spurned by David in similar terms in 2 Samuel 19:22. However, Solomon, whose very name (*shelomoh*) can be read as a play on 'peace' (*shalom*), suffers from no such mischief in the midst.

(iii)

Hiram himself must have controlled much of what we know as Lebanon. He is called "king of Tyre", which is on the coast to the south of Beirut. But his "servants" with the particular reputation for timber-working came from neighbouring Sidon (v.6) and more distant Gebal (v.18), well to the north of Beirut. Of course Phoenician skills in carpentry did not just serve architects seeking to enhance interiors with fine panelling, but were also very highly prized for ship-building. The best biblical presentation of that theme is in Ezekiel's lament over Tyre (27:3–9). It is entirely typical that Hiram in fact promises to make his deliveries by sea.

The costs of the enterprise are colossal. Hiram's household

for which food is to be supplied (vv.9-11) must be of a similar size to Solomon's own (4:22); for 60 cors per day is much the same as 20 000 cors per year. With financial arrangements of such magnitude involved, and over a period of years, it comes as little surprise that the monetary deal was required to be undergirded by nothing less than a state treaty (v.12). And I wonder if our text is not a little defensive on this issue, when it insists at the beginning of this verse that this formal alliance with a foreigner is an outcome of nothing less than the divine wisdom.

(iv)

Yet if the woodworkers were Phoenician craftsmen enjoying some reduction in taxation because Solomon had taken over responsibility for maintaining their king's household, they were assisted by a levy of Israelite labourers. The description of their organization takes us back to some questions we posed when discussing the previous chapter. What was the "all Israel" (5:13) from which they were recruited? Did it include Judah to the south, or was that area separately and more favourably managed by the son of David from Bethlehem? By contrast with their Lebanese neighbours, these Israelites were suffering extra taxation, with the time available for their normal pursuits restricted to eight months in the year—or even less; for presumably the travelling period to and from Lebanon came off their time and not the king's!

The stonemasons too were Solomon's own, set to quarry in great quantities the lovely stone which has graced Jerusalem in every period. We cannot be sure just how large the "great, costly stones" (v.17) were which they excavated and dressed. All visitors to Jerusalem in the last twenty centuries have marvelled at the colossal and finely bordered blocks weighing many tons apiece which were typical of the grand temple architecture of Herod the Great. His work was so thorough that nothing remains of what stood before on that holy site. However it is easy to believe from this description that Solomon's was hardly less splendid.

THE TEMPLE AT THE CENTRE

1 Kings 6:1

> ¹In the four hundred and eightieth year after the people of Israel came out of the land of Egypt, in the fourth year of Solomon's reign over Israel, in the month of Ziv, which is the second month, he began to build the house of the Lord.

Before we begin to look at some of the details of the following three chapters of Kings, we should pause and consider the Temple in the wider setting suggested by this verse.

(i)

Solomon's reputation is a double one in biblical tradition. He is remembered for his wisdom and for the building of the Jerusalem Temple. The account of his reign in 1 Kings chapters 2–11 does artful justice to this two-fold claim to fame. It opens with samples of his wisdom (chs. 2–4); and returns near its end to the fabled visit of the Queen of Sheba paying court to his sagacity (ch. 10). But if it both begins and ends in that theme, it has the construction of the sanctuary at its very middle and heart (chs. 5–8).

This deliberate structuring of the biblical presentation of David's son has been successful; this is how Solomon is widely remembered. The propaganda has worked. And yet the artifice in this depiction is far from completely concealed. The sub-theme of these central chapters is Solomon's construction of a whole series of buildings, some of which were larger and took longer to build than Yahweh's "house". All this is conceded, yet almost as an aside within the detailed reports of the Temple and its furnishings.

(ii)

The opening verse of 1 Kings 6 makes another sort of claim for the importance of Solomon building the Temple. In addition to the normal and matter-of-fact dating of the start of this great project in terms of the second month of the fourth year of the king's reign (and that is all that the parallel note in 2 Chron.

3:1–2 says), the first words of the chapter measure the Temple on a scale that starts with the Exodus.

The 480 years it mentions is a round figure, and not— or not necessarily—a historical one. We may be reasonably confident that the early years of Solomon's reign belong roughly in the middle of the tenth century B.C.—not far from 950 B.C. Yet it would be a misreading and misuse of this note to deduce that the deliverance from Egypt happened somewhere in the latter part of the fifteenth century before Christ. That has to be argued on different grounds.

This note seems to me to be making two rather different points. The one is clearly a positive one; that the building of the Temple permitted a quality of life for Israel that represented a certain fulfilment. To a new degree, the promise implied by and inaugurated in the liberation from Pharaoh could be more fully enjoyed. The other point, however, I find harder to evaluate. Four hundred and eighty years are a long time! Is the negative suggestion being made that the fulfilment was long delayed? Or should we understand that a figure which is the multiple of two numbers which in themselves are round and significant (12 × 40) marks a suitably grand period for the maturation of God's plans, remembering that in his sight "a thousand years ... are but as yesterday" when they are past (Psalm 90:4)?

(iii)

The whole structure of the great speeches in the books from Joshua to Kings, those books which Jewish tradition calls the 'Former Prophets', echoes this reading of our note. Solomon's long prayer in 1 Kings chapter 8, offered at the dedication of this sanctuary, ends a series of orations that includes the farewell of Joshua (Josh. chs. 23–24), the great speech of Samuel (1 Sam. ch. 12), and the oracle of Nathan (2 Sam. ch. 7). When we compare these with the long speeches in Deuteronomy by Moses through whom the *Torah* was mediated, we notice that each major speech in the succeeding books was associated with another major divine blessing: the land of Israel (Joshua); the institution of kingship (Samuel); the validation of David

and his house (Nathan); and finally the Jerusalem Temple
(Solomon). Together with the Mosaic expression of the divine
will in the *Torah* or "Law", these varied following institutions
created the conditions for Israel's full life in her land.

So much for the argument from the literary structure of the
Deuteronomistic History. The link between Exodus and Solomon's achievement can be described another way as well. The
Book of Exodus, after charting Israel's escape from Egypt,
moves immediately to the disclosure of God's will for his
people: *first* the fundamentals of behaviour before him and in
the community (Exod. chs. 19–24), and *second* the details of
sanctuary and worship and of his presence within the congregation (Exod. chs. 25ff.).

Links have long been noted between the Solomonic building
described in Kings and Chronicles and the portable shrine
prescribed through Moses and detailed in Exodus chapters
25ff. It has seemed as if the one was an idealization of the other.
Even the role in Exodus 31ff. of the skilled craftsmen Bezalel
and Oholiab is strikingly reminiscent of the second Hiram of 1
Kings chapter 7. Twelve times forty years on from the Exodus,
Moses' ideal for worship was becoming a reality.

(iv)

All we have so far said surely represents the loudest voice to
sound through 1 Kings chapters 5–8 concerning Solomon's
achievement. And yet we can also detect an ambivalence in this
note about the 480 years. It reminds me also of part of Amos's
protest against confidence in ritual as protection against guilt:
"Did you bring to me sacrifices and offerings the forty years in
the wilderness, O house of Israel?" (Amos 5:25). For forty years
Israel had managed without some of the mechanics of religion—and some of her prophets even described that period as
her honeymoon with Yahweh. For twelve times as long, Israel
had survived without the Temple in Jerusalem. Had it all been
anxious waiting? I wonder whether this note, which may well
not have been part of the original text of Kings (why then would
it have been dropped from the Chronicler's version in 2 Chron.

3:1?), was not added as a quiet protest against the assumption that this royal Temple was the only blessing required to bring fulfilment to Israel. We shall certainly see other evidence in these chapters of more than one voice.

BUILDING THE TEMPLE

1 Kings 6:2–38

²The house which King Solomon built for the Lord was sixty cubits long, twenty cubits wide, and thirty cubits high. ³The vestibule in front of the nave of the house was twenty cubits long, equal to the width of the house, and ten cubits deep in front of the house. ⁴And he made for the house windows with recessed frames. ⁵He also built a structure against the wall of the house, running round the walls of the house, both the nave and the inner sanctuary; and he made side chambers all around. ⁶The lowest storey was five cubits broad, the middle one was six cubits broad, and the third was seven cubits broad; for around the outside of the house he made offsets on the wall in order that the supporting beams should not be inserted into the walls of the house.

⁷When the house was built, it was with stone prepared at the quarry; so that neither hammer nor axe nor any tool of iron was heard in the temple, while it was being built.

⁸The entrance for the lowest storey was on the south side of the house; and one went up by stairs to the middle storey, and from the middle storey to the third. ⁹So he built the house, and finished it; and he made the ceiling of the house of beams and planks of cedar. ¹⁰He built the structure against the whole house, each storey five cubits high, and it was joined to the house with timbers of cedar.

¹¹Now the word of the Lord came to Solomon, ¹²"Concerning this house which you are building, if you will walk in my statutes and obey my ordinances and keep all my commandments and walk in them, then I will establish my word with you, which I spoke to David your father. ¹³And I will dwell among the children of Israel, and will not forsake my people Israel."

¹⁴So Solomon built the house, and finished it. ¹⁵He lined the walls of the house on the inside with boards of cedar; from the floor of the house to the rafters of the ceiling, he covered them on the inside with wood; and he covered the floor of the house with boards

of cypress. [16]He built twenty cubits of the rear of the house with boards of cedar from the floor to the rafters, and he built this within as an inner sanctuary, as the most holy place. [17]The house, that is, the nave in front of the inner sanctuary, was forty cubits long. [18]The cedar within the house was carved in the form of gourds and open flowers; all was cedar, no stone was seen. [19]The inner sanctuary he prepared in the innermost part of the house, to set there the ark of the covenant of the Lord. [20]The inner sanctuary was twenty cubits long, twenty cubits wide, and twenty cubits high; and he overlaid it with pure gold. He also made an altar of cedar. [21]And Solomon overlaid the inside of the house with pure gold, and he drew chains of gold across, in front of the inner sanctuary, and overlaid it with gold. [22]And he overlaid the whole house with gold, until all the house was finished. Also the whole altar that belonged to the inner sanctuary he overlaid with gold.

[23]In the inner sanctuary he made two cherubim of olivewood, each ten cubits high. [24]Five cubits was the length of one wing of the cherub, and five cubits the length of the other wing of the cherub; it was ten cubits from the tip of one wing to the tip of the other. [25]The other cherub also measured ten cubits; both cherubim had the same measure and the same form. [26]The height of one cherub was ten cubits, and so was that of the other cherub. [27]He put the cherubim in the innermost part of the house; and the wings of the cherubim were spread out so that a wing of one touched the one wall, and a wing of the other cherub touched the other wall; their other wings touched each other in the middle of the house. [28]And he overlaid the cherubim with gold.

[29]He carved all the walls of the house round about with carved figures of cherubim and palm trees and open flowers, in the inner and outer rooms. [30]The floor of the house he overlaid with gold in the inner and outer rooms.

[31]For the entrance to the inner sanctuary he made doors of olivewood; the lintel and the doorposts formed a pentagon. [32]He covered the two doors of olivewood with carvings of cherubim, palm trees, and open flowers; he overlaid them with gold, and spread gold upon the cherubim and upon the palm trees.

[33]So also he made for the entrance to the nave doorposts of olivewood, in the form of a square, [34]and two doors of cypress wood; the two leaves of the one door were folding, and the two leaves of the other door were folding. [35]On them he carved cherubim and palm trees and open flowers; and he overlaid them

with gold evenly applied upon the carved work. ³⁶He built the inner court with three courses of hewn stone and one course of cedar beams.

³⁷In the fourth year the foundation of the house of the Lord was laid, in the month of Ziv. ³⁸And in the eleventh year, in the month of Bul, which is the eighth month, the house was finished in all its parts, and according to all its specifications. He was seven years in building it.

(i)

This is not an easy chapter to study closely. Its writer or (better) writers have taken considerable trouble to satisfy themselves about, and establish for posterity, the details of this sacred structure. Yet some of their technical Hebrew vocabulary is strange to us; and so the translation above is often a makeshift, and merely a best, attempt. To say all this is not just to pluck an explanation out of the skies for the difficulties in the passage. There are a few elements of more objective evidence.

The notes about dating at the beginning and end of the chapter (except for the 480 years) point in different directions at the same time. "Ziv" and "Bul" are the old Canaanite and Israelite names for months of the year, meaning 'flowers' (spring-time) and 'moisture' (the autumn rains); and they could well have figured in an official entry in Solomon's royal archives. Yet the explanations in verses 1 and 38 that these are the second and eighth months belongs to the period of Judah's exile in Babylon, when the Books of Kings themselves began to be written. It was only then that the people of the Bible adopted the Babylonian calendar, and the beginning of the year was moved from late summer/autumn to spring, just as in Roman times our year's beginning was moved to January from March, so making the names 'September' (seventh month) to 'December' (tenth month) rather odd.

Other evidence of the complexity of this tradition is provided by the different versions of it which we possess. First of all 2 Chronicles 3:1–13 provides only about half the detail found in our verses 1–28. Has the Chronicler a shortened version; or does he preserve the not-yet-expanded one? Most of the differences concern two matters: the decoration of the Temple interior apart from the holy of holies (the inner sanctuary, v. 16) and the structure that immediately surrounded the main Temple building and abutted on it. Did the Chronicler pare down his version to the bare essentials of the most holy place? Or did someone supplement the account after the fall of Jerusalem and destruction of the Temple, so producing our version in Kings lest memory of once-familiar details should fade? The fact that even the ancient Greek version of this chapter is without verses 11–13 and 18 makes me incline to a theory of gradual supplementation. This will help explain why some details are less clear than they might be.

(ii)

One of the interesting details found only in the Kings version concerns the stone used in the building (v.7). RSV makes less clear than it might that the material specified in the Hebrew is 'whole' or 'complete' stone. If we take time to follow this theme, we obtain an instructive example of the Bible's own interpretation of biblical texts.

Solomon's workers were clearly held to have paid attention to Moses' instructions in Deuteronomy 27:5–6:

> ... you shall build an altar to the Lord your God, an altar of stones; you shall lift up no iron tool upon them. You shall build an altar to the Lord your God of whole stones ....

Reporting on the earlier altar constructed for Joshua, Joshua 8:31 speaks of "an altar of unhewn [whole] stones, upon which no man has lifted an iron tool".

Deuteronomy 27 and Joshua 8 remain in the spirit of the earlier prescription in Exodus 20:25—"if you make me an altar of stone, you shall not build it of hewn stones; for if you wield your tool upon it you profane it". They all envisage what Scots call a 'dry stane' construction from materials picked up in their natural state. I suspect this was more than just the consequence of a taboo against alien imports like iron for the tools. But verse 7 in Kings 'squares its conscience' in a rather literalistic way. It interprets Deuteronomy 27:5–6 quoted above as banning only _on-site dressing_ of the blocks, which would have represented a noisy profanation of the sanctity of the place. (Interestingly the added note in verse 18 claims that once all the wood panelling was in place, none of this stone was to be seen.)

One's view of whether such flexibility in interpretation is a good or a bad thing may depend in this instance on whether (in terms of our last chapter) one thinks Solomon's Temple was a long-awaited fulfilment or an institution that was done without to no ill effect for more than 480 years.

(iii)

It is on the holiest part of the shrine that the Chronicler concentrates his attention (in this chapter it is not reached until v. 19). This occupied the rear third of the central building of the Temple; that is the part most distant from its entrance. Its space was a perfect cube with a side of some ten metres. Its furniture, which of course was not regularly seen, was a cedar altar overlaid with gold, and above it the two cherubim. Despite all that we have learned to call 'cherubic', whether from Botticelli or from numerous decorators of baroque churches, these substantial carved figures with outspread wings touching each other were winged sphinxes filling and so dominating much of the upper half of the cubic space (see 2 Chron. 3:11–13 and here, vv. 23ff.).

Their name ("cherubim") was Mesopotamian; and there it referred to a 'genie' who was both adviser to the great gods and also advocate for the faithful. Several biblical texts envisage the invisible Yahweh as riding them or enthroned upon them (_eg_ Ps. 99:1). When we come to discuss chapter 12 we shall see that this form of 'icon' or 'image' was apparently acceptable in Jerusalem, while the idea of Yahweh riding on a bull's back was not.

It was quite precisely here that the Lord chose to "dwell among the children of Israel" according to 1 Kings 6:13.

OTHER ROYAL BUILDINGS

1 Kings 7:1–12

¹Solomon was building his own house thirteen years, and he finished his entire house.

²He built the House of the Forest of Lebanon; its length was a hundred cubits, and its breadth fifty cubits, and its height thirty cubits, and it was built upon three rows of cedar pillars, with cedar beams upon the pillars. ³And it was covered with cedar above the chambers that were upon the forty-five pillars, fifteen in each row. ⁴There were window frames in three rows, and window opposite window in three tiers. ⁵All the doorways and windows had square frames, and window was opposite window in three tiers.

⁶And he made the Hall of Pillars; its length was fifty cubits, and its breadth thirty cubits; there was a porch in front with pillars, and a canopy before them.

⁷And he made the Hall of the Throne where he was to pronounce judgment, even the Hall of Judgment; it was finished with cedar from floor to rafters.

⁸His own house where he was to dwell, in the other court back of the hall, was of like workmanship. Solomon also made a house like this hall for Pharaoh's daughter whom he had taken in marriage.

⁹All these were made of costly stones, hewn according to measure, sawed with saws, back and front, even from the foundation to the coping, and from the court of the house of the Lord to the great court. ¹⁰The foundation was of costly stones, huge stones, stones of eight and ten cubits. ¹¹And above were costly stones, hewn according to measurement, and cedar. ¹²The great court had three courses of hewn stone round about, and a course of cedar beams; so had the inner court of the house of the Lord, and the vestibule of the house.

(i)

We have already drawn attention to the rather odd setting of this further and very important construction report. It follows a formal conclusion to the building of the sanctuary (6:38), but is itself followed by the story of additional temple details which are presented as if no break had occurred. There is obviously some evidence for supposing a degree of embarrassment at some stage in the tradition that Solomon had spent 13 years building his own house, but only seven building the house of the Lord. I take it that the Chronicler both recognizes and attempts to neutralize this tricky point when he abbreviates the whole issue in 2 Chronicles 8:1 to the words:

> At the end of twenty years, in which Solomon had built the house of the Lord and his own house . . .

On the other hand the erection of these several fine buildings which this first quarter of 1 Kings 7 records must have contributed handsomely to the reputation for substance and even magnificence which is an important part of the Solomonic tradition.

(ii)

Five structures are detailed in almost as many verses (2–8). However only their official names and their principal dimensions are provided; and we are unfortunately left quite ignorant of the relationships of these structures to each other and to the "house of the Lord". Each may have been free-standing; or some or all may have been sections of a more extensive structure. No certain ground-plan of the whole complex can be drawn on the basis of this chapter. Nor is other evidence readily to hand, whether biblical or not. That leads us at least to an important negative conclusion: this part of the chapter is not concerned with technical precision or architectural history.

The so-called "House of the Forest of Lebanon" we meet again a little later in the Solomon story in 1 Kings 10:17, 21 (which is paralleled in 2 Chron. 9:16, 20), and nowhere else in the Bible. There the richness of its furnishings is specified in a little greater detail; and talk of vessels distinct from Solomon's own suggests it may have been the ceremonial reception or banqueting hall. Since cedar-wood is a regular component in these buildings, the name of the hall will suggest more than just the panelling of its interior by cedar. Perhaps the Forest of Lebanon was depicted in some way, by paint or tapestry. It may be the inspiration of similar decoration in Jerusalem's Dome of the Rock.

As for the Hall of Pillars, it is referred to nowhere else by this name. The name tells us very little, for pillars were a feature of neighbouring halls as well. All we can note in passing from it is that it was less than a third of the size of Lebanon Forest Hall.

The next stop on our quick tour is a third formal chamber, called variously the Throne Room or the Judgment Hall. The related Hebrew verb (*shaphat*) and noun (*mishpat*) are often discussed by scholars, and I have referred to the discussion in connection with chapter 3 above, and at a few points in my treatment of the Book of Judges. Interest centres on whether the principal component of the word is 'rule/govern' or 'judge/ judgment/justice'. To a considerable extent the choice is a false one for the biblical period, and represents really the specialized development of larger modern states with their distinction between judicial and legislative functions.

In the more intimate and also perhaps more conservative societies of the biblical period all such responsibility lay with the king. We could say that as judge he answered appeals according to what he thought fair and right, *ie* what seemed appropriate policy; and that as ruler he pursued a policy in tune with his legal decisions. The throne was also the judgment seat. This impossibility of separating out in any consistent or final way the responsibilities of the biblical king is also one of the grounds for a Christian believer's ultimate confidence. God's 'judgment' is not distinct from, but is a part of, his 'rule' or 'reign' or 'kingdom'. If God's kingdom is as Jesus proclaimed it, then his justice and judgment are consistent with that too.

Solomon's own residence (v.8) and another for his Egyptian wife are simply said to have shared the quality of "this" Hall, which presumably means the Judgment Hall. Everything in this part of the chapter, briefly stated though it is, points to the fact that the house of the great lady was part of the same complex of buildings. Since this is so, the Chronicler's attitude to her new residence (2 Chron. 8:11) is based more on prejudice against her presence in Jerusalem at all, than on good reasoning. If she should not remain in David's former house in the lower city because the sacred ark had been brought there, why bring her to a new complex of buildings one of which was the new and permanent home of the ark?

(iii)

This brief report of the main structures within Solomon's new 'acropolis' for Jerusalem may not contain enough detail for us to sketch the ground-plan of the whole area; but it does help us to evaluate the new Temple rather better. It is clear from the dimensions that are provided for the several distinct structures, that in size at least the new shrine was only a modest element within the whole complex. It may not have been quite as tiny as Queen Margaret's Chapel within the several separate buildings that make up the Castle that dominates the skyline of much of modern Edinburgh. Yet equally it did not command Jerusalem like our medieval cathedrals and abbey churches. Its successor structures were different: the Temple of Herod the Great was, and Omar's magnificent Dome of the Rock is, an imposing public building. Solomon's Temple was more of a royal chapel, an adjunct to the palace, simply one of the buildings of state. Although they refer to another place, we might recall Amaziah's words as he warned Amos out of Bethel: "it is the king's sanctuary, and it is a temple of the kingdom" (Amos 7:13).

There are parallels in plenty, in the world of the ancient Near East and elsewhere, for the king's palace having privileged access to the main shrine. Official theology, in the Bible too, portrayed the king as a divine agent. However the architectural symbolism which our text appears to allude to almost presents Solomon as Yahweh's landlord rather than his tenant.

HIRAM THE CRAFTSMAN I—TEXT

1 Kings 7:13-51

13And King Solomon sent and brought Hiram from Tyre. 14He was the son of a widow of the tribe of Naphtali, and his father was a man of Tyre, a worker in bronze; and he was full of wisdom, understanding, and skill, for making any work in bronze. He came to King Solomon, and did all his work.

¹⁵He cast two pillars of bronze. Eighteen cubits was the height of one pillar, and a line of twelve cubits measured its circumference; it was hollow, and its thickness was four fingers; the second pillar was the same. ¹⁶He also made two capitals of molten bronze, to set upon the tops of the pillars; the height of the one capital was five cubits, and the height of the other capital was five cubits. ¹⁷Then he made two nets of chequer work with wreaths of chain work for the capitals upon the tops of the pillars; a net for the one capital, and a net for the other capital. ¹⁸Likewise he made pomegranates; in two rows round about upon the one network, to cover the capital that was upon the top of the pillar; and he did the same with the other capital. ¹⁹Now the capitals that were upon the tops of the pillars in the vestibule were of lily-work, four cubits. ²⁰The capitals were upon the two pillars and also above the rounded projection which was beside the network; there were two hundred pomegranates, in two rows round about; and so with the other capital. ²¹He set up the pillars at the vestibule of the temple; he set up the pillar on the south and called its name Jachin; and he set up the pillar on the north and called its name Boaz. ²²And upon the tops of the pillars was lily-work. Thus the work of the pillars was finished.

²³Then he made the molten sea; it was round, ten cubits from brim to brim, and five cubits high, and a line of thirty cubits measured its circumference. ²⁴Under its brim were gourds, for thirty cubits, compassing the sea round about; the gourds were in two rows, cast with it when it was cast. ²⁵It stood upon twelve oxen, three facing north, three facing west, three facing south, and three facing east; the sea was set upon them, and all their hinder parts were inward. ²⁶Its thickness was a handbreadth; and its brim was made like the brim of a cup, like the flower of a lily; it held two thousand baths.

²⁷He also made the ten stands of bronze; each stand was four cubits long, four cubits wide, and three cubits high. ²⁸This was the construction of the stands: they had panels, and the panels were set in the frames ²⁹and on the panels that were set in the frames were lions, oxen, and cherubim. Upon the frames, both above and below the lions and oxen, there were wreaths of bevelled work. ³⁰Moreover each stand had four bronze wheels and axles of bronze; and at the four corners were supports for a laver. The supports were cast, with wreaths at the side of each. ³¹Its opening was within a crown

which projected upward one cubit; its opening was round, as a pedestal is made, a cubit and a half deep. At its opening there were carvings; and its panels were square, not round. ³²And the four wheels were underneath the panels; the axles of the wheels were of one piece with the stands; and the height of a wheel was a cubit and a half. ³³The wheels were made like a chariot wheel; their axles, their rims, their spokes, and their hubs, were all cast. ³⁴There were four supports at the four corners of each stand; the supports were of one piece with the stands. ³⁵And on the top of the stand there was a round band half a cubit high; and on the top of the stand its stays and its panels were of one piece with it. ³⁶And on the surfaces of its stays and on its panels, he carved cherubim, lions, and palm trees, according to the space of each, with wreaths round about. ³⁷After this manner he made the ten stands; all of them were cast alike, of the same measure and the same form.

³⁸And he made ten lavers of bronze; each laver held forty baths, each laver measured four cubits, and there was a laver for each of the ten stands. ³⁹And he set the stands, five on the south side of the house, and five on the north side of the house; and he set the sea on the southeast corner of the house.

⁴⁰Hiram also made the pots, the shovels, and the basins. So Hiram finished all the work that he did for King Solomon on the house of the Lord: ⁴¹the two pillars, the two bowls of the capitals that were on the tops of the pillars, and the two networks to cover the two bowls of the capitals that were on the tops of the pillars; ⁴²and the four hundred pomegranates for the two networks, two rows of pomegranates for each network, to cover the two bowls of the capitals that were upon the pillars; ⁴³the ten stands, and the ten lavers upon the stands; ⁴⁴and the one sea, and the twelve oxen underneath the sea.

⁴⁵Now the pots, the shovels, and the basins, all these vessels in the house of the Lord, which Hiram made for King Solomon, were of burnished bronze. ⁴⁶In the plain of the Jordan the king cast them, in the clay ground between Succoth and Zarethan. ⁴⁷And Solomon left all the vessels unweighed, because there were so many of them; the weight of the bronze was not found out.

⁴⁸So Solomon made all the vessels that were in the house of the Lord: the golden altar, the golden table for the bread of the Presence, ⁴⁹the lampstands of pure gold, five on the south side and five on the north, before the inner sanctuary; the flowers, the lamps, and the tongs, of gold; ⁵⁰the cups, snuffers, basins, dishes for

incense, and firepans, of pure gold; and the sockets of gold, for the doors of the innermost part of the house, the most holy place, and for the doors of the nave of the temple.

⁵¹Thus all the work that King Solomon did on the house of the Lord was finished. And Solomon brought in the things which David his father had dedicated, the silver, the gold, and the vessels, and stored them in the treasuries of the house of the Lord.

HIRAM THE CRAFTSMAN II—COMMENTARY

Kings 7:13–51 (*cont'd*)

(i)

Our first surprise as we move from the brief listing of royal buildings to a much fuller account of the casting of many metal objects is the identity of the master metalworker. Chapter 5 described a relationship between Solomon and one Hiram who was "king of Tyre", who had had dealings with David his father and who apparently dealt with Solomon as an equal. And now we have Solomon summoning a Hiram from Tyre who seems to be an agent rather than an equal. Certainly no surprise is shown in the text at this second principal actor with the same name and from the same place: he is simply introduced as son of a Tyrian metalworker by a woman from Naphtali in northern Israel. The Chronicler, who spells the basic name differently, calls the king Huram and the craftsman Huram-abi, for what the distinction is worth.

He is introduced with the highest recommendation, described in superlatives (v.14): "full of wisdom, understanding, and skill, for making any work in bronze". In passing we should be reminded that the Hebrew words for "wisdom" and "understanding" are not at all confined to intellectual capabilities, but are used equally to describe practical craftsmanship. Even the distinction between 'craft' and 'art' is a fairly modern one— remember Leonardo the military engineer as well as Leonardo the painter.

We already noted in an earlier chapter some of the similarities

between Hiram's introduction here and the divine appointment of Bezalel and Oholiab in Exodus chapter 31. Oholiab is
linked with Dan, part of the north like Naphtali. (And the
Chronicler in fact calls him Huram-abi, son of a Danite!) Then
Bezalel's divine attributes lie in the same direction as Hiram's,
even if superlatively further:

> I have filled him with the Spirit of God, with ability and intelli-
> gence, with knowledge and all craftsmanship, to devise artistic
> designs, to work in gold, silver, and bronze, in cutting stones for
> setting, and in carving wood, for work in every craft.
>
> (Exod. 31:3-5)

It may well be that we are dealing here with a complex
development of tradition. Yet it does have a basis in quite
remarkable technological fact. The casting of some of the
objects described in this chapter was an unusually skilled operation—and one for which archaeology of the ancient Near East
has supplied little parallel. That should not persuade even the
most critical reader to doubt the fundamentals of the account.
To put it crudely: what is described could hardly have been
imagined had it not been known!

(ii)

Many of the details of the bronze objects are unclear; this part
of the chapter, like elements in 1 Kings 6, seems to have been
drafted in a complicated way. However some of the issues can
be presented fairly simply.

The monumental pillars (7:15-22) stood outside and in front
of the Temple. Evidence from similar columns elsewhere in the
ancient Near East suggests that smoking fire may have burned
continually from them. It may be that perpetual fire and smoke
from the top of these pillars was associated with the desert
tradition of early times; of the pillar of fire by night and the pillar
of cloud by day.

As for their names, Jachin and Boaz, the most attractive

account known to me proposes that each is the first word of the short Hebrew inscriptions on the respective pillars. On the basis of many verses in the Psalms using these words, it is suggested that Jachin began the line, "He will establish the throne of David", while Boaz opened the expression, "In the strength of Yahweh shall the king rejoice"—both affirming that particular presence of God with the king, and through him with the people, which was also symbolized by the perpetual flame on their heads.

As if the job of casting these was not enough, the creation of the molten "sea" as thick as the breadth of a hand and supported on a dozen bronze oxen was a technical triumph (vv.23-26). To be the provider of his people's water was an important role of the oriental monarch; and, beyond this, to be guarantor of the rains was an important function of his god. Yet this huge reservoir, which seems to have been set too high for the priests' ritual ablutions (despite 2 Chron. 4:6), may have symbolized even more. Yamm (or "Sea") is one of the princes vanquished by Lord Baal in Canaanite myth; and this "sea" is borne aloft by twelve oxen, the bull being part of the imagery closely associated with Baal. However, this iconography in the Jerusalem Temple is not just alien and Canaanite; for part of creation according to the beginning of Genesis consisted in God's containment of the primordial chaos waters. The great model "sea" reminded worshippers of that divine power.

The description offered (vv.27-39) of the ten "lavers" on their wheeled and hence movable stands is much more detailed, although several of these details are less clear to a Hebrew reader than the straightforward rendering of RSV suggests. Happily in their case the archaeology of the eastern Mediterranean has supplied some useful comparisons. They were for ritual washing; and the closing comment about their placing (v.39) suggests some association with the great "sea".

Much of the foregoing has been described in much greater detail than the corresponding passage in Chronicles offers. However the concluding accounts of smaller miscellaneous bronze utensils (vv.40-47) and the more precious gold-work, some of it a legacy from David (vv.48–51), reappear with hardly a difference in wording in 2 Chronicles 4:11–5:1.

If it were not for the similar and rather puzzling comment which we shall meet in 1 Kings 15:15, we could easily suppose as we read verse 51 that 'David's dedications', housed in a temporary sanctuary up to this point, were simply relocated to join these products of Solomon's munificence and Hiram's skill. Yet the later passage (which concerns King Asa) may suggest some other custom more familiar to the original readers than to ourselves.

ARK INSTALLED AND LORD'S THRONE

1 Kings 8:1–13

[1]Then Solomon assembled the elders of Israel and all the heads of the tribes, the leaders of the fathers' houses of the people of Israel, before King Solomon in Jerusalem, to bring up the ark of the covenant of the Lord out of the city of David, which is Zion. [2]And all the men of Israel assembled to King Solomon at the feast in the month Ethanim, which is the seventh month. [3]And all the elders of Israel came, and the priests took up the ark. [4]And they brought up the ark of the Lord, the tent of meeting, and all the holy vessels that were in the tent; the priests and the Levites brought them up. [5]And King Solomon and all the congregation of Israel, who had assembled before him, were with him before the the ark, sacrificing so many sheep and oxen that they could not be counted or numbered. [6]Then the priests brought the ark of the covenant of the Lord to its place, in the inner sanctuary of the house, in the most holy place, underneath the wings of the cherubim. [7]For the cherubim spread out their wings over the place of the ark, so that the cherubim made a covering above the ark and its poles. [8]And the poles were so long that the ends of the poles were seen from the holy place before the inner sanctuary; but they could not be seen from outside; and they are there to this day. [9]There was nothing in the ark except the two tables of stone which Moses put there at Horeb, where the Lord made a covenant with the people of Israel, when they came out of the land of Egypt. [10]And when the priests came out of the holy place, a cloud filled the house of the Lord, [11]so that the priests could

not stand to minister because of the cloud; for the glory of the Lord
filled the house of the Lord.

¹²Then Solomon said,
"The Lord has set the sun in the heavens,
 but has said that he would dwell in thick darkness.
¹³I have built thee an exalted house,
 a place for thee to dwell in for ever."

(i)

The final addition to the Temple before its dedication is the
"ark of the covenant". The report of its transfer to this new
royal and divine acropolis from the lower "city of David" is
described almost identically in verses 1–11 of this chapter and in
2 Chronicles 5:2–14; the Chronicler simply inserts two verses
about singers and trumpeters towards the end of the account
(11–13). However the ark is far from being simply a last or even
climactic piece of equipment. Its removal from David's city to
Solomon's new upper quarter itself constituted the change of
the national religious centre. As such, it was effected in the
presence of a fully representative selection of the leadership of
Israel (v.1).

Although this reminds us of the large company David took
with him (2 Sam. 6) to witness the transfer of the ark to
Jerusalem in the first place, the accounts are not quite parallel.
Then a new cart was used; here the ark is carried by the priests,
in a manner which reminds us of the ark's ceremonial crossing
of the Jordan to the land of promise (Josh. 3–4). Priests carry
the ark itself; and their associates, the Levites, are entrusted
with the tent that had housed it and its holy utensils. (Admittedly there is some tension between this division of labour and the
one worked out in some detail in Num. 3.)

(ii)

The ark does not make as many appearances in the earlier story of Israel as would seem to be warranted by its importance within those traditions where it does figure. The scattered witness to its role is hard to systematize. There appear in fact to be two principal components: the *first* is more prominent in some traditions, the *second* in others.

In the *first*, *ie* the traditions associated with Deuteronomy, and that of course includes Kings, the ark is foremost a box, a container. This is emphasized in 1 Kings 8:9, which insists that only the two stone tables inscribed with the ten commandments are to be found in it. (In passing we might note that Hebrews 9:4 follows a rather different tradition which held that other relics of the Exodus period were there too.) Indeed it is from this quintessential summary of the divine will that the sacred container derives its usual name; for in Deuteronomy "covenant" refers to the ten commandments, God's own immediate revelation of his will to all Israel at the holy mountain of Horeb—as opposed to his *Torah* or "law" which he provided more gradually, and through the mediation of Moses when Israel felt hazarded by his immediate presence.

Yet in other traditions it is precisely the potent *presence* of Lord Yahweh which is realized in his ark. That is why even a god falls on his face before it (1 Sam. 5:2–4), and the wretched Uzzah perishes for touching it (2 Sam. 6:6–7). That is why, when it is moved, Moses addresses himself as if to God (Num. 10:35–36). In fact a slightly closer look at what the Bible has to say about the loss of the ark to the Philistines will help explain one of the other details of our passages. For example, we read in Psalm 78:59–61:

> When God heard, he was full of wrath,
>   and he utterly rejected Israel.
> He forsook his dwelling at Shiloh,
>   the tent where he dwelt among men,
> and delivered his *power* to captivity,
>   his *glory* to the hand of the foe.

In similar vein, the wife of Phinehas responds to the same crisis by calling her baby Ichabod (*ie* Where-is-the-glory?), saying:

"The glory has departed from Israel, for the ark of God has been captured" (1 Sam. 4:21-22).

"Glory" often seems to us modern users of the word to be a warm but rather unspecific idea. It is a word which we use, but would be hard pressed to define. However, for an important biblical tradition it is quite intimately and precisely associated with God's ark. Once that was in its place in the new shrine, "the glory of the Lord filled the house of the Lord" (v.11).

The relationship of Yahweh and his ark was pictured in another way too, with the ark (and sometimes the cherubim above it) thought of as his throne or his footstool. His presence was not so much in the ark as invisibly above it. We shall return to this when discussing Jeroboam and his calves. Responding to its loss when Jerusalem fell to Babylon, Jeremiah promises that in future Jerusalem itself "shall be called the throne of the Lord", while the ark "shall not come to mind, or be remembered, or missed" (3:16-17). Biblical ideas, even those concerning central elements of religion, were far from static; and we shall see further evidence of this in 1 Kings 8.

(iii)

Solomon's first reported words on this solemn occasion (vv.12-13) are also quite distinct from the main body of what he has to say (vv.14-53). In fact the Greek version of our book places them after rather than before his lengthy blessings and prayers. They are poetic lines (indeed the Greek ascribes them to "The Book of the Song") and so compact that they are hard to interpret.

Verse 12 is an important statement of God's creativity. Over against the many peoples who have always worshipped the life-giving sun as itself divine, Solomon acknowledges that even its power and heat and light are derived from Yahweh; yet Yahweh's own choice is to shun the light and live in darkness, where he cannot be glimpsed, or comprehended, or fully known. I find it hard to decide whether Solomon's own building for this Yahweh (v.13) is fully in accord with God's wishes, or whether the king feels that God deserves better than

that which he claims for himself. Is the "exalted" (or "princely")
house he has built for God an infringement of his own modesty?
Or does Solomon think of it as a "sanctuary" for even God
himself: where he may expect to live for ever without unwelcome intrusion?

SOLOMON'S PRAYERS I—TEXT

1 Kings 8:14–50

14Then the king faced about, and blessed all the assembly of Israel,
while all the assembly of Israel stood. 15And he said, "Blessed be the
Lord, the God of Israel, who with his hand has fulfilled what he
promised with his mouth to David my father, saying, 16"Since the
day that I brought my people Israel out of Egypt, I chose no city in
all the tribes of Israel in which to build a house, that my name might
be there; but I chose David to be over my people Israel.' 17Now it
was in the heart of David my father to build a house for the name of
the Lord, the God of Israel. 18But the Lord said to David my father,
'Whereas it was in your heart to build a house for my name, you did
well that it was in your heart, 19nevertheless you shall not build the
house, but your son who shall be born to you shall build the house
for my name.' 20Now the Lord has fulfilled his promise which he
made; for I have risen in the place of David my father, and sit on the
throne of Israel, as the Lord promised, and I have built the house
for the name of the Lord, the God of Israel. 21And there I have
provided a place for the ark, in which is the covenant of the Lord
which he made with our fathers, when he brought them out of the
land of Egypt."

22Then Solomon stood before the altar of the Lord in the
presence of all the assembly of Israel, and spread forth his hands
toward heaven; 23and said, "O Lord, God of Israel, there is no God
like thee, in heaven above or on earth beneath, keeping covenant
and showing steadfast love to thy servants who walk before thee
with all their heart; 24who hast kept with thy servant David my
father what thou didst declare to him; yea, thou didst speak with
thy mouth, and with thy hand hast fulfilled it this day. 25Now
therefore, O Lord, God of Israel, keep with thy servant David my
father what thou has promised him, saying, 'There shall never fail
you a man before me to sit upon the throne of Israel, if only your

sons take heed to their way, to walk before me as you have walked before me.' ²⁶Now therefore, O God of Israel, let thy word be confirmed, which thou hast spoken to thy servant David my father.

²⁷"But will God indeed dwell on the earth? Behold, heaven and the highest heaven cannot contain thee; how much less this house which I have built! ²⁸Yet have regard to the prayer of thy servant and to his supplication, O Lord my God, hearkening to the cry and to the prayer which thy servant prays before thee this day; ²⁹that thy eyes may be open night and day toward this house, the place of which thou hast said, 'My name shall be there,' that thou mayest hearken to the prayer which thy servant offers toward this place. ³⁰And hearken thou to the supplication of thy servant and of thy people Israel, when they pray toward this place; yea, hear thou in heaven thy dwelling place; and when thou hearest, forgive.

³¹"If a man sins against his neighbour and is made to take an oath, and comes and swears his oath before thine altar in this house, ³²then hear thou in heaven, and act, and judge thy servants, condemning the guilty by bringing his conduct upon his own head, and vindicating the righteous by rewarding him according to his righteousness.

³³"When thy people Israel are defeated before the enemy because they have sinned against thee, if they turn again to thee, and acknowledge thy name, and pray and make supplication to thee in this house; ³⁴then hear thou in heaven, and forgive the sin of thy people Israel, and bring them again to the land which thou gavest to their fathers.

³⁵"When heaven is shut up and there is no rain because they have sinned against thee, if they pray toward this place, and acknowledge thy name, and turn from their sin, when thou dost afflict them, ³⁶then hear thou in heaven, and forgive the sin of thy servants, thy people Israel, when thou dost teach them the good way in which they should walk; and grant rain upon thy land, which thou hast given to thy people as an inheritance.

³⁷"If there is famine in the land, if there is pestilence or blight or mildew or locust or caterpillar; if their enemy besieges them in any of their cities; whatever plague, whatever sickness there is; ³⁸whatever prayer, whatever supplication is made by any man or by all thy people Israel, each knowing the affliction of his own heart and stretching out his hands toward this house; ³⁹then hear thou in heaven thy dwelling place, and forgive, and act, and render to each whose heart thou knowest, according to all his ways (for thou, thou

only, knowest the hearts of all the children of men); [40]that they may fear thee all the days that they live in the land which thou gavest to our fathers.

[41]"Likewise when a foreigner, who is not of thy people Israel, comes from a far country for thy name's sake [42](for they shall hear of thy great name, and thy mighty hand, and of thy outstretched arm), when he comes and prays toward this house, [43]hear thou in heaven thy dwelling place, and do according to all for which the foreigner calls to thee; in order that all the peoples of the earth may know thy name and fear thee, as do thy people Israel, and that they may know that this house which I have built is called by thy name.

[44]"If thy people go out to battle against their enemy, by whatever way thou shalt send them, and they pray to the Lord toward the city which thou hast chosen and the house which I have built for thy name, [45]then hear thou in heaven their prayer and their supplication, and maintain their cause.

[46]"If they sin against thee—for there is no man who does not sin—and thou art angry with them, and dost give them to an enemy, so that they are carried away captive to the land of the enemy, far off or near; [47]yet if they lay it to heart in the land to which they have been carried captive, and repent, and make supplication to thee in the land of their captors, saying, 'We have sinned and have acted perversely and wickedly'; [48]if they repent with all their mind and with all their heart in the land of their enemies, who carried them captive, and pray to thee toward their land, which thou gavest to their fathers, the city which thou hast chosen, and the house which I have built for thy name; [49]then hear thou in heaven thy dwelling place their prayer and their supplication, and maintain their cause [50]and forgive thy people who have sinned against thee, and all their transgressions which they have committed against thee; and grant them compassion in the sight of those who carried them captive, that they may have compassion on them . . . "

SOLOMON'S PRAYERS II—COMMENTARY

1 Kings 8:14–50 (*cont'd*)

(i)

Solomon's own "glory" may have been acknowledged by Jesus (even if rated only second best when compared with "the lilies of of the field"!). But his praying is much longer than the Master recommended, although all too typical of much leadership of public worship, ancient and modern.

He opens with a formal acknowledgment or greeting to both the people and God (vv.14-21). We often think of blessing or benediction as a solemn conclusion. Yet prayers often begin by invoking God as "blessed"; and it is clear from passages like Ruth 2:4 that this religious usage had its roots in common speech, where "the Lord bless you" was a form of greeting. The extent of the blessing of God (vv.15-21) is already a token of the length of the whole prayer.

Solomon takes us back to the anticipation of his project in the story of David and of Nathan's dynastic oracle to him (2 Sam. 7), and he blesses God for having "filled with his hand what he spoke with his mouth"—I find this literal rendering of the Hebrew more striking than RSV in verse 15. There, in a bargain of typical oriental courtesy, David suggests building a "house" for God; he replies he has no need of it, but will build one for David (now in the sense of dynastic "house")—later David's heir can build one for God. Solomon is the beneficiary of the arrangement, and has now discharged his side of the business.

(ii)

In the following passage, addressed to God with hands outstretched to heaven, Solomon builds on and seeks to clarify the divine arrangement with David (vv.22-26). The precise words, "There shall never fail you a man before me . . . if only your sons take heed . . . "(v.25), are quoted from David's last words to Solomon (2:1-4), and are not actually found in Nathan's oracle. All that Nathan says to David is that his son will not be rejected like Saul, and that, "your house and your kingdom shall be made sure for ever before me; your throne shall be established for ever" (2 Sam. 7:15-16). David on his death-bed and Solomon here, want to pin God down: to find out whether "for ever" is a rhetorical superlative, or whether it really means son following father, generation after generation. Perhaps to enable God to be more specific, they accept a condition that was absent from Nathan's words: provided David's successors follow in his footsteps. (A cynical reader might observe that that gives the royal house considerable license!) Solomon, like many of us when we are asking to have something "confirmed", is actually angling for more than was first offered.

(iii)

The next few verses (27-30) are transitional. They introduce the topic of the remainder of the prayer; but their first concern is with religious orthodoxy. The close association of Yahweh and his ark (vv.1-11) could be misunderstood. Talk of Yahweh dwelling in any place on earth, however princely and however protected by dark mystery (vv.12-13), was open to misinterpretation. And so Solomon acknowledges that such forms of words do not really literally mean what they say. Not even heaven can contain God, and not even the heaven of heavens— how much less a house on earth! For this text there are gradations in the heavens; and the language may be compared with talk of Yahweh as "King of kings, and God of gods": the gods belong to heaven, and *their* God will belong in a higher place.

This place for Yahweh's name (v.29) will be a focus for devotion. The biblical idea of "name" has two main components, both of which are still real to us. The *first* is ownership: if it has my name on it, it is mine. The *second* is access: if I know someone's name, I can get in touch with him more easily. The two ideas overlap here—the Jerusalem shrine belongs to Yahweh, and the presence of his "name" there makes prayerful access to him more easy.

The image sketched in verses 29-30 reminds me of modern communications satellite technology. Two would-be communicators become linked when each is directed to the same satellite. Similarly Solomon asks God to watch the Temple in Jerusalem night and day, so that no prayer directed towards that shrine may go unheeded.

(iv)

Various situations to which God should attend are now briefly
sketched (vv.31-50). The initial situation (31-32) presumably
concerns the sort of judicial case which cannot be settled on the
evidence of third parties; the accused may come to the altar and
protest his innocence under oath, so making God the arbiter.
Swearing by God was altogether a more terrible matter then,
than the mere formality of taking the oath on the Bible is now,
in a modern courtroom.

The next situation (33-34) also involves prayer within the
shrine: supplication after defeat in battle, and prayer for the
return of the captured. However, the following verses sketch
prayer from a distance towards the Temple rather than solemn
devotion within it, or at least in its courts. Drought, famine and
blight (35-40), all held to be consequences of misbehaviour,
may be cleared by prayer *towards* the sanctuary. (Note that
sacrifice is not called for; simply supplication towards the
shrine.) The non-Israelite too (41-43) should be encouraged to
pray in this direction to Israel's God.

Gradually the geographical context is enlarged beyond the
bounds of Solomon's own people. Armies serving abroad
(44-45) can appeal towards the Temple for help. And finally
(46-50), the nation exiled for their misbehaviour may enjoy
recourse at long distance to the same divine support. And of
course it is precisely this that the Babylonian exiles, who
treasured but also developed the ancient traditions of their
people, needed to be sure of.

This point gained, we can say a last word about verses 25-26.
There too Solomon's prayer seeks to extend old promises and
old certainties to a new and perplexing foreign situation. What
was God's will once the people were exiled and a son of David
was no more on the throne?

SOLEMNITIES CONCLUDED

1 Kings 8:50-66

50" . . . and forgive thy people who have sinned against thee, and all their transgressions which they have committed against thee; and grant them compassion in the sight of those who carried them captive, that they may have compassion on them ⁵¹(for they are thy people, and thy heritage, which thou didst bring out of Egypt, from the midst of the iron furnace). ⁵²Let thy eyes be open to the supplication of thy servant, and to the supplication of thy people Israel, giving ear to them whenever they call to thee. ⁵³For thou didst separate them from among all the peoples of the earth, to be thy heritage, as thou didst declare through Moses, thy servant, when thou didst bring our fathers out of Egypt, O Lord God."

⁵⁴Now as Solomon finished offering all this prayer and supplication to the Lord, he arose from before the altar of the Lord, where he had knelt with hands outstretched toward heaven; ⁵⁵and he stood, and blessed all the assembly of Israel with a loud voice, saying, ⁵⁶"Blessed be the Lord who has given rest to his people Israel, according to all that he promised; not one word has failed of all his good promise, which he uttered by Moses his servant. ⁵⁷The Lord our God be with us, as he was with our fathers; may he not leave us or forsake us; ⁵⁸that he may incline our hearts to him, to walk in all his ways, and to keep his commandments, his statutes, and his ordinances, which he commanded our fathers. ⁵⁹Let these words of mine, wherewith I have made supplication before the Lord, be near to the Lord our God day and night, and may he maintain the cause of his servant, and the cause of his people Israel, as each day requires; ⁶⁰that all the peoples of the earth may know that the Lord is God; there is no other. ⁶¹Let your heart therefore be wholly true to the Lord our God, walking in his statutes and keeping his commandments, as at this day."

⁶²Then the king, and all Israel with him, offered sacrifice before the Lord. ⁶³Solomon offered as peace offerings to the Lord twenty-two thousand oxen and a hundred and twenty thousand sheep. So the king and all the people of Israel dedicated the house of the Lord. ⁶⁴The same day the king consecrated the middle of the court that was before the house of the Lord; for there he offered the burnt offering and the cereal offering and the fat pieces of the peace offerings, because the bronze altar that was before the Lord was too small to receive the burnt offering and the cereal offering and the fat pieces of the peace offerings.

⁶⁵So Solomon held the feast at that time, and all Israel with him, a great assembly, from the entrance of Hamath to the Brook of Egypt, before the Lord our God, seven days. ⁶⁶On the eighth day he

sent the people away; and they blessed the king, and went to their homes joyful and glad of heart for all the goodness that the Lord had shown to David his servant and to Israel his people.

(i)

Up to the point so far discussed, the reports of Solomon's blessings and prayers in 1 Kings 8 and 2 Chronicles 6 have been virtually identical. However, different conclusions are now provided in the two accounts, each reflecting a different theological tradition. The Chronicler (2 Chron. 6:41–42) quotes with slightly altered wording part of Psalm 132 (vv.8–10):

> And now arise, O Lord God, and go to thy resting place,
>   thou and the ark of thy might.
> Let thy priests, O Lord God, be clothed with salvation,
>   and let thy saints rejoice in thy goodness.
> O Lord God, do not turn away the face of thy anointed one!
>   Remember thy steadfast love for David thy servant.

Psalm 132 fits this occasion very well, with its joint themes of the ark in Zion and of the promise to David—even if it relates even more closely to David's first introduction of the portable shrine to his new capital. In fact it is not just the occasion which it suits; it also makes more explicit than Nathan's words in 2 Samuel 7 the terms of the divine offer to David (Ps. 132:12):

> If your sons keep my covenant
>   and my testimonies which I shall teach them,
> their sons also for ever
>   shall sit upon your throne.

Just what Solomon had reported!

But our text finishes differently. 1 Kings 8:50–53 focusses less on the king and the divine guarantees to the royal line, and more on the whole people—that nation which has belonged to the Lord since its ancient deliverance from Egypt. It is typical of Chronicles to base itself on the David traditions, and Kings (like Joshua, Judges and Samuel) on the Moses story. But more than this is at stake. The people in exile may have had two minds about the value of restoring their monarchy; but they were presumably united in hoping for a new national deliverance, for a second exodus. Hence their heightened interest in Moses!

(ii)

In the tradition which both Kings and Chronicles represent as they report the happenings on this most important of days, there follows a note about Solomon ending his prayer (v.54*a* = 2 Chron. 7:1*a*) and an account of a great festal sacrifice (vv.62–66 = 2 Chron. 7:4–10). However, each book develops and modifies the tradition in a different direction. The Chronicler (7:1*b*–3) reports a spectacular divine response, with lightning (the divine fire from heaven) striking and consuming the sacrifices, and the people answering prostrate with words we know from the opening of Psalm 136. This reminds us of the way God affirmed and supported his servant Elijah in his contest with Baal on Mount Carmel (1 Kings 18:38–39).

What we find in Kings, rather strangely after the conclusion of a series of prayers, is yet another full benediction by Solomon (vv.54*b*–61). This has some late features in it, like the suggestion that the king had been kneeling in prayer—the normal Old Testament attitudes of prayer are standing with hands outstretched or prostration with the forehead on the ground. Then, like many prayers since (and perhaps before!), it selects and harmonizes some key moments in biblical tradition.

"Rest", the first of his chosen topics (v.56), is found in several parts of scripture. Sometimes it refers to a goal which is still ahead, as when Moses reminds Israel (Deut. 12:9) that the Promised Land has not yet been achieved, or as when God threatens an erring generation (Psalm 95:11) that they will not enter his rest. However, some moments of achievement, of equilibrium even, are noted. In Solomon's embassy to Tyre (1 Kings 5:4), he records that "now the Lord my God has given me rest on every side; there is neither adversary nor misfortune". Joshua's taking of Canaan is underscored in similar terms

(Josh. 21:44). It may well be that "rest" which Solomon has in mind. Certainly it is the very next verse in Joshua (21:45; cf. also 23:14) that is recalled in the next theme: 'that not one word has failed of all his good promises'.

Solomon then (v.57) uses words which are remarkably rare in the Old Testament, for all their familiarity to us. When he prays "the Lord our God be with us", he may have the refrain of Psalm 46 in mind:

> The Lord of hosts is with us;
> the God of Jacob is our refuge.

Or he might be anticipating the surprising name Immanuel, 'God-with-us', given by Isaiah (7:14) to a hoped-for more distant descendant of David. But it is the language of optimism, of the few pinnacles of religious experience. And most of us most of the time find it easier to echo Gideon's despairing response to the Lord's messenger: "Pray, sir, if the Lord is with us, why then has all this befallen us? And where are all his wonderful deeds which our fathers recounted to us . . . ?" (Judg. 6:13). Solomon hopes for a restitution of the good old days.

Finally (8:60) he reminds us again of Elijah on Carmel, and the people's response to the pyrotechnics (1 Kings 18:39): "The Lord, he is God; the Lord, he is God", adding the words from Isaiah, "[I am the Lord,] and there is no other" (Isa. 45:5–6).

(iii)

Massive sacrifices of all the main kinds, contributed by both king and people, follow as a dedication of "the house of the Lord" (vv.62ff.). They require a specially large altar in the courtyard; and some have supposed that this was on top of the rock which is still the visible focus of Omar's Dome of the Rock. In the Chronicler's view (2 Chron. 3:1), followed by Muslim tradition, this rock was none other than Mount Moriah, where Abraham had almost slaughtered his only son in solemn sacrifice (Gen. 22).

A SECOND VISION AND A SURVEY

1 Kings 9:1–28

¹When Solomon had finished building the house of the Lord and the king's house and all that Solomon desired to build, ²the Lord appeared to Solomon a second time, as he had appeared to him at Gibeon. ³And the Lord said to him, "I have heard your prayer and your supplication, which you have made before me; I have consecrated this house which you have built, and put my name there for ever; my eyes and my heart will be there for all time. ⁴And as for you, if you will walk before me, as David your father walked, with integrity of heart and uprightness, doing according to all that I have commanded you, and keeping my statutes and my ordinances, ⁵then I will establish your royal throne over Israel for ever, as I promised David your father, saying, 'There shall not fail you a man upon the throne of Israel.' ⁶But if you turn aside from following me, you or your children, and do not keep my commandments and my statutes which I have set before you, but go and serve other gods and worship them, ⁷then I will cut off Israel from the land which I have given them; and the house which I have consecrated for my name I will cast out of my sight; and Israel will become a proverb and a byword among all peoples. ⁸And this house will become a heap of ruins; everyone passing by it will be astonished, and will hiss; and they will say, 'Why has the Lord done thus to this land and to this house?' ⁹Then they will say, 'Because they forsook the Lord their God who brought their fathers out of the land of Egypt, and laid hold on other gods, and worshipped them and served them; therefore the Lord has brought all this evil upon them.'"

¹⁰At the end of twenty years, in which Solomon had built the two houses, the house of the Lord and the king's house, ¹¹and Hiram king of Tyre had supplied Solomon with cedar and cypress timber and gold, as much as he desired, King Solomon gave to Hiram twenty cities in the land of Galilee. ¹²But when Hiram came from Tyre to see the cities which Solomon had given him, they did not please him. ¹³Therefore he said, "What kind of cities are these which you have given me, my brother?" So they are called the land of Cabul to this day. ¹⁴ Hiram had sent to the king one hundred and twenty talents of gold.

¹⁵And this is the account of the forced labour which King Solomon levied to build the house of the Lord and his own house and the Millo and the wall of Jerusalem and Hazor and Megiddo

and Gezer ¹⁶(Pharaoh king of Egypt had gone up and captured Gezer and burnt it with fire, and had slain the Canaanites who dwelt in the city, and had given it as dowry to his daughter, Solomon's wife; ¹⁷so Solomon rebuilt Gezer) and Lower Bethhoron ¹⁸and Baalath and Tamar in the wilderness, in the land of Judah, ¹⁹and all the store-cities that Solomon had, and the cities for his chariots, and the cities for his horsemen, and whatever Solomon desired to build in Jerusalem, in Lebanon, and in all the land of his dominion. ²⁰All the people who were left of the Amorites, the Hittites, the Perizzites, the Hivites, and the Jebusites, who were not of the people of Israel— ²¹their descendants who were left after them in the land, whom the people of Israel were unable to destroy utterly—these Solomon made a forced levy of slaves, and so they are to this day. ²²But of the people of Israel Solomon made no slaves; they were the soldiers, they were his officials, his commanders, his captains, his chariot commanders and his horsemen.

²³These were the chief officers who were over Solomon's work: five hundred and fifty, who had charge of the people who carried on the work.

²⁴But Pharaoh's daughter went up from the city of David to her own house which Solomon had built for her; then he built the Millo.

²⁵Three times a year Solomon used to offer up burnt offerings and peace offerings upon the altar which he built to the Lord, burning incense before the Lord. So he finished the house.

²⁶King Solomon built a fleet of ships at Ezion-geber, which is near Eloth on the shore of the Red Sea, in the land of Edom. ²⁷And Hiram sent with the fleet his servants, seamen who were familiar with the sea, together with the servants of Solomon; ²⁸and they went to Ophir, and brought from there gold, to the amount of four hundred and twenty talents; and they brought it to King Solomon.

(i)

Two points of tension are resolved in the first part of this chapter. The one is quite recent: Solomon has addressed many words to his God at the formal consecration of the Temple, and some response or at least acknowledgment is called for. The other point stretches back to the beginning of chapter 3, and the embarrassment there over the location of Solomon's first vision and of the main national shrine at Gibeon. Both issues are

answered by means of a second divine vision, which we may
assume was entrusted to Solomon this time at Jerusalem.

Like its predecessor at Gibeon, this vision is reported to us,
the readers of the Books of Kings; yet we are not told that
Solomon reported it to his own people. In the previous chapter,
it is stressed again and again that Solomon is addressing God
for and in full face of the people. Yet, as so often in biblical
narrative, the divine response is less direct, more at a tangent;
and this is true here in two respects. *First* it is made only to a
representative, here the king but often a prophet. *Second*, as at
Gibeon, it is given in a dream by night; and that is an essentially
elusive and intangible means. We might compare the five
visions reported in Amos chapters 7–9, whose contents are not
part of Amos's proclamation, but which doubtless had a vital
influence on how he shaped what he had to say.

The answers to prayer, including public prayer, are regularly
less direct than the occasion itself. They require discernment
and interpretation. In short, they are a matter of faith rather
than knowledge—that faith which "is the assurance of things
hoped for, the conviction of things not seen" (Heb. 11:1).

(ii)

God's response is to accept the house Solomon has built for
him; to renew the promise made to the Davidic line, provided
Davidic standards are maintained; and to reaffirm what is the
basic demand made of the royal house—exclusive devotion to
Yahweh. "No other gods before me" (Deut. 5:7) is the first and
foremost commandment; while the "Hear, O Israel" in Deuteronomy's following chapter puts the matter more positively:
"you shall love the Lord your God with all your heart, and with
all your soul, and with all your might" (Deut. 6:5).

The divine alternative is for people and shrine to become an
unenviable talking point. We may savour some of the flavour of
verse 7, if we contrast it with part of Psalm 69 (vv.6–7, 9–11):

Let not those who hope in thee be put to shame through me,
  O Lord God of hosts;

let not those who seek thee be brought to dishonour
  through me,
O God of Israel.
For it is for thy sake that I have borne reproach,
  that shame has covered my face.
. . . .
For zeal for thy house has consumed me,
  and the insults of those who insult thee have fallen on me.
When I humbled my soul with fasting,
  it became my reproach.
When I made sackcloth my clothing,
  I became a byword to them.

The divine warning to Solomon is that if God himself is not
maintained as the sole object of his zeal, even his house and his
people will become a byword and object lesson for the world, by
divine appointment. (The exact language used in our passage is
found also in Deut. 28:37 and Jer. 24:9.)

(iii)

The remainder of this chapter reads like a miscellany of official
minutes and archives. And in fact in different ancient versions
of Kings we find these notes in different order and in different
chapters. They begin and end with Hiram of Tyre. Verses 10–14
strike a chord with many business exploits that start with
effusive compliments but less than precise and specific terms
(5:1–12). More is provided than first asked for—considerable
quantities of gold in this case. And the unnegotiated payment
(here twenty cities in coastal Galilee) proves disappointing.
Despite this—or, in terms of historical order, was it before
this?—Hiram and Solomon also collaborated in merchant
naval enterprises (vv.26–28).

Another topic relates to Solomon's treatment of foreigners in
the mass. The non-Israelite sections within his total dominions
were simply reduced to forced labour for his major public
works. These were alien "neighbours" whom Israel, in the
Chronicler's version, had not "finished" (*ie* "destroyed"; 2
Chron. 8:8). Our version claims inability to destroy them

utterly (v.21). The king now finds a use for them, and does not seek to 'complete' the national task!

This passage also contains a summary of his major construction sites. Hazor, Megiddo and Gezer share pride of place after Jerusalem (v.15). It is interesting that archaeologists in recent decades have found identical and striking city-gates of this period in exactly these three towns—and that their proportions are just those of the gates in the temple wall which are described in Ezekiel's vision (40:5–16), although unavailable for archaeological scrutiny. There were also numerous store-cities and military installations (v.19).

One foreigner received different treatment. No discontent like Hiram's is reported of Solomon's Egyptian wife. She in fact (v.24) was one of the beneficiaries, not one of the casualties, of his building programmes.

Our last point returns us to where we began in this section—the removal of the embarrassment of Gibeon. After the extended reports of its construction and dedication, verse 25 deftly makes the point that Solomon's Temple was no royal 'white elephant': it became the working focus of his people's religion. He himself superintended the sacrifices at the three major national festivals, which were, as the Chronicler reminds us, "the feast of unleavened bread, the feast of weeks, and the feast of tabernacles" (2 Chron. 8:13).

THE QUEEN OF SHEBA

1 Kings 10:1–29

¹Now when the queen of Sheba heard of the fame of Solomon concerning the name of the Lord, she came to test him with hard questions. ²She came to Jerusalem with a very great retinue, with camels bearing spices, and very much gold, and precious stones; and when she came to Solomon, she told him all that was on her mind. ³And Solomon answered all her questions; there was nothing hidden from the king which he could not explain to her. ⁴And when the queen of Sheba had seen all the wisdom of Solomon, the house that he had built, ⁵the food of his table, the seating of his officials,

and the attendance of his servants, their clothing, his cupbearers, and his burnt offerings which he offered at the house of the Lord, there was no more spirit in her.

⁶And she said to the king, "The report was true which I heard in my own land of your affairs and of your wisdom, ⁷but I did not believe the reports until I came and my own eyes had seen it; and, behold, the half was not told me; your wisdom and prosperity surpass the report which I heard. ⁸Happy are your wives! Happy are these your servants, who continually stand before you and hear your wisdom! ⁹Blessed be the Lord your God, who has delighted in you and set you on the throne of Israel! Because the Lord loved Israel for ever, he has made you king, that you may execute justice and righteousness." ¹⁰Then she gave the king a hundred and twenty talents of gold, and a very great quantity of spices, and precious stones; never again came such an abundance of spices as these which the queen of Sheba gave to King Solomon.

¹¹Moreover the fleet of Hiram, which brought gold from Ophir, brought from Ophir a very great amount of almug wood and precious stones. ¹²And the king made of the almug wood supports for the house of the Lord, and for the king's house, lyres also and harps for the singers; no such almug wood has come or been seen, to this day.

¹³And King Solomon gave to the queen of Sheba all that she desired, whatever she asked besides what was given her by the bounty of King Solomon. So she turned and went back to her own land, with her servants.

¹⁴Now the weight of gold that came to Solomon in one year was six hundred and sixty-six talents of gold, ¹⁵besides that which came from the traders and from the traffic of the merchants, and from all the kings of Arabia and from the governors of the land. ¹⁶King Solomon made two hundred large shields of beaten gold; six hundred shekels of gold went into each shield. ¹⁷And he made three hundred shields of beaten gold; three minas of gold went into each shield; and the king put them in the House of the Forest of Lebanon. ¹⁸The king also made a great ivory throne, and overlaid it with the finest gold. ¹⁹The throne had six steps, and at the back of the throne was a calf's head, and on each side of the seat were arm rests and two lions standing beside the arm rests, ²⁰while twelve lions stood there, one on each end of a step on the six steps. The like of it was never made in any kingdom. ²¹All King Solomon's drinking vessels were of gold, and all the vessels of the House of the

Forest of Lebanon were of pure gold; none were of silver, it was not considered as anything in the days of Solomon. ²²For the king had a fleet of ships of Tarshish at sea with the fleet of Hiram. Once every three years the fleet of ships of Tarshish used to come bringing gold, silver, ivory, apes, and peacocks.

²³Thus King Solomon excelled all the kings of the earth in riches and in wisdom. ²⁴And the whole earth sought the presence of Solomon to hear his wisdom, which God had put into his mind. ²⁵Every one of them brought his present, articles of silver and gold, garments, myrrh, spices, horses, and mules, so much year by year. ²⁶And Solomon gathered together chariots and horsemen; he had fourteen hundred chariots and twelve thousand horsemen, whom he stationed in the chariot cities and with the king in Jerusalem. ²⁷And the king made silver as common in Jerusalem as stone, and he made cedar as plentiful as the sycamore of the Shephelah. ²⁸And Solomon's import of horses was from Egypt and Kue, and the king's traders received them from Kue at a price. ²⁹A chariot could be imported from Egypt for six hundred shekels of silver, and a horse for a hundred and fifty; and so through the king's traders they were exported to all the kings of the Hittites and the kings of Syria.

(i)

The arrival in Solomon's court in Jerusalem of this Arabian queen has excited dramatists and artists and storytellers through the ages. This almost lone female ruler in a biblical world of men joins Egyptian Cleopatra in western minds as a symbol of the exotic east. While it has delighted its readers, this tale has also puzzled and vexed some of them: we shall see how some significant details have been altered in the different versions available to us.

The Chronicler tells us simply that the queen has heard of the fame of Solomon: she has heard tell of him and can hardly credit the reports—and yet she has believed enough to make a great expedition worth-while (2 Chron. 9:1). Our version in Kings has added a significant qualification: her impulse comes from the king's reputation *concerning the name of the Lord* (v.1). This cautiously orthodox comment insists that Solomon is not important for Solomon's sake, but only in as much as he contributes to the reputation of his God. In fact the Chronicler himself makes a rather similar point, when he has the queen bless Yahweh for setting Solomon "on his throne as king for the Lord your God" (2 Chron. 9:8) and not "on the throne of Israel" as in our verse 9.

(ii)

There are two distinct but intimately intertwined aspects to the queen's mission; and their linkage is no less vital in our own world: diplomacy and trade. There are discussions to be had, she has questions to be answered that are intricate "riddles" (a more literal rendering of "hard questions" in v.1). And yet, as we have warned before, we should not think of Solomon's "wisdom" as just expressed in talk, however clever. Verses 4 and 5 appear to list everything from the house he built to his offerings in the Temple as together summing up his "wisdom". And the treasures she brought and promised served to enhance the spectacle of his provident success.

Skilled use of striking and puzzling words was highly prized in the biblical world. Samson's riddle (Judg. 14) was as impressive as his strength, and demonstrated that he was no dumb prize-fighter. Prophecy seems often to have been deliberately ambiguous; and its use of riddles and parables is expressly mentioned in Ezekiel 17. Then that most dangerous of latter-day rulers portrayed in Daniel 8 is introduced not just as "a king of bold countenance", but also as "one who understands riddles" (v.23). And his description continues: "[he] . . . shall succeed in what he does, and destroy mighty men and the people of the saints. By his cunning he shall make deceit prosper under his hand . . . " (vv.24–25). And of course Daniel himself, like Joseph, won his political role through his reputation as an interpreter of dreams, which are quite as teasing and testing as riddles.

Arts such as these were recognized as a divine gift—they are sometimes called the gift of "the spirit", as classically in Isaiah's royal hope (11:2):

And the Spirit of the Lord shall rest upon him,
   the spirit of wisdom and understanding,
   the spirit of counsel and might,
   the spirit of knowledge and the fear of the Lord.

It is as the queen comes to full recognition of Solomon's qualities that she herself becomes quite 'dis-spirited' (v.5). This is not exactly the way we would use the expression; she is still fully able to respond generously to him (vv.6–9). Yet the battle of wills has gone his way; and she gives his God the credit for this. (Perhaps the theory is that, as with David and Saul, the divine spirit can only be with one of them.)

After the meeting of minds, and the following compliments from the foreign queen, came the resulting commercial advantages. Verse 10 reads at first like a munificent gift of exotic abundance, particularly as immediately after it the subject switches to further exploits of Phoenician Hiram. However, it seems from verse 13 that the queen managed to secure a return for her goods on her own terms.

(iii)

It is over some of the details in the account of Solomon's commercial naval exploits that ancient and modern scholars have exercised most ingenuity. The report seems a mixture of the possible and the fanciful. "Six hundred and sixty-six talents of gold" as a baseline (v.14) is an extravagant sum: on differing estimates of the ancient talent, it varies from $10 million to $30 million—as annual *income*!

It is fascinating to speculate too on how literally to take the three-yearly cargoes of the Tarshish fleet (v.22). Tarshish itself, although its location is far from certain, is usually associated with the Phoenician town on the Spanish coast which the Romans knew as Tartessus. But what did they bring? Did their cargoes include live animals, or simply artistic representations? The ancient Greek version lists simply "gold, silver, chased stone and worked wood"—and the Iberian peninsula was long famous for such work. However, the last Hebrew word in verse

22 is quite obscure, and the translators may simply have covered their ignorance in a bland phrase. The main candidates for the final item in the verse are "peacock" and "baboon". If the fleet brought ivory, apes and baboons, then these came from North Africa. Yet if they were peacocks, or even symbolic peacocks, it is more likely they came from the east. In eastern imagery they were associated with gods and kings, with their exotic tails decorated with eyes.

An interesting question of imagery lurks behind the throne of verses 18-20 as well. RSV has followed the ancient Greek translation in reading the central Hebrew word in verse 19 as *egel* or "calf". Hebrew tradition itself has preserved it as *agol* or "round". "Calf's head" or "round top"? The Chronicler seems to have known the more worrying alternative, for he opts for safety at this point and records only a "footstool" (2 Chron. 9:18). Solomon's throne in Jerusalem may have included a symbol which was to be objected to in Jeroboam's shrines!

Consistency is not always a mark of political strife—even of religious political strife!

THE END OF SOLOMON I—TEXT

1 Kings 11:1-43

¹Now King Solomon loved many foreign women: the daughter of Pharaoh, and Moabite, Ammonite, Edomite, Sidonian, and Hittite women, ²from the nations concerning which the Lord had said to the people of Israel, "You shall not enter into marriage with them, neither shall they with you, for surely they will turn away your heart after their gods"; Solomon clung to these in love. ³He had seven hundred wives, princesses, and three hundred concubines; and his wives turned away his heart. ⁴For when Solomon was old his wives turned away his heart after other gods; and his heart was not wholly true to the Lord his God, as was the heart of David his father. ⁵For Solomon went after Ashtoreth the goddess of the Sidonians, and after Milcom the abomination of the Ammonites. ⁶So Solomon did what was evil in the sight of the Lord, and did not wholly follow the Lord, as David his father had done. ⁷Then Solomon built a high place for Chemosh the abomination of Moab, and for Molech the

abomination of the Ammonites, on the mountain east of Jerusalem. 8And so he did for all his foreign wives, who burned incense and sacrificed to their gods.

9And the Lord was angry with Solomon, because his heart had turned away from the Lord, the God of Israel, who had appeared to him twice, 10and had commanded him concerning this thing, that he should not go after other gods; but he did not keep what the Lord commanded. 11Therefore the Lord said to Solomon, "Since this has been your mind and you have not kept my covenant and my statutes which I have commanded you, I will surely tear the kingdom from you and will give it to your servant. 12Yet for the sake of David your father I will not do it in your days, but I will tear it out of the hand of your son. 13However I will not tear away all the kingdom; but I will give one tribe to your son, for the sake of David my servant and for the sake of Jerusalem which I have chosen."

14And the Lord raised up an adversary against Solomon, Hadad the Edomite; he was of the royal house in Edom. 15For when David was in Edom, and Joab the commander of the army went up to bury the slain, he slew every male in Edom 16(for Joab and all Israel remained there six months, until he had cut off every male in Edom); 17but Hadad fled to Egypt, together with certain Edomites of his father's servants, Hadad being yet a little child. 18They set out from Midian and came to Paran, and took men with them from Paran and came to Egypt, to Pharaoh king of Egypt, who gave him a house, and assigned him an allowance of food, and gave him land. 19And Hadad found great favour in the sight of Pharaoh, so that he gave him in marriage the sister of his own wife, the sister of Tahpenes the queen. 20And the sister of Tahpenes bore him Genubath his son, whom Tahpenes weaned in Pharaoh's house; and Genubath was in Pharaoh's house among the sons of Pharaoh. 21But when Hadad heard in Egypt that David slept with his fathers and that Joab the commander of the army was dead, Hadad said to Pharaoh, "Let me depart, that I may go to my own country." 22But Pharaoh said to him, "What have you lacked with me that you are now seeking to go to your own country?" And he said to him, "Only let me go."

23God also raised up as an adversary to him, Rezon the son of Eliada, who had fled from his master Hadadezer king of Zobah. 24And he gathered men about him and became leader of a marauding band, after the slaughter by David; and they went to Damascus, and dwelt there, and made him king in Damascus. 25He was an adversary of Israel all the days of Solomon, doing mischief as Hadad did; and he abhorred Israel, and reigned over Syria.

²⁶Jeroboam the son of Nebat, an Ephraimite of Zeredah, a servant of Solomon, whose mother's name was Zeruah, a widow, also lifted up his hand against the king. ²⁷And this was the reason why he lifted up his hand against the king. Solomon built the Millo, and closed up the breach of the city of David his father. ²⁸The man Jeroboam was very able, and when Solomon saw that the young man was industrious he gave him charge over all the forced labour of the house of Joseph. ²⁹And at that time, when Jeroboam went out of Jerusalem, the prophet Ahijah the Shilonite found him on the road. Now Ahijah had clad himself with a new garment; and the two of them were alone in the open country. ³⁰Then Ahijah laid hold of the new garment that was on him, and tore it into twelve pieces. ³¹And he said to Jeroboam, "Take for yourself ten pieces; for thus says the Lord, the God of Israel, 'Behold, I am about to tear the kingdom from the hand of Solomon, and will give you ten tribes ³²(but he shall have one tribe, for the sake of my servant David and for the sake of Jerusalem, the city which I have chosen out of all the tribes of Israel), ³³because he has forsaken me, and worshipped Ashtoreth the goddess of the Sidonians, Chemosh the god of Moab, and Milcom the god of the Ammonites, and has not walked in my ways, doing what is right in my sight and keeping my statutes and my ordinances, as David his father did. ³⁴Nevertheless I will not take the whole kingdom out of his hand; but I will make him ruler all the days of his life, for the sake of David my servant whom I chose, who kept my commandments and my statutes; ³⁵but I will take the kingdom out of his son's hand, and will give it to you, ten tribes. ³⁶Yet to his son I will give one tribe, that David my servant may always have a lamp before me in Jerusalem, the city where I have chosen to put my name. ³⁷And I will take you, and you shall reign over all that your soul desires, and you shall be king over Israel. ³⁸And if you will hearken to all that I command you, and will walk in my ways, and do what is right in my sight by keeping my statutes and my commandments, as David my servant did, I will be with you, and will build you a sure house, as I built for David, and I will give Israel to you. ³⁹And I will for this afflict the descendants of David, but not for ever.'" ⁴⁰Solomon sought therefore to kill Jeroboam; but Jeroboam arose, and fled into Egypt, to Shishak king of Egypt, and was in Egypt until the death of Solomon.

⁴¹Now the rest of the acts of Solomon, and all that he did, and his

wisdom, are they not written in the book of the acts of Solomon? ⁴²And the time that Solomon reigned in Jerusalem over all Israel was forty years. ⁴³And Solomon slept with his fathers, and was buried in the city of David his father; and Rehoboam his son reigned in his stead.

THE END OF SOLOMON II—COMMENTARY

1 Kings 11:1-43 (*cont'd*)

(i)

The most trenchant criticism of Solomon is left to the end of the report. We have sensed at various points in the previous chapters an undertow of critique; but now it is on the surface and in the open. Women are said to have been his undoing— and many of the worldly wise will wag their heads and say that little more could be expected of someone who was offspring of a man prepared to kill to cover the traces of an illicit liaison and a woman who made no protest at the "honour" done her. The whole chapter (to v.40), we should note, is absent from 2 Chronicles.

The marriage to the Egyptian princess of which we have already been told was unique only in the eminence of her father. There were apparently more representatives from the neighbouring nations in his harem than official emissaries from them in his court. And our author charges these women with being all too successful ambassadors for their own cults and gods. We have to be careful not to label the writer anti-feminine— Deuteronomy 7:1-5, which verse 2 quotes, prohibits intermarriage with foreign men or women. It seems to me that such a ruling reflects loss of national self-esteem after defeat and exile, rather than the thrusting self-confidence we naturally associate with the periods of David and Solomon, or indeed Moses and Joshua. Solomon was less than proverbially wise if he was so readily led astray!

(ii)

"To whom much is given, of him will much be required" (Luke

12:48). Solomon's default in loyalty hurts God not just because an order has been disobeyed, but even more in that he had entrusted the king with two visions of himself. Solomon's was not just a taught religion: he had had the benefit of personal experience of God. Yet the divine anger is doubly moderated— and all of us benefit regularly from that. The loss of Israel will be delayed until the reign of his son; and Jerusalem will not be lost with Israel. We are not told how the king learns of the divine decision, nor indeed how it will be effected—except that its agent will be a "servant" (v.11). With this mystery promised, our author now reports mischief from three of the king's vassals.

There are several ironies in the story of Hadad (vv.14–22), Solomon's *first* reported *satan* (cf. comments on 5:4). It was the needless barbarism of one of David's officers on a burial detail which was now rebounding in resentment against David's son. Egypt, for Hadad as well as for Jacob and Joseph, was a place of refuge and even of personal advancement. The great power (Egypt) which had joined Solomon in marriage alliance was also harbouring a would-be alternative government in exile. (How many contemporary examples of that can we count?) We are told less of the *second satan*, Rezon (vv.23–25): his base was Damascus—and again it was a slaughter by David that had turned him into a guerrilla leader.

Jeroboam, by contrast, was a rebel from within (vv.26–40). It was Solomon himself who had recognized Jeroboam's abilities, and given him responsibility for the corvée workers from the central highlands on one of the royal projects in Jerusalem. And, in further distinction from the two other adversaries, Jeroboam received an explicit divine mandate for his rebellion, from the prophet Ahijah from Shiloh.

(iii)

Like others of the Bible's prophetic figures, Ahijah communi-cates by action as well as word (v.30). Since the action concerns a garment, the parallel that comes most immediately to mind is with Jeremiah and the wasted loin-cloth (Jer.13:1–11). Our difficulty as readers consists in the fact that such symbolic actions are even harder to interpret than the ancient words associated with them. It is the numbers involved (vv.31–32) that have baffled commentators through the ages: in what sort of divine mathematics does ten plus one make twelve?

Despite the familiar English translations, including RSV above, we should probably put out of our heads any idea that "twelve" points to the ancient *tribal* structure of Israel. We met a total of twelve most recently when discussing the organization of Solomon's kingdom (1 Kings 4:7–19); as the number of districts in northern Israel *excluding Judah*. The ancient Greek Bible is probably more helpful, in this royal context, when it offers "sceptre" as a translation rather than "tribe". This may sound nonsense at first! However, the same Hebrew word is used for both: *shebet* is the general word for "rod/stick/staff/sceptre"—and also for "tribe". When it was used to denote a "tribe", it was probably because a tribal chief or ruler had a ceremonial staff as badge of office. Usually it is clear which way it should be rendered, but not here. Nevertheless I feel sure that Ahijah is promising Jeroboam ten times more (*ie* overwhelmingly much more) power and responsibility than will be enjoyed by the contemporary son of David. After all, he says God is "about to tear the kingdom from the hand of Solomon" (v.31).

God, however, has prior commitments to David and Jerusalem —and these must be maintained in however attenuated a form. The language of verse 36, "that David my servant may always have a lamp before me in Jerusalem," reminds us of 2 Samuel 21:17 where, after David had a near escape in battle, his warriors said to him: "You shall no more go out with us to battle, lest you quench the lamp of Israel". God's commitment to Jerusalem will prove fateful for Jeroboam—it is to "the city where I have chosen to put my name."

It is a very rich offer which is made to Jeroboam; a fresh start on similar terms to David (v.38). Indeed it is expressed in the words of Abigail's good wishes to David: "the Lord will certainly make my lord a sure house, because my lord is fighting the battles of the Lord" (1 Sam. 25:28). However, Solomon's suspicions are aroused, and Jeroboam too has to seek sanctuary in Egypt.

After all this talk in chapter 11 of troubles in his realms, the formal notice at the end of our passage concerning Solomon's death and burial seems rather an anti-climax. This king of so great promise seems almost a spent force before his time is finished.

REHOBOAM ADVISED AND GOLDEN CALVES
1 Kings 12:1–33

[1]Rehoboam went to Shechem, for all Israel had come to Shechem to make him king. [2]And when Jeroboam the son of Nebat heard of it (for he was still in Egypt, whither he had fled from King Solomon), then Jeroboam returned from Egypt. [3]And they sent and called him; and Jeroboam and all the assembly of Israel came and said to Rehoboam, [4]"Your father made our yoke heavy. Now therefore lighten the hard service of your father and his heavy yoke upon us, and we will serve you." [5]He said to them, "Depart for three days, then come again to me." So the people went away.

[6]Then King Rehoboam took counsel with the old men, who had stood before Solomon his father while he was yet alive, saying, "How do you advise me to answer this people?" [7]And they said to him, "If you will be a servant to this people today and serve them, and speak good words to them when you answer them, then they will be your servants for ever." [8]But he forsook the counsel which the old men gave him, and took counsel with the young men who had grown up with him and stood before him. [9]And he said to them, "What do you advise that we answer this people who have said to me, 'Lighten the yoke that your father put upon us'?" [10]And the young men who had grown up with him said to him, "Thus shall you speak to this people who said to you, 'Your father made our yoke heavy, but do you lighten it for us'; thus shall you say to them, 'My little finger is thicker than my father's loins. [11]And now, whereas my father laid upon you a heavy yoke, I will add to your yoke. My father chastised you with whips, but I will chastise you with scorpions.'"

[12]So Jeroboam and all the people came to Rehoboam the third

day, as the king said, "Come to me again the third day." ¹³And the king answered the people harshly, and forsaking the counsel which the old men had given him, ¹⁴he spoke to them according to the counsel of the young men, saying, "My father made your yoke heavy, but I will add to your yoke; my father chastised you with whips, but I will chastise you with scorpions." ¹⁵So the king did not hearken to the people; for it was a turn of affairs brought about by the Lord that he might fulfil his word, which the Lord spoke by Ahijah the Shilonite to Jeroboam the son of Nebat.

¹⁶And when all Israel saw that the king did not hearken to them, the people answered the king,

"What portion have we in David?
　We have no inheritance in the son
　　of Jesse.
To your tents, O Israel!
　Look now to your own house,
　　David."

So Israel departed to their tents. ¹⁷But Rehoboam reigned over the people of Israel who dwelt in the cities of Judah. ¹⁸Then King Rehoboam sent Adoram, who was taskmaster over the forced labour, and all Israel stoned him to death with stones. And King Rehoboam made haste to mount his chariot, to flee to Jerusalem. ¹⁹So Israel has been in rebellion against the house of David to this day. ²⁰And when all Israel heard that Jeroboam had returned, they sent and called him to the assembly and made him king over all Israel. There was none that followed the house of David, but the tribe of Judah only.

²¹When Rehoboam came to Jerusalem, he assembled all the house of Judah, and the tribe of Benjamin, a hundred and eighty thousand chosen warriors, to fight against the house of Israel, to restore the kingdom to Rehoboam the son of Solomon. ²²But the word of God came to Shemaiah the man of God: ²³"Say to Rehoboam the son of Solomon, king of Judah, and to all the house of Judah and Benjamin, and to the rest of the people, ²⁴'Thus says the Lord, You shall not go up or fight against your kinsmen the people of Israel. Return every man to his home, for this thing is from me.'" So they hearkened to the word of the Lord, and went home again, according to the word of the Lord.

²⁵Then Jeroboam built Shechem in the hill country of Ephraim, and dwelt there; and he went out from there and built Penuel. ²⁶And Jeroboam said in his heart, "Now the kingdom will turn back to the

house of David; [27]if this people go up to offer sacrifices in the house of the Lord at Jerusalem, then the heart of this people will turn again to their lord, to Rehoboam king of Judah, and they will kill me and return to Rehoboam king of Judah." [28]So the king took counsel, and made two calves of gold. And he said to the people, "You have gone up to Jerusalem long enough. Behold your gods, O Israel, who brought you up out of the land of Egypt." [29]And he set one in Bethel, and the other he put in Dan. [30]And this thing became a sin, for the people went to the one at Bethel and to the other as far as Dan. [31]He also made houses on high places, and appointed priests from among all the people, who were not of the Levites. [32]And Jeroboam appointed a feast on the fifteenth day of the eighth month like the feast that was in Judah, and he offered sacrifices upon the altar; so he did in Bethel, sacrificing to the calves that he had made. And he placed in Bethel the priests of the high places that he had made. [33]He went up to the altar which he had made in Bethel on the fifteenth day in the eighth month, in the month which he had devised of his own heart; and he ordained a feast for the people of Israel, and went up to the altar to burn incense.

(i)

The dual nature of the monarchy of David and Solomon is nowhere made plainer than in the transition from 11:43 to 12:1. Rehoboam falls heir without question or hitch to his father's throne in his grandfather's city. But, although king of Judah in Jerusalem, he is not yet king of Israel. We might compare the situation of the Stuarts in Scotland and England after the union of the crowns in 1603. The hiatus after Charles I's death was shorter in Scotland, where Charles II was crowned in 1651—yet this conferred no automatic rights to the southern crown, and it was not until 1660 that he assumed the English throne.

It rather looks from verse 1 that Rehoboam's visit some 40 miles north to Shechem was a mere formality: Israel was convening there for his investiture. However, Jeroboam's arrival produced a surprise. We all know the situation at a wedding, or an ordination, when objections are invited—but has anyone seen any offered? Like the dramatic intervention at the wedding service in Charlotte Brontë's *Jane Eyre*, the coronation at Shechem was interrupted—with some questions about the prospective king's policy. Was he to continue in his father's ways?

(ii)

Our narrator is quite transparent in his antipathy to the young bloods around the new king. RSV is altogether too kind to them in verses 8 and 10 where it calls them "the young men"—the Hebrew more tellingly dubs them "the children"! And these cubs are also coarse. If we remember that "hand" is the standard euphemism in Hebrew for the male member, we will detect the flavour of the end of verse 10. Rehoboam seems at least to have had enough good sense to delete that bawdy introduction from his policy statement.

I find it much harder to know what to make of those who had formerly advised Solomon (v.7). "If you will be a servant to this people today and serve them" is a rather redundant phrase, and is quite without parallel in the Hebrew Bible. The Chronicler offers the no less unique, "if you will be kind to this people and please them" (2 Chron. 10:7). Are these older courtiers intended to sound vacuous and unimpressive, so that the young king is bound to turn elsewhere for advice?

We have, I think, to read both sets of advice in the light of verse 24: "for this thing has been brought about by me" (following the rather better rendering of similar Hebrew in 1:27). God has willed the punishment of the Davidic house; and the courtiers are part of the means by which Rehoboam alienates Israel. The strength of popular feeling in Shechem can be judged from the lynching of Adoram the forced labour chief (v.18)—a post Jeroboam had earlier held (11:28), but presumably with greater acceptance.

(iii)

In verses 25-33, a portion which is not part of the Chronicler's report, we come to the heart of the religious problem of the northern kingdom of Israel as presented in the Books of Kings. It is hard not to sympathize with Jeroboam on several counts.

What we have just read presents him in an attractive light; yet from this point his name is abhorred on many pages of our text.

From our reading of chapters 6 and 7 above we can appreciate what verses 26–27 do not spell out. Continued worship by northerners at the Temple in Jerusalem would mean regular dealings with—and even religious control by—the house of David. The Temple was not just anywhere in now hostile Judah; it was actually part of the palace complex in Jerusalem. It is for similar reasons that most Muslims have dropped Jerusalem and Hebron, since these cities came under Israeli control in 1967, from the itinerary of the pilgrimage to Mecca, although they are the third and fourth most holy cities of Islam.

An alternative national shrine was called for, and Jeroboam selected the twin foci of the ancient holy city of Bethel (literally "God's House") near his southern frontier, and Dan in the far north. It was easy enough to build or rebuild shrines. But the ark, potent symbol of God's journeying presence in the people's past, was in Jerusalem, with Yahweh invisibly over the winged cherubim above it.

We may suppose a good deal of later Judean and Jewish prejudice in verse 28. A number of ancient Near Eastern deities are represented as standing on, or riding on, the back of a bull. Jeroboam's statues had in fact been devised for a similar function to the Jerusalem ark and cherubim: a throne or pedestal for the invisible Yahweh. If he did say "Behold your God . . . ," he was pointing to the space above the golden calf, and not to the statue itself. But it was very easy for a hostile and much later narrator to misrepresent the scene.

It is clear that there are the closest of links between this story and Aaron's making of the golden calf according to Exodus chapter 32. Each one reflects on the other. In the Bible as we know it, it is because we are familiar with the ancient scandal at the very mountain of God that we sense the futility of Jeroboam making the same mistake over again. The historical realities behind these linked Biblical texts are probably beyond our grasp: at best we can offer an informed guess.

In both Exodus and Kings the making of the 'true' shrine is reported first and in greatest detail (Exod. 25–31 and 1 Kings 5–8), then the 'distortion' more briefly (Exod. 32 and 1 Kings 12). Both texts are designed to legitimate the shrine in Jerusalem, and its furniture, and its priesthood (cf. v.31).

All in all, it is this whole chapter which gives us our best clue so far to the interests of the scribes who refashioned their people's traditions into the Books of Kings. They supported the House of David—yet rather as a residual ongoing ideal than as a major political force. However, in their view, the Jerusalem Temple was the only proper religious focus.

THE MAN OF GOD FROM JUDAH

1 Kings 13:1–10

[1]And behold, a man of God came out of Judah by the word of the Lord to Bethel. Jeroboam was standing by the altar to burn incense. [2]And the man cried against the altar by the word of the Lord, and said, "O altar, altar, thus says the Lord: 'Behold, a son shall be born to the house of David, Josiah by name; and he shall sacrifice upon you the priests of the high places who burn incense upon you, and men's bones shall be burned upon you.'" [3]And he gave a sign the same day, saying, "This is the sign that the Lord has spoken: 'Behold, the altar shall be torn down, and the ashes that are upon it shall be poured out.'" [4]And when the king heard the saying of the man of God, which he cried against the altar at Bethel, Jeroboam stretched out his hand from the altar, saying, "Lay hold of him." And his hand, which he stretched out against him, dried up, so that he could not draw it back to himself. [5]The altar also was torn down, and the ashes poured out from the altar, according to the sign which the man of God had given by the word of the Lord. [6]And the king said to the man of God, "Entreat now the favour of the Lord your God, and pray for me, that my hand may be restored to me." And the man of God entreated the Lord; and the king's hand was restored to him, and became as it was before. [7]And the king said to the man of God, "Come home with me, and refresh yourself, and I will give you a reward." [8]And the man of God said to the king, "If you give me half your house, I will not go in with you. And I will not

eat bread or drink water in this place; ⁹for so was it commanded me by the word of the Lord, saying, 'You shall neither eat bread, nor drink water, nor return by the way that you came.'" ¹⁰So he went another way, and did not return by the way that he came to Bethel.

(i)

This tale of the mission to Bethel of a man of God from Judah is rich in undertones and overtones. It takes its occasion from the end of chapter 12 with Jeroboam at the altar of his southern state sanctuary burning incense. To some literally-minded readers such action might appear blameworthy in itself; in that cultic ministry was priestly business. However, no less is said of Solomon himself (9:25). We must suppose either that the king was himself a cultic functionary, or that these texts assume that he had at least general responsibility for worship arrangements. In any case it is not what Jeroboam himself did or did not do at this altar that is at stake here—the problem is rather the existence of the altar at all as an official alternative to the one in Jerusalem. The unnamed emissary confronts the villain at the very scene of his crime.

The climax of the twin Books of Kings comes just before their conclusion, with the account of the religious reforms of good King Josiah in 2 Kings chapters 22–23. We shall find in these chapters a remedy for every single one of the cultic abuses perpetrated during the separate monarchies of Judah and Israel. Jeroboam's illicit altars are the worst of such abuses to be reported. It is here, in token for all the others that will be compendiously narrated in chapters to come, that their future remedy is signalled. The cure is violent and bloody: the only sacrifice pleasing to God on this altar will be the human one of the very priests that have ministered there.

(ii)

Often the truth is harder to hear from the wrong person. And we are mostly over-sensitive to criticism from outsiders. If we can persuade ourselves that the speaker is bound to be partisan and unsympathetic, then we can save ourselves examining what

he actually says on its own merits. Jeroboam signals the arrest
of the meddler from Judah (v.4). The tale then takes a dramatic
turn.

The man of God has promised a "wonder" (v.3): an imminent
collapse of the offending altar which will anticipate its final
destruction in Josiah's time. This in fact occurs; but is now
supplemented by a manifestation of divine power on the very
person of the king who has failed to recognize the emissary's
words as God's own message. And of course this immediate
demonstration of God's ability both to maim (v.4) and to heal
(v.6) serves to underscore the seriousness of the man of God's
mission. What can happen to the king himself can also happen
to his whole dynasty and all its physical trappings, including the
altar at Bethel.

I have deliberately used "wonder" at the beginning of the last
paragraph, in preference to "sign" which RSV uses in verses 3
and 5 to translate Hebrew *mopheth*. "Sign" normally renders
the Hebrew *oth*. Most often we find these two words as a pair,
especially in the language of Deuteronomy. While they do
overlap in sense, each has its own contribution to make: one
that can be best assessed in the biblical passages where each
appears separately. The Book of Exodus is the best resource for
such a study. "Signs" there require an element of discernment to
see the hand of God in them; when such discrimination is there,
they serve to build up faith and confidence in him. Forms of
religious observance can also be called signs—such as worship-
ping at the holy mountain after the exodus (Exod. 3:12), or
observing the sabbath (Exod. 31:13,17): these too nourish
faith.

But a "wonder" or a "portent" (*mopheth*) is a demonstration
of divine power that compels assent—or at least that would do
so if an equal and opposite restraint was not put in the way. A
good example of this is Exodus 4:21, where RSV translates the
key word as "miracle":

And the Lord said to Moses, "When you go back to Egypt, see that
you do before Pharaoh all the miracles which I have put in your

power; but I will harden his heart, so that he will not let the people
go.

That is the nature of the "wondrous" collapse of the altar in our
story; and, reinforced by the king's own suffering, it does
produce some result.

(iii)

The end of this part of the story gives us much to ponder. Is it
spontaneous and natural generosity and gratitude that we
should detect in Jeroboam's invitation to the man of God (v.7)?
Is it relief about his arm, and possibly the beginnings of
recognition of the higher credentials of his southern critic?
Or is it a plot: like "'come into my parlour', said the
spider to the fly'"? It is not clear whether it helps or hinders that
we are immediately reminded of other biblical stories. Certainly
King Herod's dealings with the eastern visitors to baby Jesus,
and the divine warning to them to choose another route home
encourage us to smell foul play here. But I suspect that is unfair
to Jeroboam.

The links have long been noted between this story and the
brief narrative about Amos and Amaziah (Amos 7:10–17).
Both concern Bethel and a divine emissary from Judah. In both
stories the king of Israel is a Jeroboam. Both concern the
possible conflict between divine and royal authority. And both
talk of "eating bread". Why the prohibition of tasting food or
water during the man of God's mission to Bethel? Was the
northern kingdom of Israel, or at least the area of Bethel, so
polluted that any social contact would prove contaminating? I
find no warrant for supposing this. Was the intention to prevent
him accepting royal hospitality? Just possibly, yet the prohibition is given before the invitation is offered.

I think the point may just be a simple demonstration of
obedience. At times a flexible approach to a changing situation
is appropriate. Yet attention to God's specific prohibitions and
wishes is also to be commended! The simple obedience of the
man of God was itself a useful "sign" for King Jeroboam to
ponder.

.. AND THE PROPHET FROM BETHEL

1 Kings 13:11–34

¹¹Now there dwelt an old prophet in Bethel. And his sons came and told him all that the man of God had done that day in Bethel; the words also which he had spoken to the king, they told to their father. ¹²And their father said to them, "Which way did he go?" And his sons showed him the way which the man of God who came from Judah had gone. ¹³And he said to his sons, "Saddle the ass for me." So they saddled the ass for him and he mounted it. ¹⁴And he went after the man of God, and found him sitting under an oak; and he said to him, "Are you the man of God who came from Judah?" And he said, "I am." ¹⁵Then he said to him, "Come home with me and eat bread." ¹⁶And he said, "I may not return with you, or go in with you; neither will I eat bread nor drink water with you in this place; ¹⁷for it was said to me by the word of the Lord, 'You shall neither eat bread nor drink water there, nor return by the way that you came.'" ¹⁸And he said to him, "I also am a prophet as you are, and an angel spoke to me by the word of the Lord, saying, 'Bring him back with you into your house that he may eat bread and drink water.'" But he lied to him. ¹⁹So he went back with him, and ate bread in his house, and drank water.

²⁰And as they sat at the table, the word of the Lord came to the prophet who had brought him back; ²¹and he cried to the man of God who came from Judah, "Thus says the Lord, 'Because you have disobeyed the word of the Lord, and have not kept the commandment which the Lord your God commanded you, ²²but have come back, and have eaten bread and drunk water in the place of which he said to you, "Eat no bread, and drink no water"; your body shall not come to the tomb of your fathers.'" ²³And after he had eaten bread and drunk, he saddled the ass for the prophet whom he had brought back. ²⁴And as he went away a lion met him on the road and killed him. And his body was thrown in the road, and the ass stood beside it; the lion also stood beside the body. ²⁵And behold, men passed by, and saw the body thrown in the road, and the lion standing by the body. And they came and told it in the city where the old prophet dwelt.

²⁶And when the prophet who had brought him back from the way heard of it, he said, "It is the man of God, who disobeyed the word of the Lord; therefore the Lord has given him to the lion, which has

torn him and slain him, according to the word which the Lord spoke to him." ²⁷And he said to his sons, "Saddle the ass for me." And they saddled it. ²⁸And he went and found his body thrown in the road, and the ass and the lion standing beside the body. The lion had not eaten the body or torn the ass. ²⁹And the prophet took up the body of the man of God and laid it upon the ass, and brought it back to the city, to mourn and to bury him. ³⁰And he laid the body in his own grave; and they mourned over him, saying, "Alas, my brother!" ³¹And after he had buried him, he said to his sons, "When I die, bury me in the grave in which the man of God is buried; lay my bones beside his bones. ³²For the saying which he cried by the word of the Lord against the altar in Bethel, and against all the houses of the high places which are in the cities of Samaria, shall surely come to pass."

³³After this thing Jeroboam did not turn from his evil way, but made priests for the high places again from among all the people; any who would, he consecrated to be priests of the high places. ³⁴And this thing became sin to the house of Jeroboam, so as to cut it off and to destroy it from the face of the earth.

(i)

Unhappily, having jumped the first fence successfully, God's "man" failed miserably at the second. And which of his servants has not suffered that experience? Whatever else we are to make of our unfortunate hero's second encounter in Bethel, one thing is clear. This story must have conveyed a powerful and important warning to the religious community in shrunken Judah after the exile. It was not enough to tell themselves that they were well rid of heretical northern Israel and its apostate shrines. I was not enough even to remember that their own former kings had not always served them or their God well. We all need to be reminded that the security of our own religious community around its own religious symbols is in fact no security. God's own "man" from Judah failed the second test.

(ii)

Part of what this story is about is a warning about the claims of prophecy. We tend to think of biblical prophets as, in general at least, 'the good guys'. And such an attitude is all too easy to understand. Much of the early Christian message is presented in terms of fulfilment of prophecy. It is not just the Christian Bible which has exalted the role of the "prophets". The Hebrew Bible too, as we have already noted, describes as "The Former Prophets" the very section from Joshua to Kings, part of which we are studying. All this is true; and yet it is also true that several traditions *within* the Old Testament or Hebrew Bible are more cautious, and even hostile, in what they have to say about prophets. Over the biblical period the meaning of the word "prophet" changed—in fact improved. Many of the figures whom we know as "prophets" are called so only in the *titles* of the books associated with them, and not *within* the books themselves, where they are styled differently. This story is one of the cautious ones; and it also contains one nice piece of evidence for the change in meaning of "prophet" that I have mentioned.

Our hero is a "man of God": it is the fellow from Bethel who is a "prophet". We need not suppose the latter to have been a very bad man; he was simply intrigued by the news brought to him by his sons of the altercation at the altar. Perhaps wanting to learn something of benefit to his own 'trade', or possibly simply wishing to offer someone he took to be a fellow professional some hospitality when he was a visitor in town, he saddled his ass and rode to catch up with him on the way south.

Still loyal to the divine orders, his would-be guest refuses the invitation—and explains his reasons. The prophet of Bethel then claims equal status as a "prophet" (v.18), and goes on to pile authority on authority asserting (1) that he had received "the word of the Lord", and (2) that this had been directly from an "angel" or divine ambassador. What could an exhausted "man of God" do, but to accept further divine instructions for the day—especially when these would reward his earlier loyalty with some attention to his bodily needs?

However, the old man had (what many of us would call) 'bent the truth'—the end of verse 18 is crisper and more straightforward. The point of the story is not that "prophets" are necessarily perfidious. As the story develops, the prophet does receive the divine "word" which he then passes to his guest (vv.20–22). A prophet *may* be an ambassador for God. The problem is how to know for sure on any given occasion that his credentials are what he claims them to be.

(iii)

The Book of Deuteronomy addresses itself to a similar issue:

> If a prophet arises among you, or a dreamer of dreams, and gives you a sign or a wonder, and the sign or wonder which he tells you comes to pass, and if he says, "Let us go after other gods", which you have not known, "and let us serve them", you shall not listen to the words of that prophet or to that dreamer of dreams; for the Lord your God is testing you, to know whether you love the Lord your God with all your heart and with all your soul.
>
> (Deut. 13:1–3)

We can note a relationship in both directions between our story and this rule. On the one hand, it is this rule that vindicates the behaviour of our hero before Jeroboam at the altar. It was precisely to call Jeroboam back to the already revealed "means of grace", back to the existing place of worship, that "God's man" employed his successful "portent". On the other hand, we should detect in Deuteronomy's general principle the same basic message as we described at the end of the previous portion. Obedience to what we already know from God is to be preferred to new disclosures—however powerful, and apparently divine, the 'visual aids' employed to present them.

Of course this sounds a most unexciting charter for stuffy conservatism. It certainly marked an important step on the way towards the pre-eminence accorded to the Books of Moses in normative Judaism over the other parts of Scripture: everything in the rest of the Bible has to be tested by, and understood in, the light of Mosaic *torah*. Questioned about the relevance or good sense of traditional Jewish practices, rabbis have often made the attractively direct response: it is not because we understand or can explain this that we do it, but because it is *torah*.

And of course this has been a key issue for the mission of

Jesus and then the Church from the beginning vis-à-vis Judaism. Does Jesus' teaching enhance and reinforce the hallowed instruction about God and his ways for man in the Hebrew Bible? Or does it seek to divert faithful Jews, by various powerful demonstrations, into false channels? Arguments from miracles are always dangerous.

JEROBOAM AND REHOBOAM AGAIN

1 Kings 14:1–31

[1]At that time Abijah the son of Jeroboam fell sick. [2]And Jeroboam said to his wife, "Arise, and disguise yourself, that it be not known that you are the wife of Jeroboam, and go to Shiloh; behold, Ahijah the prophet is there, who said of me that I should be king over this people. [3]Take with you ten loaves, some cakes, and a jar of honey, and go to him; he will tell you what shall happen to the child."

[4]Jeroboam's wife did so; she arose, and went to Shiloh, and came to the house of Ahijah. Now Ahijah could not see, for his eyes were dim because of his age. [5]And the Lord said to Ahijah, "Behold, the wife of Jeroboam is coming to inquire of you concerning her son; for he is sick. Thus and thus shall you say to her."

When she came, she pretended to be another woman. [6]But when Ahijah heard the sound of her feet, as she came in at the door, he said, "Come in, wife of Jeroboam; why do you pretend to be another? For I am charged with heavy tidings for you. [7]Go, tell Jeroboam, 'Thus says the Lord, the God of Israel: "Because I exalted you from among the people, and made you leader over my people Israel, [8]and tore the kingdom away from the house of David and gave it to you; and yet you have not been like my servant David, who kept my commandments, and followed me with all his heart, doing only that which was right in my eyes, [9]but you have done evil above all that were before you and have gone and made for yourself other gods, and molten images, provoking me to anger, and have cast me behind your back; [10]therefore behold, I will bring evil upon the house of Jeroboam, and will cut off from Jeroboam every male, both bond and free in Israel, and will utterly consume the house of Jeroboam, as a man burns up dung until it is all gone. [11]Any one belonging to Jeroboam who dies in the city the dogs shall eat; and any one who dies in the open country the birds of the air shall eat; for the Lord has spoken it."' 12Arise therefore, go to your house. When your feet enter the city, the child shall die. 13And all Israel shall mourn for him, and bury him; for he only of Jeroboam shall come to the grave, because in him there is found something pleasing to the Lord, the God of Israel, in the house of Jeroboam. 14Moreover the Lord will raise up for himself a king over Israel, who shall cut off the house of Jeroboam today. And henceforth 15the Lord will smite Israel, as a reed is shaken in the water, and root up Israel out of this good land which he gave to their fathers, and scatter them beyond the Eu-phrates, because they have made their Asherim, provoking the Lord to anger. 16And he will give Israel up because of the sins of Jeroboam, which he sinned and which he made Israel to sin."

17Then Jeroboam's wife arose, and departed, and came to Tirzah. And as she came to the threshold of the house, the child died. 18And all Israel buried him and mourned for him, according to the word of the Lord, which he spoke by his servant Ahijah the prophet. 19Now the rest of the acts of Jeroboam, how he warred and how he reigned, behold, they are written in the Book of the Chronicles of the Kings of Israel. 20And the time that Jeroboam reigned was twenty-two years; and he slept with his fathers, and Nadab his son reigned in his stead.

21Now Rehoboam the son of Solomon reigned in Judah. Rehoboam was forty-one years old when he began to reign, and he reigned seventeen years in Jerusalem, the city which the Lord had chosen out of all the tribes of Israel, to put his name there. His mother's name was Naamah the Ammonitess. 22And Judah did what was evil in the sight of the Lord, and they provoked him to jealousy with their sins which they committed, more than all that their fathers had done. 23For they also built for themselves high places, and pillars, and Asherim on every high hill and under every green tree; 24and there were also male cult prostitutes in the land. They did according to all the abominations of the nations which the Lord drove out before the people of Israel.

25In the fifth year of King Rehoboam, Shishak king of Egypt came up against Jerusalem; 26he took away the treasures of the house of the Lord and the treasures of the king's house; he took away everything. He also took away all the shields of gold which Solomon had made; 27and King Rehoboam made in their stead shields of bronze, and committed them to the hands of the officers of the guard, who kept the door of the king's house. ²⁸And as often as the king went into the house of the Lord, the guard bore them and brought them back to the guardroom.

²⁹Now the rest of the acts of Rehoboam, and all that he did, are they not written in the Book of the Chronicles of the Kings of Judah? ³⁰And there was war between Rehoboam and Jeroboam continually. ³¹And Rehoboam slept with his fathers and was buried with his fathers in the city of David. His mother's name was Naamah the Ammonitess. And Abijam his son reigned in his stead.

(i)

Readers who are at all familiar with the contemporary practice by eastern women of respectable public life behind the veil may be surprised that there was any need for Jeroboam's wife to disguise herself before visiting Ahijah at Shiloh. We are not in fact very well informed about dressing habits in the biblical world. I suspect women were not normally veiled. There is some evidence (Gen. 38:14–15) that a veil, or at least a distinctive headscarf, was in fact the 'uniform' of a harlot. However, we are dealing here with the king's wife: disguise for her would involve not so much a masking of the features as a removal of regal vestments. Yet her precautions are doubly in vain. Blind Ahijah could not have recognized her in any case; but he did have an impeccable 'source'.

Particularly with a series of healing stories just ahead of us in Kings, related about Elijah and Elisha, we should observe that it is not for a cure that the prophet is being visited—but for information. It is rather like Saul visiting Samuel to find where his father's animals have strayed (1 Sam. 9); or indeed Jeremiah being approached on behalf of Zedekiah (Jer. 37:3–10). Not only ministers and priests, but many other professionals as well, are still regularly expected to have 'second sight' over a wide range of topics.

It is not made clear whether it was dynastic concerns or simple family worry that impelled Jeroboam and his wife to take counsel from Ahijah—the serious illness of a prince must always remind a palace of the fragility of the succession. But the prophetic answer certainly encompasses Jeroboam's "house" and all its doings! Like David, he had been promoted from the ranks; like David's successors, but unlike David, he had not kept faith: in fact he is charged with doing "evil above all that were before you" (v.9)—and his "house" will suffer a far worse fate.

The invective in verses 10–16 is striking in its intensity, but far from unparalleled. It is in fact the first of a whole series of linked passages with stereotyped phrases which are more effective at first meeting than when they become more familiar. It begins coarsely, and not altogether clearly. Modern English versions prefer euphemisms like "every male" (RSV and Jerusalem Bible) or "every mother's son" (NEB) to AV's literal rendering of the Hebrew—"him that pisseth against the wall" (v.10). It seems to me even more *improper* that translators should tidy up and apologize for the Bible, than that they should risk upsetting its readers with its 'improprieties'. A matter of interpretation is at stake too. The following phrase, "bond and free" (v.10), is a puzzling description for members of the royal household. The two Hebrew words normally mean "restrained" and "abandoned"—and I tend to follow the suggestion that they develop the coarse expression already begun: "all that piss on a wall—decently or openly". The association of ideas that leads the prophet on to the topic of "dung" is all too obvious.

The wretched woman is sent away with some comfort, but it is very cold comfort. Abijah's sickness and imminent death will at least ensure decent burial and proper mourning for one member of her husband's house. All the rest will be disposed of by mother nature's own scavengers. As a 'bonus', Ahijah informs her not just that another Israelite dynasty will replace Jeroboam's, but that the kingdom of Israel itself will in the end pay the price of her husband's apostasy. The death of the child exactly as promised makes this long-term menace all the more potent—like the sign of the altar and the maiming of the king in the previous chapter.

(ii)

With the end of the section on Jeroboam (vv.19–20) we begin
the running series of formulaic notes on the kings of Israel and
Judah that characterize the Books of Kings and Chronicles.
They are brief and stereotyped, like official minutes; and they
are either derived from, or at least seek to imitate, the original
state "chronicles".

Rehoboam's "chronicle" is introduced next—rather strangely in that we have already met him in chapter 12. We learn now
(v.21) that he was far from a 'child'—at least in years (cf. our
comments on 12:8 when he negotiated so ineptly in Shechem!).
We also learn that the queen mother was from Ammon. For all
that we are told of Solomon, we learn nothing about the details
of his family. Clearly the daughter of Pharaoh, however
prominent in her husband's building operations, was not the
mother of his heir. She may simply have had no son. Yet there
may be more at stake: Shishak's campaign (vv.26–27) points
clearly to the end of the alliance which that marriage had
embodied. Our chronicler seems to insist on queen mother
Naamah's origins, for he repeats his note at the end of the
chapter (vv.21,31). This quietly links Rehoboam's failures to
his father's indulgence in foreign liaisons (11:1–8). There is no
question of 'safety in numbers' in such matters!

Even after the graphic detail of Ahijah's message to Jeroboam's wife, our author's comments on religion in Judah are
memorable. The second Book of Chronicles at this point
contents itself with, "And he did evil, for he did not set his heart
to seek the Lord" (12:14). But Kings lists several of its standard
complaints. God's "jealousy" (v.22) is one of his essential
attributes, according to the Ten Commandments; and what
triggers the divine vexation is precisely any hint of apostasy.

We see this language used classically in two poetic contexts.
First briefly in Psalm 78(v.58):

> For they provoked him to anger with their high places;
>   they moved him to jealousy with their graven images.

And then, *second*, developed more fully in Deuteronomy 32:16–22, *eg*:

> They have stirred me to jealousy with what is no god;
>   they have provoked me with their idols.
> So I will stir them to jealousy with those who are no people;
>   I will provoke them with a foolish nation.
>
> (Deut. 32:21)

Even the reform of long-distant Josiah would prove a failed last-ditch stand. Judah's behaviour under Rehoboam was already pregnant with this bitter future.

NINE KINGS OF JUDAH AND ISRAEL I—TEXT

1 Kings 15:1–16:34

¹Now in the eighteenth year of King Jeroboam the son of Nebat, Abijam began to reign over Judah. ²He reigned for three years in Jerusalem. His mother's name was Maacah the daughter of Abishalom. ³And he walked in all the sins which his father did before him; and his heart was not wholly true to the Lord his God, as the heart of David his father. ⁴Nevertheless for David's sake the Lord his God gave him a lamp in Jerusalem, setting up his son after him, and establishing Jerusalem; ⁵because David did what was right in the eyes of the Lord, and did not turn aside from anything that he commanded him all the days of his life, except in the matter of Uriah the Hittite. ⁶Now there was war between Rehoboam and Jeroboam all the days of his life. ⁷The rest of the acts of Abijam, and all that he did, are they not written in the Book of the Chronicles of the Kings of Judah? And there was war between Abijam and Jeroboam. ⁸And Abijam slept with his fathers; and they buried him in the city of David. And Asa his son reigned in his stead.

⁹In the twentieth year of Jeroboam king of Israel Asa began to reign over Judah, ¹⁰and he reigned forty-one years in Jerusalem. His mother's name was Maacah the daughter of Abishalom. ¹¹And Asa did what was right in the eyes of the Lord, as David his father had done. ¹²He put away the male cult prostitutes out of the land, and removed all the idols that his fathers had made. ¹³He also removed Maacah his mother from being queen mother because she had an abominable image made for Asherah; and Asa cut down her

image and burned it at the brook Kidron. ¹⁴But the high places were not taken away. Nevertheless the heart of Asa was wholly true to the Lord all his days. ¹⁵And he brought into the house of the Lord the votive gifts of his father and his own votive gifts, silver, and gold, and vessels.

¹⁶And there was war between Asa and Baasha king of Israel all their days. ¹⁷Baasha king of Israel went up against Judah, and built Ramah, that he might permit no one to go out or come in to Asa king of Judah. ¹⁸Then Asa took all the silver and the gold that were left in the treasures of the house of the Lord and the treasures of the king's house, and gave them into the hands of his servants; and King Asa sent them to Ben-hadad the son of Tabrimmon, the son of Hezi-on, king of Syria, who dwelt in Damascus, saying, ¹⁹"Let there be a league between me and you, as between my father and your father: behold, I am sending to you a present of silver and gold; go, break your league with Baasha king of Israel, that he may withdraw from me." ²⁰And Ben-hadad hearkened to King Asa, and sent the commanders of his armies against the cities of Israel, and conquered Ijon, Dan, Abel-beth-maacah, and all Chin-neroth, with all the land of Naphtali. ²¹And when Baasha heard of it, he stopped building Ramah, and he dwelt in Tirzah. ²²Then King Asa made a proclamation to all Judah, none was exempt, and they carried away the stones of Ramah and its timber, with which Baasha had been building; and with them King Asa built Geba of Benjamin and Mizpah. ²³Now the rest of all the acts of Asa, all his might, and all that he did, and the cities which he built, are they not written in the Book of the Chronicles of the Kings of Judah? But in his old age he was diseased in his feet. ²⁴And Asa slept with his fathers, and was buried with his fathers in the city of David his father; and Jehoshaphat his son reigned in his stead.

²⁵Nadab the son of Jeroboam began to reign over Israel in the second year of Asa king of Judah; and he reigned over Israel two years. ²⁶He did what was evil in the sight of the Lord, and walked in the way of his father, and in his sin which he made Israel to sin.

²⁷Baasha the son of Ahijah, of the house of Issachar, conspired against him; and Baasha struck him down at Gibbethon, which belonged to the Philistines; for Nadab and all Israel were laying siege to Gibbethon. ²⁸So Baasha killed him in the third year of Asa king of Judah, and reigned in his stead. ²⁹And as soon as he was king, he killed all the house of Jeroboam; he left to the house of Jeroboam not one that breathed, until he had destroyed it, accord-

ing to the word of the Lord which he spoke by his servant Ahijah the Shilonite; ³⁰it was for the sins of Jeroboam which he sinned and which he made Israel to sin, and because of the anger to which he provoked the Lord, the God of Israel.

³¹Now the rest of the acts of Nadab, and all that he did, are they not written in the Book of the Chronicles of the Kings of Israel? ³²And there was war between Asa and Baasha king of Israel all their days.

³³In the third year of Asa king of Judah, Baasha the son of Ahijah began to reign over all Israel at Tirzah, and reigned twenty-four years. ³⁴He did what was evil in the sight of the Lord, and walked in the way of Jeroboam and in his sin which he made Israel to sin.

¹And the word of the Lord came to Jehu the son of Hanani against Baasha, saying, ²"Since I exalted you out of the dust and made you leader over my people Israel, and you have walked in the way of Jeroboam, and have made my people Israel to sin, provoking me to anger with their sins, ³behold, I will utterly sweep away Baasha and his house, and I will make your house like the house of Jeroboam the son of Nebat. ⁴Any one belonging to Baasha who dies in the city the dogs shall eat; and any one of his who dies in the field the birds of the air shall eat."

⁵Now the rest of the acts of Baasha, and what he did, and his might, are they not written in the Book of the Chronicles of the Kings of Israel? ⁶And Baasha slept with his fathers, and was buried at Tirzah; and Elah his son reigned in his stead. ⁷Moreover the word of the Lord came by the prophet Jehu the son of Hanani against Baasha and his house, both because of all the evil that he did in the sight of the Lord, provoking him to anger with the work of his hands, in being like the house of Jeroboam, and also because he destroyed it.

⁸In the twenty-sixth year of Asa king of Judah, Elah the son of Baasha began to reign over Israel in Tirzah, and reigned two years. ⁹But his servant Zimri, commander of half his chariots, conspired against him. When he was at Tirzah, drinking himself drunk in the house of Arza, who was over the household in Tirzah, ¹⁰Zimri came in and struck him down and killed him, in the twenty-seventh year of Asa king of Judah, and reigned in his stead.

¹¹When he began to reign, as soon as he had seated himself on his throne, he killed all the house of Baasha; he did not leave him a single male of his kinsmen or his friends. ¹²Thus Zimri destroyed all the house of Baasha, according to the word of the Lord, which he

spoke against Baasha by Jehu the prophet, ¹³for all the sins of Baasha and the sins of Elah his son which they sinned, and which they made Israel to sin, provoking the Lord God of Israel to anger with their idols. ¹⁴Now the rest of the acts of Elah, and all that he did, are they not written in the Book of the Chronicles of the Kings of Israel?

¹⁵In the twenty-seventh year of Asa king of Judah, Zimri reigned seven days in Tirzah. Now the troops were encamped against Gibbethon, which belonged to the Philistines, ¹⁶and the troops who were encamped heard it said, "Zimri has conspired, and he has killed the king"; therefore all Israel made Omri, the commander of the army, king over Israel that day in the camp. ¹⁷So Omri went up from Gibbethon, and all Israel with him, and they besieged Tirzah. ¹⁸And when Zimri saw that the city was taken, he went into the citadel of the king's house, and burned the king's house over him with fire, and died, ¹⁹because of his sins which he committed, doing evil in the sight of the Lord, walking in the way of Jeroboam, and for his sin which he committed, making Israel to sin. ²⁰Now the rest of the acts of Zimri, and the conspiracy which he made, are they not written in the Book of the Chronicles of the Kings of Israel?

²¹Then the people of Israel were divided into two parts; half of the people followed Tibni the son of Ginath, to make him king, and half followed Omri. ²²But the people who followed Omri overcame the people who followed Tibni the son of Ginath; so Tibni died, and Omri became king. ²³In the thirty-first year of Asa king of Judah, Omri began to reign over Israel, and reigned for twelve years; six years he reigned in Tirzah. ²⁴He bought the hill of Samaria from Shemer for two talents of silver; and he fortified the hill, and called the name of the city which he built, Samaria, after the name of Shemer, the owner of the hill.

²⁵Omri did what was evil in the sight of the Lord, and did more evil than all who were before him. ²⁶For he walked in all the way of Jeroboam the son of Nebat, and in the sins which he made Israel to sin, provoking the Lord, the God of Israel, to anger by their idols. ²⁷Now the rest of the acts of Omri which he did, and the might that he showed, are they not written in the Book of the Chronicles of the Kings of Israel? ²⁸And Omri slept with his fathers, and was buried in Samaria; and Ahab his son reigned in his stead.

²⁹In the thirty-eighth year of Asa king of Judah, Ahab the son of Omri began to reign over Israel, and Ahab the son of Omri reigned over Israel in Samaria twenty-two years. ³⁰And Ahab the son of

Omri did evil in the sight of the Lord more than all that were before
him. ³¹And as if it had been a light thing for him to walk in the sins
of Jeroboam the son of Nebat, he took for wife Jezebel the daughter
of Ethbaal king of the Sidonians, and went and served Baal, and
worshipped him. ³²He erected an altar for Baal in the house of Baal,
which he built in Samaria. ³³And Ahab made an Asherah. Ahab did
more to provoke the Lord, the God of Israel, to anger than all the
kings of Israel who were before him. ³⁴In his days Hiel of Bethel
built Jericho; he laid its foundation at the cost of Abiram his
firstborn, and set up its gates at the cost of his youngest son Segub,
according to the word of the Lord, which he spoke by Joshua the
son of Nun.

NINE KINGS OF JUDAH AND ISRAEL II—
COMMENTARY

1 Kings 15:1–16:34 (*cont'd*)

(i)

For many less sympathetic readers these two chapters represent
'quintessential Kings'. Nine monarchs are passed over—if not
in silence then at least more than succinctly—at an average of
seven and a half verses per head! No attempt is made to assess
the character of each, as a historian or biographer might. And
this is all the more disappointing after the deft characterizations
we have all enjoyed of Saul, David, Solomon, and even
Rehoboam and Jeroboam.

Part of the explanation may simply be the availability of
information to our historian—or the lack of it—some four
centuries after these kings reigned. For details on those kings
whose actions had not lived on in the ripples of popular story-
telling the historian had to depend on the terse entries from the
archives. We all know his situation well. Any Scot knows many
stories about King Robert the Bruce, but would be hard pressed
to say much about his immediate successors. Everyone knows
about King Henry VIII and his matrimonial troubles, but much
less about his Tudor forebears. Some characters of our own
times too are much larger than their entries in the archives—for
others we have to content ourselves with the cryptic entries in
Who's Who.

Before we content ourselves with that explanation, we have
to note at least that the author of Chronicles did find more to
say about many of the kings of Judah. Yet few of his special
narratives have the force of those in Kings: they seem to be
more 'pious legends' than 'good stories'! But there is another
and more positive reason too for our author's approach in
Kings. The title we use for these books is not his: we have
already remarked that *Kings and Prophets* or *Why did Jerusalem Fall?* might have been more suitable. He is concerned to
show that that final collapse had age-old causes that went back
almost to the roots of monarchy in Judah and Israel. Already in
the time of Jeroboam and Rehoboam his people were set on
course for disaster. Detailed documentation of all their successors, even if it were to hand, is hardly necessary.

(ii)

Rehoboam's two successors in Judah (Abijam and Asa)
spanned almost half a century. The Chronicler makes a lot of
the war between the first of these and Jeroboam (2 Chron. 13):
Judah's resounding victory is punishment for Israel's apostasy.
For our historian, Abijam is only tolerated for the sake of his
great-grandfather; he himself is no better than his bad father.
Both accounts will tell us a lot about the views of their authors,
and how little hard information they had.

Their estimates vary too over the long reign of Asa. For our
author, Asa is a good king, almost without qualification. He
undid most of the religious wrongs of his predecessors: although sanctuaries other than the Jerusalem Temple were
retained, Judah's religion was purged of idols—even at the cost
of his own mother's removal from court. The burning of her
sacred pole by the waters of the Kidron (15:13) reminds us of
the fate of the golden calf in Deuteronomy 9:21. No value is put
on his warring with Baasha of Israel "all their days" (v.32). No
blame is attached even to the ailment in his "feet" in his old age
(v.23). But for the Chronicler (2 Chron. chs. 14–16) Asa starts
well and then declines. The wars with the north begin only after
thirty-five years peace, and are marred by Asa buying Syrian

help. His ailment is only one symptom of his loss ɔf trust in the Lord.

(iii)

These two chapters, (1 Kings 15–16), partly through the 'accident' of Asa's long reign, provide us with a typical first impression of the greater stability of the ongoing house of David in Judah when compared with the regular dynastic upsets in northern Israel. For the several kings of Israel in the same half-century we have to rely only on the testimony of Kings: the northern apostates are only given passing mention in Chronicles when they impinge directly on the affairs of Judah.

Several of these short scenes from Israel aptly illustrate the principle that the sins of the fathers are visited on the sons. Rehoboam had to settle Solomon's account; and the model was followed. Jeroboam's son Nadab (vv.25–27) failed in the eyes of our historian to live up to the promise of his name, which means 'generous' or 'noble': he did not give up his father's religious innovations. Baasha overthrew him when in the field against Israel's arch-enemy, the Philistines—and proceeded to root out the whole family (v.29).

He himself was to reign for nearly a quarter-century, but made no alteration to his victim's religious policy. Accordingly Jehu ben-Hanani repeats against him precisely the threat made by Ahijah against Jeroboam (16:2ff.). And the threat is executed in similar fashion—on Baasha's son Elah. Baasha himself comes to a peaceful death and burial. Verse 7 of 1 Kings 16 is worth pondering. Baasha came under judgment, not for destroying the house of Jeroboam, but for doing so and being no better himself. We might compare Amos's denunciation of Israel (Amos chs. 1–2) for being no better than the nations around her.

Elah (vv.8ff.) is not with his troops outside Philistine Gibbethon when Zimri disposes of him, but is a drunken guest of his own royal chamberlain. However, the army in the field were to have nothing to do with the usurper: a quick march to Tirzah and a short seige of the capital led to his suicide (v.18) after only seven days. The situation remained unstable, with Tibni ruling over part of Israel; but the army's candidate Omri finally had the upper hand.

The rich court of Omri and his son Ahab provides the background to the career of Elijah, and we shall discuss them more fully in the portions that follow. Here we note simply that Elijah enters the stage as the divine response to the king, "[who] did more to provoke the Lord, the God of Israel, to anger than all the kings of Israel who were before him" (16:33).

ELIJAH INTRODUCED

1 Kings 17:1–24

¹Now Elijah the Tishbite, of Tishbe in Gilead, said to Ahab, "As the Lord the God of Israel lives, before whom I stand, there shall be neither dew nor rain these years, except by my word." ²And the word of the Lord came to him, ³"Depart from here and turn eastward, and hide yourself by the brook Cherith, that is east of the Jordan. ⁴You shall drink from the brook, and I have commanded the ravens to feed you there." ⁵So he went and did according to the word of the Lord; he went and dwelt by the brook Cherith that is east of the Jordan. ⁶And the ravens brought him bread and meat in the morning, and bread and meat in the evening; and he drank from the brook. ⁷And after a while the brook dried up, because there was no rain in the land.

⁸Then the word of the Lord came to him, ⁹"Arise, go to Zarephath, which belongs to Sidon, and dwell there. Behold, I have commanded a widow there to feed you." ¹⁰So he arose and went to Zarephath; and when he came to the gate of the city, behold, a widow was there gathering sticks; and he called to her and said, "Bring me a little water in a vessel, that I may drink." ¹¹And as she was going to bring it, he called to her and said, "Bring me a morsel of bread in your hand." ¹²And she said, "As the Lord your God lives, I have nothing baked, only a handful of meal in a jar, and a little oil in a cruse; and now, I am gathering a couple of sticks, that I may go in and prepare it for myself and my son, that we may eat it, and die." ¹³And Elijah said to her, "Fear not; go and do as you have said; but first make me a little cake of it and bring it to me, and afterward make for yourself and your son. ¹⁴For thus says the Lord

the God of Israel, 'The jar of meal shall not be spent, and the cruse of oil shall not fail, until the day that the Lord sends rain upon the earth.'" [15]And she went and did as Elijah said; and she, and he, and her household ate for many days. [16]The jar of meal was not spent, neither did the cruse of oil fail, according to the word of the Lord which he spoke by Elijah.

[17]After this the son of the woman, the mistress of the house, became ill; and his illness was so severe that there was no breath left in him. [18]And she said to Elijah, "What have you against me, O man of God? You have come to me to bring my sin to remembrance, and to cause the death of my son!" [19]And he said to her, "Give me your son." And he took him from her bosom, and carried him up into the upper chamber, where he lodged, and laid him upon his own bed. [20]And he cried to the Lord, "O Lord my God, hast thou brought calamity even upon the widow with whom I sojourn, by slaying her son?" [21]Then he stretched himself upon the child three times, and cried to the Lord, "O Lord my God, let this child's soul come into him again." [22]And the Lord hearkened to the voice of Elijah; and the soul of the child came into him again, and he revived. [23]And Elijah took the child, and brought him down from the upper chamber into the house, and delivered him to his mother; and Elijah said, "See, your son lives." [24]And the woman said to Elijah, "Now I know that you are a man of God, and that the word of the Lord in your mouth is truth."

(i)

We encounter here one of the Bible's most majestic figures. The Elijah traditions are not extensive: they occupy only the next few chapters of our text. But the 'hero' they sketch is commanding, and even monumental, without ceasing for a moment to be utterly human, and even fragile. The last words of our Old Testament (Mal. 4:5–6) denote an expectation of his return before the coming day of the Lord; and he is a wholly worthy precursor of Jesus of Nazareth in point after point of comparison.

Elijah is an outsider in the capital. Gilead is away on the other (eastern) side of the Jordan, and Tishbe we know only as Elijah's home. When he confronts King Ahab in all the magnificence we now know was Samaria, his status comes not from his background but from his God. "Before whom I stand" (v.1) is his claim to authority: it is a technical phrase used of a king's

first or 'prime' minister—his confidant and chief executive.
And his oath is tied to the very life-force of his Lord Yahweh. If
he truly lives, his threat of no rain is an awesome one. The
gauntlet is thrown down; and God's very life is on the line. But
the contest is not yet; and prudent withdrawal is appropriate for
God's champion (or perhaps rather his 'second'?).

(ii)

Elijah is first (vv.2ff.) sent back east across the Jordan, to hide
by a watercourse named Cherith, which is as unknown to us as
Tishbe. From it he can drink; and food will be supplied by the
'crybym—which read one way means 'ravens' and pronounced another way means 'Arabs' (which originally means
'beduin', people who know how to live in the desert). But once
the brook dries up, neither can help him.

He is sent next (vv.8ff.) north-east to what we know as the
Lebanese coast, to one of the ports between Tyre and Sidon,
there to live a little longer, courtesy of a widow of the town.
Many of us who have known the story of her jar of meal and
cruse of oil from the days of childhood, when we were also read
folk tales of magic and marvellous deeds, will see God's
miraculous intervention here too; and we may be right. But this
story also may be read another way—and quite as fairly. A lot
hangs on whether Elijah's would-be landlady told the whole
truth at their first meeting (v.12), or whether she did not start by
prevaricating a little over the extent of her supplies—to protect
her family of course! The important thing is that in the end she
does respond to his plea and to his assurance: she takes him on
trust *before* she has any evidence. It is this point that is brought
out clearly at the end of the chapter, where she is finally able to
say, "Now I know . . . ".

Readers may bring their own preferences to these feeding
stories and opt either for birds or for beduin, for a renewing
store or a stock that was always just sufficient. But what we all
must see is that normal relationships are being overturned
around Elijah. Both ravens and the people of the desert have
reputations as scroungers, not suppliers. And a widow and her

orphan son might have expected to be the beneficiaries of charity, not its providers. Arab beduin and a Lebanese widow both caring for an Israelite man of God out of their meagre resources—the theme is too close to several episodes in Jesus' parables for us easily to avoid the master's repeated imperative: "You go and do the same!"

(iii)

When disaster strikes the vicinity of Elijah next (vv.17ff.), it is not the loss of the water-supply but calamity in the household of his hostess. It is true that Hebrew, even more than English, talks of people "reviving", without implying that they had been physically dead. It is true that the story-teller does not actually confirm brain death or the absence of heart beat. But the lady of the house takes the lad for dead and blames Elijah, and he takes him for dead and blames God.

The woman assumes, or knows, that the tragedy is her own fault—could she even be referring in verse 18 to having misled Elijah at first over whether she could feed him? And much biblical tradition and indeed much popular morality too agree with her analysis. You reap what you sow. You get what you deserve. You pay for doing wrong. Yet Elijah himself (v.20) takes a rather different tack with his God. Like Naomi (Ruth 1:21), and like Job (2:10), Elijah simply protests against the malevolence of Yahweh who brings calamity as well as blessing—even when no moral reason can be glimpsed. He intercedes on the lad's behalf, and he also seeks to coax the boy's life-force back into his still frame. Never having commented on the mother's claim that the boy was dead nor on her proposal that she was the cause, he is now able simply to hand him back alive.

The mother's response is rather mixed up and entirely natural. Elijah was already "man of God" to her when she blamed him for the boy's death (v.18); and she now "knows" he is "a man of God" because he has returned her lad alive; and as a bonus she is also sure that Yahweh's word in his mouth is to be relied on. Does that refer back to the divine promise that food would not run out until rain came (v.14)?

(iv)

One last word. The Books of Chronicles are as silent about the stories of Elijah and Elisha as they are about the Kings of the northern kingdom of Israel. This loud silence makes it all the more likely that these tales come from a different source from the royal annals shared by Kings and Chronicles. They are appropriate exactly here in the Books of Kings, not just because bad King Ahab is their anti-hero, but because we have just been reminded in the last verse of chapter 16 of an earlier servant of God. Joshua's public vindication as an accurate bearer of the divine word has had to wait many hundreds of years.

ELIJAH AND AHAB

1 Kings 18:1–19

¹After many days the word of the Lord came to Elijah, in the third year, saying, "Go, show yourself to Ahab; and I will send rain upon the earth." ²So Elijah went to show himself to Ahab. Now the famine was severe in Samaria. ³And Ahab called Obadiah who was over the household. (Now Obadiah revered the Lord greatly; ⁴and when Jezebel cut off the prophets of the Lord, Obadiah took a hundred prophets and hid them by fifties in a cave, and fed them with bread and water.) ⁵And Ahab said to Obadiah, "Go through the land to all the springs of water and to all the valleys; perhaps we may find grass and save the horses and mules alive, and not lose some of the animals." ⁶So they divided the land between them to pass through it; Ahab went in one direction by himself, and Obadiah went in another direction by himself.

⁷And as Obadiah was on the way, behold, Elijah met him; and Obadiah recognised him, and fell on his face, and said, "Is it you, my lord Elijah?" ⁸And he answered him, "It is I. Go, tell your lord, 'Behold, Elijah is here.'" ⁹And he said, "Wherein have I sinned, that you would give your servant into the hand of Ahab, to kill me? ¹⁰As the Lord your God lives, there is no nation or kingdom whither my lord has not sent to seek you; and when they would say, 'He is not here,' he would take an oath of the kingdom or nation, that they had not found you. ¹¹And now you say, 'Go, tell your lord, "Behold, Elijah is here."' ¹²And as soon as I have gone from you, the Spirit of

the Lord will carry you whither I know not; and so, when I come
and tell Ahab and he cannot find you, he will kill me, although I
your servant have revered the Lord from my youth. ¹³Has it not
been told my lord what I did when Jezebel killed the prophets of the
Lord, how I hid a hundred men of the Lord's prophets by fifties in a
cave, and fed them with bread and water? ¹⁴And now you say, 'Go,
tell your lord, "Behold, Elijah is here"'; and he will kill me." ¹⁵And
Elijah said, "As the Lord of hosts lives, before whom I stand, I will
surely show myself to him today." ¹⁶So Obadiah went to meet
Ahab, and told him; and Ahab went to meet Elijah.

¹⁷When Ahab saw Elijah, Ahab said to him, "Is it you, you
troubler of Israel?" ¹⁸And he answered, "I have not troubled Israel;
but you have, and your father's house, because you have forsaken
the commandments of the Lord and followed the Baals. ¹⁹Now
therefore send and gather all Israel to me at Mount Carmel, and the
four hundred and fifty prophets of Baal and the four hundred
prophets of Asherah, who eat at Jezebel's table."

(i)

After the three episodes of 1 Kings 17:2–24, we are brought
back to the opening theme of that chapter: control of the rains.
In the interim, some considerable time has passed and the
famine is now severe (v.2). In the meantime too, our knowledge
of God's "man" in this crisis has grown. He himself has been
unusually preserved, and has himself acted to preserve life. He
is now instructed to bring the good news to King Ahab.

The king is at the same time issuing instructions to his
chamberlain. The bracketed verses (3b–4) take pains to point
out to us that this official did live up to his name: like the Arabic
and Muslim Abdullah, Obadiah means 'servant/worshipper of
God'. We have to make up our own minds whether the problem
of fodder for the royal horses was simply top of Ahab's agenda
that day, or whether his stables took precedence over his
people.

The meeting of the two loyal followers of Yahweh (vv.7ff.)
makes an interesting scene. Obadiah's uncertainty as to whether he should believe the evidence of his own eyes (v.7) is
explained in verse 10. And Elijah's rather brusque dismissal of

the official to announce his own arrival (v.11) produces in the poor man a reaction like the widow's (17:18)—death ought to be the consequence of sin. In fact Obadiah had been fairly confident up to this point that he had not transgressed, and he stresses his past good record to Elijah (v.13). Yet, like his divine master, the latter is more concerned with present obedience than with past loyalty. However, he does guarantee on oath that he will "show [him] self" before the king that day (v.15).

This expression is nicely chosen. On one level it is a perfectly regular phrase for meeting or presenting oneself before someone. But on another it is also used to express the manifestation of divine envoys and the phenomena of visions. Elijah neatly side-steps Obadiah's suggestion (v.12) that God's "Spirit" (or is it his "wind"?) plays vanishing tricks with him.

(ii)

Nothing is told of how Ahab received his official's report: bearing strange news to our chief is not always as terrifying in the event as we fear in advance! Perhaps the king had been expecting Elijah's next "word" (17:1) from the very beginning. He does not wait to receive him, but goes to meet him.

The protagonists trade insults. Each blames the other in identical terms (18:17–18) for the national "disaster"—and I choose the word quite deliberately in preference to RSV's "trouble". I have discussed the question already in connection with Joshua chapter 7 and the sin of Achan: "troubles" we can have many of, but *'achar* talks of what brings us to "ruin". Is the mortal threat to Israel posed by malevolent mischief with the divine word on the part of Elijah, or by disloyal apostasy from the nation's God by Ahab and the royal family he heads?

The specific problem of rain is not yet openly broached, but only alluded to when each blames the other for the disaster. The tension is increased as Elijah *instructs* (v.19) the king to call a national assembly on Mount Carmel. Obviously this could only be a representative assembly. It is interesting to speculate whether Elijah reckoned the 850 prophets of Baal and Asherah *among* the members of his assembled nation, or *additional to*

them. At any rate he does not hold his king responsible for their
upkeep. That he describes (diplomatically?) as a charge on
Ahab's foreign queen.

(iii)

Elijah's analysis of the situation is very similar to that of our
historian in Kings. We can detect this in the narrator's introduction of Ahab in 1 Kings 16:29–34, from his significant addition to
the standard format. Ahab did not just continue in Jeroboam's
ways, which were already deemed apostasy (itself the most
heinous national sin), but made things worse by adopting
formally the worship of Baal in a new temple in the new capital
city of Samaria. This disastrous religious policy was associated
with his marriage with Jezebel, daughter of Ethbaal of Sidon.
As with Obadiah, the original Hebrew readers of this account
would have seen all revealed in the very names of the Phoenician father and daughter: Ethbaal signifies "Baal exists" or
"Baal is with him"; and Jezebel means "Where is the Prince?"—
a name taken from a Canaanite liturgy bewailing the summer-
long absence of Prince Baal, god of storm and rain.

It is over Ahab and his father Omri (who only gets a short
paragraph: 16:21–28) that the interests of the biblical narrator
in Kings diverge most radically from the concerns of his non-
biblical counterparts in both ancient and modern times. In the
great empires round about, Omri's name was used in preference
to the national name—the Assyrians, for example, continued to
call northern Israel 'the house of Omri' long after his dynasty
had been toppled by another. And archaeology in the last half-
century has amply confirmed the justice of this. Ahab and
Omri's new capital of Samaria was substantially and impres-
sively constructed. Its beautifully preserved decorative carvings
in ivory are perhaps the most haunting exhibits in Jerusalem's
museums. And a number of today's researchers are convinced
that some of the great public works in other northern cities of
Israel once ascribed to Solomon a century earlier are in fact
further evidence of the achievements of Omri and Ahab.

But in none of this does the narrator of Kings take any

interest at all! Omri simply continued in Jeroboam's bad way. And the additional detail at the end of 16:26 deflates his reputation even more effectively than RSV suggests. "Idols" implies construction and activity. The Hebrew word literally means an 'insubstantial puff of wind': 'empty impotences' might better capture our writer's scorn. And Ahab did the same but worse. The monumental and beautiful construction work over which they presided is passed over in silence which (at least beyond the formal record in 16:24 of Samaria's fortification) is total—unless we suppose that these efforts too are deftly snubbed by the shocking report of the rebuilding of Jericho at the cost of human sacrifice (16:34).

THE CONTEST ON CARMEL

1 Kings 18:20–46

20So Ahab sent to all the people of Israel, and gathered the prophets together at Mount Carmel. 21And Elijah came near to all the people, and said, "How long will you go limping with two different opinions? If the Lord is God, follow him; but if Baal, then follow him." And the people did not answer him a word. 22Then Elijah said to the people, "I, even I only, am left a prophet of the Lord; but Baal's prophets are four hundred and fifty men. 23Let two bulls be given to us; and let them choose one bull for themselves, and cut it in pieces and lay it on the wood, but put no fire to it; and I will prepare the other bull and lay it on the wood, and put no fire to it. 24And you call on the name of your god and I will call on the name of the Lord; and the God who answers by fire, he is God." And all the people answered, "It is well spoken." 25Then Elijah said to the prophets of Baal, "Choose for yourselves one bull and prepare it first, for you are many; and call on the name of your god, but put no fire to it." 26And they took the bull which was given them, and they prepared it, and called on the name of Baal from morning until noon, saying, "O Baal, answer us!" But there was no voice, and no one answered. And they limped about the altar which they had made. 27And at noon Elijah mocked them, saying, "Cry aloud, for he is a god; either he is musing, or he has gone aside, or he is on a journey, or perhaps he is asleep and must be awakened." 28And they cried aloud, and cut themselves after their custom with swords and lances, until the blood gushed out upon them. ²⁹And as midday passed, they raved on until the time of the offering of the oblation, but there was no voice; no one answered, no one heeded.

³⁰Then Elijah said to all the people, "Come near to me"; and all the people came near to him. And he repaired the altar of the Lord that had been thrown down; ³¹Elijah took twelve stones, according to the number of the tribes of the sons of Jacob, to whom the word of the Lord came, saying, "Israel shall be your name"; ³²and with the stones he built an altar in the name of the Lord. And he made a trench about the altar, as great as would contain two measures of seed. ³³And he put the wood in order, and cut the bull in pieces and laid it on the wood. And he said, "Fill four jars with water, and pour it on the burnt offering, and on the wood." ³⁴And he said, "Do it a second time"; and they did it a second time. And he said, "Do it a third time"; and they did it a third time. ³⁵And the water ran round about the altar, and filled the trench also with water.

³⁶And at the time of the offering of the oblation, Elijah the prophet came near and said, "O Lord, God of Abraham, Isaac, and Israel, let it be known this day that thou art God in Israel, and that I am thy servant, and that I have done all these things at thy word. ³⁷Answer me, O Lord, answer me, that this people may know that thou, O Lord, art God, and that thou hast turned their hearts back." ³⁸Then the fire of the Lord fell, and consumed the burnt offering, and the wood, and the stones, and the dust, and licked up the water that was in the trench. ³⁹And when all the people saw it, they fell on their faces; and they said, "The Lord, he is God; the Lord, he is God." ⁴⁰And Elijah said to them, "Seize the prophets of Baal; let not one of them escape." And they seized them; and Elijah brought them down to the brook Kishon, and killed them there.

⁴¹And Elijah said to Ahab, "Go up, eat and drink; for there is a sound of the rushing of rain." ⁴²So Ahab went up to eat and to drink. And Elijah went up to the top of Carmel; and he bowed himself down upon the earth, and put his face between his knees. ⁴³And he said to his servant, "Go up now, look toward the sea." And he went up and looked, and said, "There is nothing." And he said, "Go again seven times." ⁴⁴And at the seventh time he said, "Behold, a little cloud like a man's hand is rising out of the sea." And he said, "Go up, say to Ahab, 'Prepare your chariot and go down, lest the rain stop you.'" ⁴⁵And in a little while the heavens grew black with clouds and wind, and there was a great rain. And

Ahab rode and went to Jezreel. ⁴⁶And the hand of the Lord was on Elijah; and he girded up his loins and ran before Ahab to the entrance of Jezreel.

(i)

Only now do we reach the climax of the action inaugurated in Elijah's opening words: "[no] rain . . . except by my word" (1·7:1). And yet to say this may already be to court misunderstanding. Elijah's most important words are his very first ones: "as the Lord the God of Israel lives". The contest on Carmel is not, as often billed, between Elijah and the prophets of Baal: it is between his Lord Yahweh himself and Lord Baal. The humans are involved only as 'seconds'. And even if the seconds on one side pay with their lives for being on the losing side, and it is Elijah who precedes the king on his journey home, the people are right to proclaim Yahweh alone (v.39): "The Lord, he is God; the Lord, he is God". Their confession may remind us of the regular opening to Muslim prayer: "There is no God but God . . . and Muhammad is his messenger"—yet their silence about Elijah is eloquent. I suspect the biblical tradition has not been altogether faithful to them, and that part of the original point of the story was against "prophesying" in general, and not just about false prophecy in the name of Baal. We discussed aspects of this situation above in connection with 1 Kings 13 (p.94).

RSV catches but also conceals the issue well when it offers the translation "raved on" in verse 29. It catches the author's scorn of religious devotion that requires self-laceration. But it leaves the reader unaware that the Hebrew verb being translated is the normal one for "prophesying". At least in the earlier biblical period, that word had more to do with extravagant behaviour than with exalted communication. This is nicely illustrated in the two stories about King Saul falling in with bands of "prophets" (1 Sam. 10:1–13; 19:20–24). The position is similar towards the end of the puzzling narrative in Numbers 11, where at least some of the notables in the community found the behaviour of Eldad and Medad reprehensible.

These passages show that "prophesying" itself was a problem, not just the fact that it was being done in devotion to Baal. This helps me deduce that when Elijah himself is twice called "prophet", we are dealing with modifications to the original story. The one case (v.36) is not reflected in the old Greek Bible. And the other (v.22) is not repeated in Elijah's words in the next chapter (19:10, 14)—there he implies he is the only worshipper or servant left to Yahweh, not the only "prophet". And that makes more effective sense in chapter 18 as well.

(ii)

Such words may depict Elijah as exaggerating the situation in his pessimism, but they are consistent with other parts of the record. Obadiah would not have agreed with him (vv.3–4, 9); yet Elijah hardly acknowledges him as an ally, perhaps deeming him compromised through remaining in the king's service. And this was his specific complaint about the people at large. Their condition was a clinical one: their attempt to acknowledge two religious traditions at the same time was not a liberating, tolerating, life-enhancing pluralism—it was simply maiming them (v.21). The two horses they were trying to ride were running not in parallel, but in different, directions. Their resulting antics were quite as ungainly as the limping or hopping dances of Baal's prophets round their altar (v.26)— *and quite as useless.*

Of course Elijah does exaggerate. Like most of us when we are mocking others, he is less than fair. When he talks of Baal as absent, or busy, or even asleep, we smile and think, "How primitive!" And yet the Biblical psalms also talk of God in similar pictures:

Then the Lord awoke as from sleep,
  like a strong man shouting because of wine.
And he put his adversaries to rout;
  he put them to everlasting shame.

                              (Ps. 78:65–66)

Rouse thyself! Why sleepest thou, O Lord?
Awake! Do not cast us off for ever!
Why dost thou hide thy face?
Why dost thou forget our affliction and oppression?

(Ps. 44:23–24)

(iii)

The issue between Yahweh and Baal was control of the skies
and the weather.

Among the gods of Canaan, Baal was worshipped as the god
who rode on the clouds, the god who understood lightning, and
the god who set his thunder-bolt in the heavens. Each one of
these various characteristics is alluded to in the course of our
passage.

Elijah turns his people's neutrality or indifference between
Yahweh and Baal to his own advantage. They become umpire
or jury. It is to them, and not directly to the prophets of Baal,
that Elijah proposes the terms of the contest (vv.23–24); and
they deem them fair: "the God who answers by fire, he is God".
The God who can focus his lightning on a small altar on
Carmel, like a precisely controlled laser weapon, is worthy to be
called "God". Then, when we learn after a day of unceasing
effort that there is no response from Baal (v.29), the first
intimation is "there was no voice". And that would have
conveyed to the ancient Hebrew reader that not even a distant
rumble of "thunder" was heard. Finally "Baal's" clouds make
their appearance in the closing episode of our chapter
(vv.41–46).

Point by point, the expertise claimed for Baal is shown to be
defective. When Yahweh's power is demonstrated, the people
acclaim him not simply as being worthy of being called "a god".
The Hebrew of verse 39 rendered rather more literally than in
RSV has them say: "Yahweh, he is *the* god". They recognize
him now as "the [sole] god"—or simply, as RSV has it, as
"God" with a capital 'G'. This claims for Yahweh rather more
than their ancestors had, when they declared before Joshua at
Shechem "[Yahweh] is *our* God" (Josh. 24:18).

It is often said that this divine contest was fundamentally a territorial dispute: which god controlled Carmel—what was the frontier between Israel and Canaan? I suspect that that approach limits this story too much. We have already read in the previous chapter about Yahweh's care for Elijah's needs east of Jordan and in a port on the Canaanite coast. As Yahweh's power was not limited to Israel, so too this demonstration oᶠ Baal's impotence had implications beyond Israel's limits.

ELIJAH TO HOREB

1 Kings 19:1-10

¹Ahab told Jezebel all that Elijah had done, and how he had slain all the prophets with the sword. ²Then Jezebel sent a messenger to Elijah, saying, "So may the gods do to me, and more also, if I do not make your life as the life of one of them by this time tomorrow." ³Then he was afraid, and he arose and went for his life, and came to Beer-sheba, which belongs to Judah, and left his servant there.

⁴But he himself went a day's journey into the wilderness, and came and sat down under a broom tree; and he asked that he might die, saying, "It is enough; now, O Lord, take away my life; for I am no better than my fathers." ⁵And he lay down and slept under a broom tree; and behold, an angel touched him, and said to him, "Arise and eat." ⁶And he looked, and behold, there was at his head a cake baked on hot stones and a jar of water. And he ate and drank, and lay down again. ⁷And the angel of the Lord came again a second time, and touched him, and said, "Arise and eat, else the journey will be too great for you." ⁸And he arose, and ate and drank, and went in the strength of that food forty days and forty nights to Horeb the mount of God.

⁹And there he came to a cave, and lodged there; and behold, the word of the Lord came to him, and he said to him, "What are you doing here, Elijah?" ¹⁰He said, "I have been very jealous for the Lord, the God of hosts; for the people of Israel have forsaken thy covenant, thrown down thy altars, and slain thy prophets with the sword; and I, even I only, am left; and they seek my life, to take it away."

(i)

Elijah is on any count one of the giants among biblical characters; and at the same time—like Jeremiah—one with whom we very readily identify. After the heights of triumph come the depths of despair. And it is often when in this second state that we are rather more open to fundamental new learning.

He may have been only the Lord's second in his contest with Baal; yet all the members of a boxer's team share some of the glory of the victory. We have noted how Elijah preceded the king on his ride to Jezreel (18:46). (And where better to journey after this divine end to the drought—for its very name means "God sows"!) However, Elijah now has neither strength nor courage to stand up to Jezebel's rage.

We are left to wonder whether, quite naturally, he was simply exhausted by his recent efforts, and no longer able to face even a lesser challenge—or whether there was a quality to Jezebel's fury before which even an Elijah quailed. The 'power behind the throne'—whether consort or other counsellor—is regularly much harder to deal with than the monarch himself. Unlike the king, she is not bound by constitutional niceties like attention to the rule of law. Like the Queen of Hearts, or the chief of a 'dirty tricks' department, she may simply declare, "Off with his head!".

Jezebel's role as *éminence grise* is made still harder to handle because she is a foreigner. And biblical tradition states with particular eloquence our near-universal suspicion of strangers. The Book of Proverbs writes eloquently of the pitfalls in dealing with the "foreign woman". And the figure of Jezebel both embodies and reinforces that popular suspicion.

(ii)

Elijah heads south, right across or past Judah to its southern town of Beersheba, hallowed by its associations with his people's first fathers. We know from Amos 5:4–6 that it also had a sanctuary of the rank of Bethel and Gilgal. What starts as flight from Jezebel's wrath takes on the character of pilgrimage to the places of his very roots. A journey of this kind is essentially a private, personal one. His servant is left in Beersheba, as he himself heads further into the southern wilderness. Jesus too was to require space and distance from even his closest followers.

Having wrested from Jezebel the chance to have him assassinated, he now bares his neck to God and asks him to be the executioner! He claims that he is no better than his fathers (v.4). The words of someone in mortal despair deserve very close attention, but are not always to be taken at face value. It is interesting to wonder whom he means by "[his] fathers". Perhaps on Carmel he had begun to trust that he had special capabilities; and now his fear before Jezebel had 'cut him down to size'? Perhaps he had even begun to rank himself above the first fathers of his faith into whose territory he was now moving. To take more deliberate steps towards suicide would not have been acceptable. He is simply exhausted and at the end of his tether. He lies down in the shade of a bush with the prayer that Jonah was to repeat in his frustration outside Nineveh (Jonah 4:3)—the prayer that many have quietly repeated since: not to wake up again in the morning.

The initial part of the divine answer (v.5) was neither explanation nor demonstration: plenty of that was to follow! Elijah's first need was simply care and food. (And so it is with most of those who ask for God's release.) He is cared for now in the southern wilderness, as he had been east of the Jordan, and in a northern foreign port (ch.17). And the same questions rise in many minds here as there: was Elijah served by a natural or a supernatural agency? To help clear the ground, we must first protest against RSV and other translations using the word "angel" in verses 5 and 7: to choose that term settles the discussion. Yet the Hebrew word in these verses is simply the common term for "messenger", and is used in the Bible for human and divine emissaries and ambassadors and ordinary servants without distinction. The very word "angel" predisposes our minds to think of aliens with wings and white robes, although in gratitude we do sometimes say to someone, 'You're an angel', when they have surprised us by their love and care.

Most often, when the Old Testament talks of "God's *messenger*" it is quite uninterested in the background of the servant; it is concerned, as here, only to assert that God himself was behind the action performed. The theological point is rather like the one we noted towards the end of the previous chapter (v.39). The people's confession, when it comes, is of God only—Elijah's role is *quite properly not* included. "To God alone be the glory!"

(iii)

At his second meal (v.7) Elijah learns that he is not simply being revived, but is being prepared for a journey—it is not said where. The route Elijah takes, in the strength of the food, is actually further into the wilderness—to the very mountain where first Moses (Exod. 3) and then his whole people (Exod. 20) were addressed directly by the Lord himself. On arrival he takes up residence in a cave, until God addresses him in his own time (v.9): "What are you doing here?" It is rather like learning to ride in the army, with a cavalry sergeant bellowing at the unfortunate on the ground: "Who gave you permission to dismount?"! To excuse his presence at the mountain, Elijah blames not Jezebel but the whole sorry national situation, and claims that he alone constitutes the tiny remnant loyal to Yahweh.

Diversion this journey may be. But God ensures that the visit to Horeb is not a complete distraction.

ELIJAH AT HOREB

1 Kings 19:11–21

¹¹And he said, "Go forth, and stand upon the mount before the Lord." And behold, the Lord passed by, and a great and strong wind rent the mountains, and broke in pieces the rocks before the Lord, but the Lord was not in the wind; and after the wind an

earthquake, but the Lord was not in the earthquake; ¹²and after the earthquake a fire, but the Lord was not in the fire; and after the fire a still small voice. ¹³And when Elijah heard it, he wrapped his face in his mantle and went out and stood at the entrance of the cave. And behold, there came a voice to him, and said, "What are you doing here, Elijah?" ¹⁴He said, "I have been very jealous for the Lord, the God of hosts; for the people of Israel have forsaken thy covenant, thrown down thy altars, and slain thy prophets with the sword; and I, even I only, am left; and they seek my life, to take it away." ¹⁵And the Lord said to him, "Go, return on your way to the wilderness of Damascus; and when you arrive, you shall anoint Hazael to be king over Syria; ¹⁶and Jehu the son of Nimshi you shall anoint to be king over Israel; and Elisha the son of Shaphat of Abel-meholah you shall anoint to be prophet in your place. ¹⁷And him who escapes from the sword of Hazael shall Jehu slay; and him who escapes from the sword of Jehu shall Elisha slay. ¹⁸Yet I will leave seven thousand in Israel, all the knees that have not bowed to Baal, and every mouth that has not kissed him."

¹⁹So he departed from there, and found Elisha the son of Shaphat, who was ploughing, with twelve yoke of oxen before him, and he was with the twelfth. Elijah passed by him and cast his mantle upon him. ²⁰And he left the oxen, and ran after Elijah, and said, "Let me kiss my father and my mother, and then I will follow you." And he said to him, "Go back again; for what have I done to you?" ²¹And he returned from following him, and took the yoke of oxen, and slew them, and boiled their flesh with the yokes of the oxen, and gave it to the people, and they ate. Then he arose and went after Elijah, and ministered to him.

(i)

There is a great gap in time and space and situation and style between the classical (so-called 'writing') prophets of the Old Testament, beginning with Amos and Hosea and Isaiah and Micah, and Moses whom the Bible presents as the ideal, archetypal prophet. Yet the gap is not complete: parts of the space are occupied by the two transitional figures of Samuel and Elijah. Both continue, in a diminishing way, Moses' role as national leader: Samuel hands over the task to a king, while Elijah is simply king-maker (vv.15–16). The classical prophets, while deeply concerned about the conduct of their nation, have less power over it. Moreover, considerable interest is taken throughout in the direct experience of God and the address by him enjoyed by these few men.

The story of Moses' glimpse of God's back (Exod. 33:19–23) is our best point of comparison and of contrast with Elijah:

> And he said, "I will make all my goodness pass before you, and will proclaim before you my name 'The Lord'... But", he said, "you cannot see my face; for man shall not see me and live." And the Lord said, "Behold there is a place by me where you shall stand upon the rock; and while my glory passes by I will put you in a cleft of the rock, and I will cover you with my hand until I have passed by; then I will take away my hand, and you shall see my back; but my face shall not be seen."

Both men require the protection of a cave from the terror of what they experience. Both men learn that in glimpsing his glory or cowering before wind, earthquake and fire, they have not fully comprehended God. Moses sees only God's back, and it is in the peace *after* the storm that Elijah is addressed.

I suspect that this is where the ways divide. Had Moses seen more of the same, had he more than just glimpsed God's back, he would have been annihilated. The ancient Advent hymn catches the mood well in these familiar words (*The Church Hymnary*, Third Edition, Hymn 165, v.2):

> O come, O come, thou Lord of might,
> Who to thy tribes on Sinai's height,
> In ancient times didst give the law
> In cloud and majesty and awe.

Yet God does not disclose himself to Elijah in fearful display. What could have destroyed him did not in fact contain God's presence: the Lord was not in the wind, or the earthquake, or the fire.

Anticipating the theology of later and more fastidious times, our text finds it safer to make clear statements about where God is *not*, rather than where he *is*. When it moves from the negative to the positive, it turns from explicit statements to hints and suggestions. The end of verse 12 does not actually say that the Lord was in the "still small voice". However, when "a voice" does address Elijah (v.13), it is in exactly the same words and meets exactly the same response (v.14) as when "*the word of the Lord* came to him" (vv.9–10). That earlier phrase also shows the reluctance of the text to say simply that the Lord spoke to Elijah.

(ii)

The familiar "still small voice" of the Authorized Version, retained by RSV, is an attempt to render what the Hebrew also tries to catch in three words: an opportunity of which many have had experience, but all find hard to put into words. Literally attempted, the Hebrew means "a voice [or sound] of fine [or thin] silence [or quietness]". It is that pregnant silence in which one can hear the proverbial pin drop—and yet (much more important) in which one feels oneself challenged, and knows one has been addressed. It is that total yet audible stillness which is for many a necessary part of communion with God.

We are familiar enough with the witness of spiritual giants and faithful mystics who have testified that their most intimate experience of God has occurred in the peace and silence that have followed long privation or intense struggle. Silence is an important element in real worship, including public worship. It is so vital alongside its words and music and action, and yet so seldom properly provided for.

(iii)

The divine response (vv.15–18) comes at something of a tangent to Elijah's repeated complaint. After "What are you doing here, Elijah?", it underscores the suggestion that our hero's 'pilgrimage' in fact constitutes a not entirely welcome distraction from his proper business. It is not at all clear that the anointing of Hazael, Jehu and Elisha, represents an immediate answer to the details of Israel's apostasy as reported by Elijah. Elijah is being asked instead to participate in *God's* plan.

Only verse 18 requires some modification of what I have just written. Elijah is assured that even after the depredations (on Israel) of Hazael, Jehu and Elisha, there will remain 7000 faithful who have not apostasized from Yahweh to Baal. It seems to me that this is a deft but firm riposte to his fearful analysis that only he is left faithful to Israel's God.

We have some time to wait for the accomplishment of the whole mission—2 Kings (chs. 8–9) is relevant to the first two items. But the third is acted upon more immediately. Elijah recruits his attendant and successor at the workplace, as Jesus was to do with many of his followers. Elijah puts the whole onus on Elisha. The young man rightly understands the receipt of Elijah's mantle as a summons. Yet the master parries his request for immediate compassionate leave with the suggestion that he has made no claim on him. And in fact Luke 9:57–62 makes a clear allusion to this passage, and demands of Jesus' followers a more immediate and radical break with the past than is accepted in the case of Elisha here—compare also Matthew 8:18–22.

AHAB AND BEN-HADAD I—TEXT

1 Kings 20:1–43

[1]Ben-hadad the king of Syria gathered all his army together; thirty-two kings were with him, and horses and chariots; and he went up and besieged Samaria, and fought against it. [2]And he sent messengers into the city to Ahab king of Israel, and said to him, "Thus says Ben-hadad: [3]Your silver and your gold are mine; your fairest wives and children also are mine.'" [4]And the king of Israel answered, "As you say, my lord, O king, I am yours, and all that I have." [5]The messengers came again, and said, "Thus says Ben-hadad: 'I sent to you, saying, "Deliver to me your silver and your gold, your wives and your children"; [6]nevertheless I will send my servants to you tomorrow about this time, and they shall search your house and the

houses of your servants, and lay hands on whatever pleases them, and take it away.'"

⁷Then the king of Israel called all the elders of the land, and said, "Mark, now, and see how this man is seeking trouble; for he sent to me for my wives and my children, and for my silver and my gold, and I did not refuse him." ⁸And all the elders and all the people said to him, "Do not heed or consent." ⁹So he said to the messengers of Ben-hadad, "Tell my lord the king, 'All that you first demanded of your servant I will do; but this thing I cannot do.'" And the messengers departed and brought him word again. ¹⁰Ben-hadad sent to him and said, "The gods do so to me, and more also, if the dust of Samaria shall suffice for handfuls for all the people who follow me." ¹¹And the king of Israel answered, "Tell him, 'Let not him that girds on his armour boast himself as he that puts it off.'" ¹²When Ben-hadad heard this message as he was drinking with the kings in the booths, he said to his men, "Take your positions." And they took their positions against the city.

¹³And behold, a prophet came near to Ahab king of Israel and said, "Thus says the Lord, Have you seen all this great multitude? Behold, I will give it into your hand this day; and you shall know that I am the Lord." ¹⁴And Ahab said, "By whom?" He said, "Thus says the Lord, By the servants of the governors of the districts." Then he said, "Who shall begin the battle?" He answered, "You." ¹⁵Then he mustered the servants of the governors of the districts, and they were two hundred and thirty-two; and after them he mustered all the people of Israel, seven thousand.

¹⁶And they went out at noon, while Ben-hadad was drinking himself drunk in the booths, he and the thirty-two kings who helped him. ¹⁷The servants of the governors of the districts went out first. And Ben-hadad sent out scouts, and they reported to him, "Men are coming out from Samaria." ¹⁸He said, "If they have come out for peace, take them alive; or if they have come out for war, take them alive."

¹⁹So these went out of the city, the servants of the governors of the districts, and the army which followed them. ²⁰And each killed his man; the Syrians fled and Israel pursued them, but Ben-hadad king of Syria escaped on a horse with horsemen. ²¹And the king of Israel went out, and captured the horses and chariots, and killed the Syrians with a great slaughter.

²²Then the prophet came near to the king of Israel, and said to him, "Come, strengthen yourself, and consider well what you have

to do; for in the spring the king of Syria will come up against you."

²³And the servants of the king of Syria said to him, "Their gods are gods of the hills, and so they were stronger than we; but let us fight against them in the plain, and surely we shall be stronger than they. ²⁴And do this: remove the kings, each from his post, and put commanders in their places; ²⁵and muster an army like the army that you have lost, horse for horse, and chariot for chariot; then we will fight against them in the plain, and surely we shall be stronger than they." And he hearkened to their voice, and did so.

²⁶In the spring Ben-hadad mustered the Syrians, and went up to Aphek, to fight against Israel. ²⁷And the people of Israel were mustered, and were provisioned, and went against them; the people of Israel encamped before them like two little flocks of goats, but the Syrians filled the country. ²⁸And a man of God came near and said to the king of Israel, "Thus says the Lord, 'Because the Syrians have said, "The Lord is a god of the hills but he is not a god of the valleys," therefore I will give all this great multitude into your hand, and you shall know that I am the Lord.'" ²⁹And they encamped opposite one another seven days. Then on the seventh day the battle was joined; and the people of Israel smote of the Syrians a hundred thousand foot soldiers in one day. ³⁰And the rest fled into the city of Aphek; and the wall fell upon twenty-seven thousand men that were left.

Ben-hadad also fled, and entered an inner chamber in the city. ³¹And his servants said to him, "Behold now, we have heard that the kings of the house of Israel are merciful kings; let us put sackcloth on our loins and ropes upon our heads, and go out to the king of Israel; perhaps he will spare your life." ³²So they girded sackcloth on their loins, and put ropes on their heads, and went to the king of Israel and said. "Your servant Ben-hadad says, 'Pray, let me live.'" And he said, "Does he still live? He is my brother." ³³Now the men were watching for an omen, and they quickly took it up from him and said, "Yes, your brother Ben-hadad." Then he said, "Go and bring him." Then Ben-hadad came forth to him; and he caused him to come up into the chariot. ³⁴And Ben-hadad said to him, "The cities which my father took from your father I will restore; and you may establish bazaars for yourself in Damascus, as my father did in Samaria." And Ahab said, "I will let you go on these terms." So he made a covenant with him and let him go.

³⁵And a certain man of the sons of the prophets said to his fellow at the command of the Lord, "Strike me, I pray." But the man

refused to strike him. ³⁶Then he said to him, "Because you have not obeyed the voice of the Lord, behold, as soon as you have gone from me, a lion shall kill you." And as soon as he had departed from him, a lion met him and killed him. ³⁷Then he found another man, and said, "Strike me, I pray." And the man struck him, smiting and wounding him. ³⁸So the prophet departed, and waited for the king by the way, disguising himself with a bandage over his eyes. ³⁹And as the king passed, he cried to the king and said, "Your servant went out into the midst of the battle; and behold, a soldier turned and brought a man to me, and said, 'Keep this man; if by any means he be missing, your life shall be for his life, or else you shall pay a talent of silver.' ⁴⁰And as your servant was busy here and there, he was gone." The king of Israel said to him, "So shall your judgment be; you yourself have decided it." ⁴¹Then he made haste to take the bandage away from his eyes; and the king of Israel recognised him as one of the prophets. ⁴²And he said to him, "Thus says the Lord, 'Because you have let go out of your hand the man whom I had devoted to destruction, therefore your life shall go for his life, and your people for his people.'" ⁴³And the king of Israel went to his house resentful and sullen, and came to Samaria.

AHAB AND BEN-HADAD II—COMMENTARY

1 Kings 20:1-43 (*cont'd*)

The whole cycle of Elijah stories is both interrupted and reinforced by this lengthy episode. Elijah himself neither appears nor is even hinted at. However, this report immediately confirms that Elijah has repeatedly exaggerated his lone status as loyal servant of Yahweh (18:22; 19:10,14).

(i)

The teller of this tale paints a delightful picture of a royal bully engineering his own come-uppance. Ben-hadad's influence and arrogance are depicted in terms rather like those in which Isaiah sketches and also deflates the king of Assyria:

Are not my commanders all kings?
Is not Calno like Carchemish?
　Is not Hamath like Arpad?
　Is not Samaria like Damascus?
　. . . .
By the strength of my hand I have done it,
　and by my wisdom, for I have understanding;
I have removed the boundaries of peoples,
　and have plundered their treasures;
　like a bull I have brought down
　　those who sat on thrones.
My hand has found like a nest
　the wealth of the peoples;
and as men gather eggs that have been forsaken
　so I have gathered all the earth;
and there was none that moved a wing,
　or opened the mouth or chirped.

　　　　　　　　　　　　　　　　　　　(Isa.10:8-14)

To all of which Isaiah simply responds:

Shall the axe vaunt itself over him who hews with it,
　or the saw magnify itself against him who wields it?

　　　　　　　　　　　　　　　　　　　(Isa.10:15*a*)

It is from a position of strength, with his army already encir-
cling Israel's capital city, that the Syrian monarch claims his
rights as overlord. Ahab accepts the terms of the first demand,
but apparently understands them differently from Ben-hadad.
Ahab concedes that he is the vassal of his lord, and that this
implies that everything he owns belongs to his superior. Either
he is playing for time, or he hopes that this general assurance
will satisfy the boastful Ben-hadad and save him putting the
forces of his coalition to a test.

　Yet Ben-hadad is not satisfied: he wants his 'bird in the
hand'—and *generously* offers to arrange carriage himself (v.6)!
His demand that his staff be given free rein to loot Samaria,
forces Ahab to consult within the city. He now admits to the
elders of his people that he had been prepared to buy off Ben-

hadad at his own royal expense. They urge a negative reply to the aggressor, without polite qualification: "Do not heed or consent". The actual message sent is that Ahab will honour his first undertaking, but will not accept the second demand. At this point insults begin to be traded (vv.10–11) and the nonchalant Syrian orders battle to commence.

An unnamed prophet now promises Ahab success, and insists that this success will confirm the significance and importance of the Lord. He apparently represents that tradition of national prophet who promises success against the odds. Beyond simple encouragement he also offers Ahab tactical advice. Ben-hadad and his retinue of royalty are already too drunk by mid-day to offer more than careless orders (vv.16–18); and the inevitable Israelite victory results. Yet the prophet is quite clear that this is but the end of the first battle, and not the end of the war. The Syrians will be back (as the Hebrew has it in v.22) "at the [re]turn of the year": not at the new year, as our idiom has it, but when the year which set out at the end of the summer has completed more than half its course and is on the way home. 2 Samuel 11:1 tells us that this is the season "when kings go forth to battle"—with the bad weather and much of the agricultural work behind. RSV translates in both passages, accurately but prosaically; "in the spring".

(ii)

The Syrian 'experts' have two explanations for their defeat, and recipes for future success (vv.23–24). Israel's god(s) belonged in the hills: a low-lying campaign would be more to Syria's advantage. Then professional officers would make better commanders than petty monarchs getting drunk with their overlord (and who might well benefit more from Ben-hadad's downfall than from his greater success). Battle is joined on these terms at one of the several places in the Bible called Aphek—almost certainly the one near present-day Ein Gev on the coast of the Sea of Galilee just opposite Tiberias.

A "man of God" gives further encouragement to the king of Israel: a second victory will be required to expose the Syrian misjudgment that Yahweh is but a mountain god. It is nowhere made clear what lies behind this mistake. Is it simply a Syrian deduction from the fact that Israel's heartlands were in her hilly areas? Or did it actually betray knowledge of some of Israel's religious traditions which associated her god with peaks such as Sinai/Horeb and Seir in southern Transjordan? In any case, just as the contest on Carmel demonstrated that Yahweh not Baal ruled the skies and the weather, so this battle would show that he was master of all sorts of earthly terrain.

(iii)

When bully Ben-hadad becomes suppliant, he is advised about the high reputation of the kings of Israel—yet not for "mercy", as RSV has it in verse 31: rather for "loyalty". He should take it on trust, not that Ahab will spare him, but that he will honour any pledge he makes. The king of Israel in fact does treat him with fraternal respect, and secures territorial and commercial concessions.

The confrontation between one of the prophets and Ahab that concludes this chapter (vv.35ff.) reminds us of some other biblical scenes. The grisly fate of the prophet who refuses a prophetic instruction given "by the word of the Lord" takes us back to the lion which halted the return from Bethel of the man of God from Judah (1 Kings 13). And the impaling of the king on the hook of his own judicial decision is reminiscent of Nathan's tactics before David (2 Sam. 12).

The final judgment on Ahab (v.42) indicates some irony in the earlier talk of "loyalty" (v.31) as characteristic of kings of Israel. The Hebrew word *hesed* is frequently used of the loyalty God both shows and requires. Ahab's *hesed* may not be in doubt—except for its orientation!

NABOTH'S VINEYARD

1 Kings 21:1-29

¹Now Naboth the Jezreelite had a vineyard in Jezreel, beside the

palace of Ahab king of Samaria. ²And after this Ahab said to Naboth, "Give me your vineyard, that I may have it for a vegetable garden, because it is near my house; and I will give you a better vineyard for it; or, if it seems good to you, I will give you its value in money." ³But Naboth said to Ahab, "The Lord forbid that I should give you the inheritance of my fathers." ⁴And Ahab went into his house vexed and sullen because of what Naboth the Jezreelite had said to him; for he had said, "I will not give you the inheritance of my fathers." And he lay down on his bed, and turned away his face, and would eat no food.

⁵But Jezebel his wife came to him, and said to him, "Why is your spirit so vexed that you eat no food?" ⁶And he said to her, "Because I spoke to Naboth the Jezreelite, and said to him, 'Give me your vineyard for money; or else, if it please you, I will give you another vineyard for it'; and he answered, 'I will not give you my vineyard.'" ⁷And Jezebel his wife said to him, "Do you now govern Israel? Arise, and eat bread, and let your heart be cheerful; I will give you the vineyard of Naboth the Jezreelite."

⁸So she wrote letters in Ahab's name and sealed them with his seal, and she sent the letters to the elders and the nobles who dwelt with Naboth in his city. ⁹And she wrote in the letters, "Proclaim a fast, and set Naboth on high among the people; ¹⁰and set two base fellows opposite him, and let them bring a charge against him, saying, 'You have cursed God and the king.' Then take him out, and stone him to death." ¹¹And the men of his city, the elders and the nobles who dwelt in his city, did as Jezebel had sent word to them. As it was written in the letters which she had sent to them, ¹²they proclaimed a fast, and set Naboth on high among the people. ¹³And the two base fellows came in and sat opposite him; and the base fellows brought a charge against Naboth, in the presence of the people, saying, "Naboth cursed God and the king." So they took him outside the city, and stoned him to death with stones. ¹⁴Then they sent to Jezebel, saying, "Naboth has been stoned; he is dead."

¹⁵As soon as Jezebel heard that Naboth had been stoned and was dead Jezebel said to Ahab, "Arise, take possession of the vineyard of Naboth the Jezreelite, which he refused to give you for money; for Naboth is not alive, but dead." ¹⁶And as soon as Ahab heard that Naboth was dead, Ahab arose to go down to the vineyard of Naboth the Jezreelite, to take possession of it.

¹⁷Then the word of the Lord came to Elijah the Tishbite, saying, ¹⁸"Arise, go down to meet Ahab king of Israel, who is in Samaria;

behold, he is in the vineyard of Naboth, where he has gone to take possession. ¹⁹And you shall say to him, 'Thus says the Lord, "Have you killed, and also taken possession?"' And you shall say to him, 'Thus says the Lord: "In the place where dogs licked up the blood of Naboth shall dogs lick your own blood."'"

²⁰Ahab said to Elijah, "Have you found me, O my enemy?" He answered, "I have found you, because you have sold yourself to do what is evil in the sight of the Lord. ²¹Behold, I will bring evil upon you; I will utterly sweep you away, and will cut off from Ahab every male, bond or free, in Israel; ²²and I will make your house like the house of Jeroboam the son of Nebat, and like the house of Baasha the son of Ahijah, for the anger to which you have provoked me, and because you have made Israel to sin. ²³And of Jezebel the Lord also said, 'The dogs shall eat Jezebel within the bounds of Jezreel.' ²⁴Any one belonging to Ahab who dies in the city the dogs shall eat; and any one of his who dies in the open country the birds of the air shall eat."

²⁵(There was none who sold himself to do what was evil in the sight of the Lord like Ahab, whom Jezebel his wife incited. ²⁶He did very abominably in going after idols, as the Amorites had done, whom the Lord cast out before the people of Israel.)

²⁷And when Ahab heard those words, he rent his clothes, and put sackcloth upon his flesh, and fasted and lay in sackcloth, and went about dejectedly. ²⁸And the word of the Lord came to Elijah the Tishbite, saying, ²⁹"Have you seen how Ahab has humbled himself before me? Because he has humbled himself before me, I will not bring the evil in his days; but in his son's days I will bring the evil upon his house."

(i)

It is only now that we learn why it was to Jezreel (18:46) that Elijah preceded Ahab from Carmel: the king had a palace there. He also had an awkward neighbour there, who was prepared to take a stand on an issue of principle.

A very high value was placed on the continuity of a family's tenure of its ancestral land. And this of course is an important component in the continuing Jewish insistence on the vital place in its life of the land of Israel. Family land and national land, family fate and national fate, are linked in Amos's terrible curse on Amaziah:

Your wife—she shall be a harlot in the city;
and your sons and daughters—they shall fall by the sword;
and your land—it shall be divided up by line;
and yourself—you shall die in an unclean land;
and Israel—it shall go into certain exile off its land.

(Amos 7:17)

Part of the purpose of the institution of redemption (see our discussion in the sister volume on *Ruth*) was to prevent the alienation of property through a family's reduced circumstances. The continued holding of one's own land was to be desired. Yet the purchase or exchange of land was by no means excluded: Ahab's proposal to Naboth was not in itself improper.

Naboth may have been a sullen unhelpful fellow—the ease with which his elimination was contrived suggests he was not the most popular man in Jezreel. Yet his rejection of Ahab's bid strikes some significant chords. A vineyard, like an olive-orchard, is not just land that may have been in the family for a long time: it represents a high investment in many years of unfruitful care before it reaches maturity. And Ahab would have rubbished all this for vegetables—here today and gone tomorrow! In other and even more important ways too, Ahab and Jezebel had given long-nurtured national traditions short shrift. Perhaps only an Elijah had the courage or the freedom to accuse Ahab outright of "troubling Israel" (18:18). Yet the very phrasing of Naboth's answer, "the inheritance of my fathers" (v.3), is ambiguous enough to contain the jibe that Ahab wants to make free with more than Naboth's land.

Two further considerations seem to me to underscore this. The one is that he repeats Naboth's very words to himself in his sullen vexation (v.4), but suppresses them when he tells his wife (v.6) that his neighbour has refused a simple transaction. The other is that "vexed and sullen" is what the king of Israel became at the end of the previous story (the Hebrew expression is identical in 20:43), after criticism he recognized as prophetic. Ahab too is not unaware of the wider ramifications of what is being said to him. And he knows he is defeated.

(ii)

Not so Jezebel. Often wives and husbands seem more jealous of
their spouses' reputations than are the principals themselves.
Sometimes wives and husbands *are* the principal characters!
This lady's actions speak louder than her words. "Is it not you
that exercise kingship over Israel?" is what she says (v.7)—and
despatch letters over his name and under his royal seal is what
she does (v.8). And all the while he should take his royal ease
and be merry!

Naboth is to have a capital charge brought against him
falsely at a solemn public occasion in his own town. He is to be
prominently placed: he will not be able to melt away; and,
having honoured him, the elders of the town will not appear
accomplices. More than enough adult males will be present to
constitute a judicial quorum. And the necessary minimum of
two witnesses will testify. The elders will recognize the importance to the economy of their town of the royal palace. The local
community will be aware of the tensions over the vineyard.
And—at a solemn fast, where religious blame is being confessed
and explored—they will be ready to believe a charge of blasphemy. No wonder that some say the devil reads the scriptures
most closely: they contain such diabolically clever schemes!

In the heightened emotion of the fast, Naboth is quickly
despatched. Jezebel is able to report a bonus to her husband.
What he could not buy he may now have free: presumably the
estates of the executed wretch were forfeit, with any of his
family joining in his punishment.

(iii)

Elijah now enters the scene to demonstrate the principle that
justice fits the crime. A double charge was brought against
Naboth: of blasphemy, and of cursing a ruler of his people
(v.10; see Exod. 22:28). A double charge is made against Ahab
(v.19): of murder and of theft. Where Jezreel's scavenging
hounds licked Naboth's blood, they will also lick Ahab's. Just
as not only Naboth suffered, so all Ahab's male line will be
destroyed—the same coarse expression is used (v.21) as we

discussed in connection with 14:10 above (p. 99). Jezebel too will meet a similar fate in the same proper place: "God sows" in more ways than just by simply bringing the rain (18:41–46).

Ahab draws the heaviest criticism of all the kings of Israel (v.25*a*). To sell yourself is quite literally to become someone's slave—Deuteronomy 28:68 reminds us that this implied for Israel a return to the conditions of Egypt from which God had delivered her through freedom and through law, through freedom under law. And yet judgment is not the last word we hear on Ahab. His humble response following Elijah's intervention (v.27) leads to a stay of execution for his house. And the powerful complicity of Jezebel is noted in mitigation (v.25*b*). Is it suggested that in marriage he had sold himself in slavery to her? In any case it is as idolater and apostate that our narrator writes his epitaph (v.26).

MICAIAH BEN IMLAH

1 Kings 22:1–53

[1]For three years Syria and Israel continued without war. [2]But in the third year Jehoshaphat the king of Judah came down to the king of Israel. [3]And the king of Israel said to his servants, "Do you know that Ramoth-gilead belongs to us, and we keep quiet and do not take it out of the hand of the king of Syria?" [4]And he said to Jehoshaphat, "Will you go with me to battle at Ramoth-gilead?" And Jehoshaphat said to the king of Israel, "I am as you are, my people as your people, my horses as your horses."

[5]And Jehoshaphat said to the king of Israel, "Inquire first for the word of the Lord." [6]Then the king of Israel gathered the prophets together, about four hundred men, and said to them, "Shall I go to battle against Ramoth-gilead, or shall I forbear?" And they said, "Go up; for the Lord will give it into the hand of the king." [7]But Jehoshaphat said, "Is there not here another prophet of the Lord of whom we may inquire?" [8]And the king of Israel said to Jehoshaphat, "There is yet one man by whom we may inquire of the Lord, Micaiah the son of Imlah; but I hate him, for he never prophesies

good concerning me, but evil." And Jehoshaphat said, "Let not the king say so." ⁹Then the king of Israel summoned an officer and said, "Bring quickly Micaiah the son of Imlah." ¹⁰Now the king of Israel and Jehoshaphat the king of Judah were sitting on their thrones, arrayed in their robes, at the threshing floor at the entrance of the gate of Samaria; and all the prophets were prophesying before them. ¹¹And Zedekiah the son of Chenaanah made for himself horns of iron, and said, "Thus says the Lord, 'With these you shall push the Syrians until they are destroyed.'" ¹²And all the prophets prophesied so, and said, "Go up to Ramoth-gilead and triumph; the Lord will give it into the hand of the king."

¹³And the messenger who went to summon Micaiah said to him, "Behold, the words of the prophets with one accord are favourable to the king; let your word be like the word of one of them, and speak favourably." ¹⁴But Micaiah said, "As the Lord lives, what the Lord says to me, that I will speak." ¹⁵And when he had come to the king, the king said to him, "Micaiah, shall we go to Ramoth-gilead to battle, or shall we forbear?" And he answered him, "Go up and triumph; the Lord will give it into the hand of the king." ¹⁶But the king said to him, "How many times shall I adjure you that you speak to me nothing but the truth in the name of the Lord?" ¹⁷And he said, "I saw all Israel scattered upon the mountains, as sheep that have no shepherd; and the Lord said, 'These have no master; let each return to his home in peace.'" ¹⁸And the king of Israel said to Jehoshaphat, "Did I not tell you that he would not prophesy good concerning me, but evil?" ¹⁹And Micaiah said, "Therefore hear the word of the Lord: I saw the Lord sitting on his throne, and all the host of heaven standing beside him on his right hand and on his left; ²⁰and the Lord said, 'Who will entice Ahab, that he may go up and fall at Ramoth-gilead?' And one said one thing, and another said another. ²¹Then a spirit came forward and stood before the Lord, saying, 'I will entice him.' ²²And the Lord said to him, 'By what means?' And he said, 'I will go forth, and will be a lying spirit in the mouth of all his prophets.' And he said, 'You are to entice him, and you shall succeed; go forth and do so.' ²³Now therefore behold, the Lord has put a lying spirit in the mouth of all these your prophets; the Lord has spoken evil concerning you."

²⁴Then Zedekiah the son of Chenaanah came near and struck Micaiah on the cheek, and said, "How did the Spirit of the Lord go from me to speak to you?" ²⁵And Micaiah said, "Behold you shall see on that day when you go into an inner chamber to hide

yourself." 26And the king of Israel said, "Seize Micaiah, and take him back to Amon the governor of the city and to Joash the king's son; 27and say, 'Thus says the king, "Put this fellow in prison and feed him with scant fare of bread and water, until I come in peace."'" 28And Micaiah said, "If you return in peace, the Lord has not spoken by me." And he said, "Hear, all you peoples!"

29So the king of Israel and Jehoshaphat the king of Judah went up to Ramoth-gilead. 30And the king of Israel said to Jehoshaphat, "I will disguise myself and go into battle, but you wear your robes." And the king of Israel disguised himself and went into battle. 31Now the king of Syria had commanded the thirty-two captains of his chariots, "Fight with neither small nor great, but only with the king of Israel." 32And when the captains of the chariots saw Jehoshaphat, they said, "It is surely the king of Israel." So they turned to fight against him; and Jehoshaphat cried out. 33And when the captains of the chariots saw that it was not the king of Israel, they turned back from pursuing him. 34But a certain man drew his bow at a venture, and struck the king of Israel between the scale armour and the breastplate; therefore he said to the driver of his chariot, "Turn about, and carry me out of the battle, for I am wounded." 35And the battle grew hot that day, and the king was propped up in his chariot facing the Syrians, until at evening he died; and the blood of the wound flowed into the bottom of the chariot. 36And about sunset a cry went through the army, "Every man to his city, and every man to his country!"

37So the king died, and was brought to Samaria; and they buried the king in Samaria. 38And they washed the chariot by the pool of Samaria, and the dogs licked up his blood, and the harlots washed themselves in it, according to the word of the Lord which he had spoken. 39Now the rest of the acts of Ahab, and all that he did, and the ivory house which he built, and all the cities that he built, are they not written in the Book of the Chronicles of the Kings of Israel? 40So Ahab slept with his fathers; and Ahaziah his son reigned in his stead.

41Jehoshaphat the son of Asa began to reign over Judah in the fourth year of Ahab king of Israel. 42Jehoshaphat was thirty-five years old when he began to reign, and he reigned twenty-five years in Jerusalem. His mother's name was Azubah the daughter of Shilhi. 43He walked in all the way of Asa his father; he did not turn aside from it, doing what was right in the sight of the Lord; yet the high places were not taken away, and the people still sacrificed and

burned incense on the high places. ⁴⁴Jehoshaphat also made peace
with the king of Israel.

⁴⁵Now the rest of the acts of Jehoshaphat, and his might that he
showed, and how he warred, are they not written in the Book of the
Chronicles of the Kings of Judah? ⁴⁶And the remnant of the male
cult prostitutes who remained in the days of his father Asa, he
exterminated from the land.

⁴⁷There was no king in Edom; a deputy was king. ⁴⁸Jehoshaphat
made ships of Tarshish to go to Ophir for gold; but they did not go,
for the ships were wrecked at Ezion-geber. ⁴⁹Then Ahaziah the son
of Ahab said to Jehoshaphat, "Let my servants go with your
servants in the ships," but Jehoshaphat was not willing. ⁵⁰And
Jehoshaphat slept with his fathers, and was buried with his fathers
in the city of David his father; and Jehoram his son reigned in his
stead.

⁵¹Ahaziah the son of Ahab began to reign over Israel in Samaria
in the seventeenth year of Jehoshaphat king of Judah, and he
reigned two years over Israel. ⁵²He did what was evil in the sight of
the Lord, and walked in the way of his father, and in the way of his
mother, and in the way of Jeroboam the son of Nebat, who made
Israel to sin. ⁵³He served Baal and worshipped him, and provoked
the Lord, the God of Israel, to anger in every way that his father had
done.

(i)

After a number of chapters in which Judah has not rated a
mention in our text, we come now to a fascinating tale whose
background is provided by a joint military venture by Israel and
Judah across in Transjordan. An almost identical account of
the bulk of the action has also been preserved by the Chronicler:
1 Kings 22:5–35*a* differs hardly at all from 2 Chronicles
18:4–34. This very fact makes the variations in the introductory
verses all the more interesting.

The opening of our chapter (vv.1–4) resumes the issue of
Israelite/Syrian relations from chapter 20. No explanation is
offered for the arrival in Israel of Jehoshaphat of Judah;
however, he readily agrees to Israel's proposal to 'liberate'
Ramoth. Calling it Ramoth-*gilead* underlined Israel's claim to

a town which lay in natural border territory: its name is probably preserved in Ramtha on the present border between Jordan and Syria. The Chronicler in his first three verses tells us that Jehoshaphat's acquisition of wealth was followed by a marriage alliance with Ahab, who pressed him at a great party to join him against Syria. Jehoshaphat's answer, "I am as you are, my people as your people", appears in both texts, but only the Chronicler supplies its background. However, it is clear that it expresses the cordiality appropriate to a guest rather than a final official decision; for Jehoshaphat goes on to recommend consulting God first. It is this that provides the opportunity for the introduction of Micaiah son of Imlah.

GOD'S LYING SPIRIT

1 Kings 22:1–53 (*cont'd*)

(ii)

The story of Micaiah is told with much humour—and like many humorous stories it is quite partisan, mocking the general phenomenon of prophecy in Israel and the king of Israel too. The king had already consulted his own servants about his policy (v.3). To satisfy his 'brother' in Judah, he now assembles those who might be expected to be servants of the Lord—as many as 400. They promise full divine support. Jehoshaphat had requested the divine word; his colleague provided prophets. Jehoshaphat now asks specifically for "a prophet *of the Lord*" (v.7).

By his very name (meaning "Who is like Yahweh?") Micaiah sounds a suitable candidate, whereas his opponent Zedekiah ("Yahweh is my right") unhappily does not live up to the promise of his Yahweh-name. Micaiah's past record in opposition makes him unwelcome to his king. Jehoshaphat protests gently at such a sentiment, and a summons is duly issued to Micaiah. As he is being fetched, loyalist fervour is built up at a rally in front of both kings at the main gate of Samaria, with

Zedekiah and "all the prophets" (v.12) enacting the coming victory in anticipation.

Briefed on the situation by the officer sent to fetch him, Micaiah replies on his dignity that he will be loyal to Yahweh. Yet on arrival in the assembly he surprises us by agreeing with the 400 "prophets" (v.15): has his courage failed him, or does this answer in fact represent loyalty to the Lord's designs? The king of Israel, like many a spoiled child—including grown-up spoiled children!—has a shrewd hunch that getting his own way and being told what he wants to hear is not what is best for him (v.16).

There is the further problem that Micaiah's positive oracle is out of character—and that does not simply mean that his support for the king does not tally with his own 'track record'. There is a very similar discussion in story form of how to distinguish between true and false prophecy in the Book of Jeremiah. In response to a promise by Hananiah of doom for Babylon that will result in the restoration to Jerusalem of both temple vessels and the royal Davidic line (28:2–4), Jeremiah responds in the assembly (28:6–9):

> Amen! May the Lord do so; may the Lord make the words which you have prophesied come true . . . Yet hear now this word which I speak in your hearing and in the hearing of all the people. The prophets who preceded you and me from ancient times prophesied war, famine, and pestilence against many countries and great kingdoms. As for the prophet who prophesies peace, when the word of that prophet comes to pass, then it will be known that the Lord has truly sent the prophet.

Bad news is 'par for the course' from a good prophet; good news probably comes from a bad prophet. Under royal challenge, Micaiah changes his tune. Instead of a promise of victory he offers a nightmare image of a scattered and leaderless Israel (v.17). And the threatened king of Israel says to his royal guest: 'I told you so'.

Now we have a double teaser for our talents, a two-fold test of our theological sensibilities. The initial part was relatively easy: the actual structure of the story made it more likely that lone Micaiah, "prophet of the Lord", was to be preferred to the multitude of prophets first appealed to by the king of Israel. But when Micaiah says two opposite things, are we so sure that we should prefer him—and in any case, which Micaiah are we to choose?

(iii)

We can start again by restating our question. The nub of our problem is well expressed in the king of Israel's successive reactions to Micaiah. First comes his exasperated, "How many times shall I adjure you that you speak to me nothing but the truth in the name of the Lord?" (v.16). Then follows his triumphant, "Did I not tell you that he would not prophesy good concerning me, but evil?" (v.18). What are "true" and "good" for *that* king: to hear what he wants, but to go and perish; or to be saved from disaster by Micaiah's nightmare forebodings? We have to remind ourselves that the Hebrew word for "truth" has less to do with accuracy and more to do with reliability and faithfulness. "Truth" in Hebrew describes the relationship involved. And in fact in English too we know well enough that our "true" friend may still make mistakes and be in error concerning ourselves.

Our tendency in assessing the biblical prophet's words would be to opt for a Micaiah who foretells accurately what is to happen. Yet such a preference is shaped more by the members of the young Christian community who proclaimed their Lord and some of their own institutions as the culmination and fulfilment of scriptural prophecies, than by the clues the Old Testament itself gives us about the function and purpose of prophecy. A very important strand within the Hebrew Scriptures is much more concerned with the *effect* of a prophet's message than with the confirmation of what he actually says.

The Book of Jonah mocks its 'hero' for his annoyance at Nineveh's repentance. After a disobedient start, he had finally gone there and proclaimed its overthrow after 40 days. When, on its humble repentance, God spares it, his emissary is furious.

He neatly rationalizes his earlier attempt to evade his mission by claiming he knew all the time that God was merciful and slow to anger. Yet the message had to be proclaimed to achieve the desired result.

Similarly, when Jeremiah is about to be executed for promising ill in Yahweh's name towards the Temple in Jerusalem, some rural elders speak in his defence as follows:

> Micah of Moresheth prophesied in the days of Hezekiah king of Judah, and said to all the people of Judah: "Thus says the Lord of hosts,
>
> > Zion shall be ploughed as a field;
> >
> > Jerusalem shall become a heap of ruins,
> >
> > and the mountain of the house a wooded height."
>
> Did Hezekiah king of Judah and all Judah put him to death? Did he not fear the Lord and entreat the favour of the Lord, and did not the Lord repent of the evil which he had pronounced against them? But we are about to bring great evil upon ourselves.
>
> (Jer. 26:18-19)

(iv)

One of the most interesting elements in this whole narrative is Micaiah's vision (vv.19ff.). It is very similar in content to the much more famous vision of Isaiah (Isa.6). Both talk of seeing God on his throne within his court. Both report a mission of deception (see Isa. 6:9-10). And it seems likely that these two features, each of which is unusual within reports of biblical visions, are in fact closely linked. To attempt to make credible their claim that God was involved in deception, both Isaiah and Micaiah had to provide the assurance that they had been privy to his very council in heaven.

Micaiah reports God seeking the appropriate means to "entice" Ahab. We find the Hebrew word translated elsewhere "deceive" or "seduce"—we could also simply use "dupe". In his own bitterest complaint against his Master, Jeremiah protested (20:7):

O Lord, thou hast deceived me,
  and I was deceived;
thou art stronger than I,
  and thou hast prevailed.
I have become a laughingstock all the day;
  every one mocks me.

After various motions have been advanced, the spirit, who then comes forward, volunteers to become a lying spirit in the mouth of all his prophets (vv.21–22). Two points are worth stressing here. The Jerusalem Bible is right to render "*the* spirit" as against RSV's "*a* spirit"—we could equally well translate "the wind", or even (shades of the original *Star Wars*) "the force". Then the duped prophets are said to be "his", *ie* Ahab's, not Yahweh's. Remember the earlier distinction between "the prophets" and Micaiah, "a prophet of the Lord".

Zedekiah is better aware than the RSV translator that the spirit/wind/force is one and undivided (v.24). Yet he rather misses the drift of Micaiah's claim. He rejects and punishes an impudent suggestion that the divine spirit had forsaken him for Micaiah. The latter of course had said that the divine spirit was indeed speaking through Zedekiah—but speaking deliberate lies. As for the test of his words, Micaiah fears that his nightmare will have to be experienced to be believed—and so it turns out.

With nice irony, Micaiah's picture of Zedekiah cowering in an inner room to escape the disaster, is the trigger for the king of Israel to have Micaiah imprisoned in Samaria on a torturing, tantalizing shortness of rations until the king returns in peace. Not yet intimidated, Micaiah retorts: "Not [if Yahweh has] spoken by me!" (v.28). And that is the last we learn of the character who has dominated the chapter to this point: his end, or the next stage in his career, goes unreported. He has done what he had to do. Many of the Bible's most significant prophets appear on stage in only one scene. Many of us too will be called on only once to do something really significant—may we respond to the cue when it comes!

(v)

The remainder of the chapter (vv.29ff.) does tie up some loose ends, yet opens up others. Even Ahab's attempt to conceal his identity (and draw greater danger on the apparently gullible Jehoshaphat), fails to ward off his fate. He is buried with his fathers and succeeded by his son (v.40); yet he can hardly be said to have escaped the punishment promised to him before his humble submission, as the end of chapter 21 expected. Similarly the help of the dogs of Samaria in cleaning up his bloody chariot does not appear to fit the scene of the crime against Naboth in Jezreel (see 21:19). And yet to quibble over such details would be to miss the point of our discussion above concerning the purpose of prophecy in the Old Testament. Micaiah in this chapter is given a probing rather than a forecasting role.

Only in the summary of his career (v.39) do we receive a first hint of Ahab's monumental and beautiful architectural contribution to Israel's heritage (see above pp. 115–116)—yet the context is hardly complimentary. The final verses of this chapter (and of the first "Book" of Kings) sketch the career of Ahab's southern colleague Jehoshaphat (41–50), and introduce us to Ahab's son Ahaziah (51–53).

ELIJAH AND THE FIRE OF HEAVEN I—TEXT

2 Kings 1:1–2:25

[1]After the death of Ahab, Moab rebelled against Israel.

[2]Now Ahaziah fell through the lattice in his upper chamber in Samaria, and lay sick; so he sent messengers, telling them, "Go, inquire of Baal-zebub, the god of Ekron, whether I shall recover from this sickness." [3]But the angel of the Lord said to Elijah the Tishbite, "Arise, go up to meet the messengers of the king of Samaria, and say to them, 'Is it because there is no God in Israel that you are going to inquire of Baal-zebub, the god of Ekron?' [4]Now therefore thus says the Lord, 'You shall not come down from the bed to which you have gone, but you shall surely die.'" So Elijah went.

⁵The messengers returned to the king, and he said to them, "Why have you returned?" ⁶And they said to him, "There came a man to meet us, and said to us, 'Go back to the king who sent you, and say to him, Thus says the Lord, Is it because there is no God in Israel that you are sending to inquire of Baal-zebub, the god of Ekron? Therefore you shall not come down from the bed to which you have gone, but shall surely die.'" ⁷He said to them, "What kind of man was he who came to meet you and told you these things?" ⁸They answered him, "He wore a garment of haircloth, with a girdle of leather about his loins." And he said, "It is Elijah the Tishbite."

⁹Then the king sent to him a captain of fifty men with his fifty. He went up to Elijah, who was sitting on the top of a hill, and said to him, "O man of God, the king says, 'Come down.'" ¹⁰But Elijah answered the captain of fifty, "If I am a man of God, let fire come down from heaven and consume you and your fifty." Then fire came down from heaven, and consumed him and his fifty.

¹¹Again the king sent to him another captain of fifty men with his fifty. And he went up and said to him, "O man of God, this is the king's order, 'Come down quickly!'" ¹²But Elijah answered them. "If I am a man of God, let fire come down from heaven and consume you and your fifty." Then the fire of God came down from heaven and consumed him and his fifty.

¹³Again the king sent the captain of a third fifty with his fifty. And the third captain of fifty went up, and came and fell on his knees before Elijah, and entreated him, "O man of God, I pray you, let my life, and the life of these fifty servants of yours, be precious in your sight. ¹⁴Lo, fire came down from heaven, and consumed the two former captains of fifty men with their fifties; but now let my life be precious in your sight." ¹⁵Then the angel of the Lord said to Elijah, "Go down with him; do not be afraid of him." So he arose and went down with him to the king, ¹⁶and said to him, "Thus says the Lord, 'Because you have sent messengers to inquire of Baal-zebub, the god of Ekron—is it because there is no God in Israel to inquire of his word?—therefore you shall not come down from the bed to which you have gone, but you shall surely die.'"

¹⁷So he died according to the word of the Lord which Elijah had spoken. Jehoram, his brother, became king in his stead in the second year of Jehoram the son of Jehoshaphat, king of Judah, because Ahaziah had no son. ¹⁸Now the rest of the acts of Ahaziah which he did, are they not written in the Book of the Chronicles of the Kings of Israel?

¹Now when the Lord was about to take Elijah up to heaven by a whirlwind, Elijah and Elisha were on their way from Gilgal. ²And Elijah said to Elisha, "Tarry here, I pray you; for the Lord has sent me as far as Bethel." But Elisha said, "As the Lord lives, and as you yourself live, I will not leave you." So they went down to Bethel. ³And the sons of the prophets who were in Bethel came out to Elisha, and said to him, "Do you know that today the Lord will take away your master from over you?" And he said, "Yes, I know it; hold your peace."

⁴Elijah said to him, "Elisha, tarry here, I pray you; for the Lord has sent me to Jericho." But he said, "As the Lord lives, and as you yourself live, I will not leave you." So they came to Jericho. ⁵The sons of the prophets who were at Jericho drew near to Elisha and said to him, "Do you know that today the Lord will take away your master from over you?" And he answered, "Yes, I know it; hold your peace."

⁶Then Elijah said to him, "Tarry here, I pray you; for the Lord has sent me to the Jordan." But he said, "As the Lord lives, and as you yourself live, I will not leave you." So the two of them went on. ⁷Fifty men of the sons of the prophets also went, and stood at some distance from them, as they both were standing by the Jordan. ⁸Then Elijah took his mantle, and rolled it up, and struck the water, and the water was parted to the one side and to the other, till the two of them could go over on dry ground.

⁹When they had crossed, Elijah said to Elisha, "Ask what I shall do for you, before I am taken from you," And Elisha said, "I pray you, let me inherit a double share of your spirit." ¹⁰And he said, "You have asked a hard thing; yet, if you see me as I am being taken from you, it shall be so for you; but if you do not see me, it shall not be so." ¹¹And as they still went on and talked, behold, a chariot of fire and horses of fire separated the two of them. And Elijah went up by a whirlwind into heaven. ¹²And Elisha saw it and he cried, "My father, my father! the chariots of Israel and its horsemen!" And he saw him no more.

Then he took hold of his own clothes and rent them in two pieces. ¹³And he took up the mantle of Elijah that had fallen from him, and went back and stood on the bank of the Jordan. ¹⁴Then he took the mantle of Elijah that had fallen from him, and struck the water, saying, "Where is the Lord, the God of Elijah?" And when he had struck the water, the water was parted to the one side and to the other; and Elisha went over.

¹⁵Now when the sons of the prophets who were at Jericho saw him over against them, they said, "The spirit of Elijah rests on Elisha." And they came to meet him, and bowed to the ground before him. ¹⁶And they said to him, "Behold now, there are with your servants fifty strong men; pray, let them go, and seek your master; it may be that the Spirit of the Lord has caught him up and cast him upon some mountain or into some valley." And he said, "You shall not send." ¹⁷But when they urged him till he was ashamed, he said, "Send." They sent therefore fifty men; and for three days they sought him but did not find him. ¹⁸And they came back to him, while he tarried at Jericho, and he said to them, "Did I not say to you, Do not go?"

¹⁹Now the men of the city said to Elisha, "Behold, the situation of this city is pleasant, as my lord sees; but the water is bad, and the land is unfruitful." ²⁰He said, "Bring me a new bowl, and put salt in it." So they brought it to him. ²¹Then he went to the spring of water and threw salt in it, and said, "Thus says the Lord, I have made this water wholesome; henceforth neither death nor miscarriage shall come from it." ²²So the water has been wholesome to this day, according to the word which Elisha spoke.

²³He went up from there to Bethel; and while he was going up on the way, some small boys came out of the city and jeered at him, saying, "Go up, you baldhead! Go up, you baldhead!" ²⁴And he turned around, and when he saw them, he cursed them in the name of the Lord. And two she-bears came out of the woods and tore forty-two of the boys. ²⁵From there he went on to Mount Carmel, and thence he returned to Samaria.

ELIJAH AND THE FIRE OF HEAVEN II
—COMMENTARY

2 Kings 1:1–2:25 (*cont'd*)

(i)

The end of the previous chapter mentioned relations between Judah and Edom to its east and south. Our section begins with a break in relations between Israel and Transjordanian Moab, although the story is not developed until chapter 3. Before that continuation, we must take our leave of Elijah in the first two chapters of 2 Kings.

Ahaziah's accidental exit through a window sets our first scene. From his bed he sends emissaries to Philistine Ekron for a prognosis. It is almost certain that our storyteller takes the opportunity to make incidental fun of the name of the god consulted. Zebul is a well known and honorific title of Baal from ancient times (we discussed it above in connection with Jezebel's name; see p. 115); *zebub* is the Hebrew for the common "fly". It is just within the bounds of possibility that a god called "Lord of the Flies" was resorted to for help at times of insect plagues—but much more likely that a Hebrew narrator has simply been taking a side-swipe at one of his divine enemies. We may suppose that Baal Zebul, or at least the staff of his shrine at Ekron, had a high reputation in matters of healing. The reputation of this god was to last for a very long time: detractors of Jesus were to attribute some of his healings to possession by "Beelzebul" (Mark 3:22; AV has "Beelzebub"). Ahaziah, whose very name *ahaz-yahu* included the name of Yahweh God of Israel, had not, of course, intended to desert his god: merely to seek the best advice available.

Elijah's name too ("Yahweh is God") was a perpetual confession. This Yahweh now despatches an emissary to brief him to intercept the king's emissaries. His authority is enough to make them turn back—and enough also to make the king realize that it is now with Elijah he has to deal. Yet, having first approached the wrong god, he now approaches the right god's "man" the wrong way—with orders and military discipline (v.9). Elijah, like his God, is to be entreated, and not commanded. There is a fine but untranslatable pun in his response to the first two captains (vv.10,12): "If I am a man [*ish*] of God, let fire [*esh*] come down from heaven".

A more respectful form of address (v.13) does not ameliorate the divine verdict on the king. But it does save other innocent lives. And it may be tragic truth that the first two detachments had to perish before the king was receptive to Elijah's authority.

Ahaziah died in his second year of office, and was succeeded by Jehoram.

(ii)

Elijah's mantle, prominent in the scene of Elisha's call (1 Kings 19:19–21), figures again at their parting. Quite as prominent is Elijah's insistence that Elisha take full responsibility for his own actions. Since notice of Elijah's removal by whirlwind is signalled at the outset (2:1) and not delayed until the dramatically appropriate moment, we may suppose that that fact— however remarkable—is not of greatest concern to the story-teller.

If this is true, it was not to continue to be the case in developing biblical and post-biblical tradition. Elijah's removal from his follower and from the wider Israelite scene in mysteriously powerful circumstances was partly anticipated by the pious but worried Obadiah (1 Kings 18:10–12), who never knew where Elijah would be "taken" next. When later tradition looked back on these narratives, it was to speculate on the availability of an Elijah who had not died to return for further service, as in the very last words of our Old Testament (Mal. 4:5–6):

> Behold I will send you Elijah the prophet before the great and terrible day of the Lord comes. And he will turn the hearts of fathers to their children and the hearts of children to their fathers, lest I come and smite the land with a curse.

The followers of Jesus and John the Baptist were to discuss whether either of their masters fitted the criteria for the returned Elijah (Matt. 11:2–15). The earthly 'ends' of Enoch (Gen. 5:24) and Moses (Deut. 34:5–6) were also covered in mystery—and they too flourished in later legend. It is not surprising that it was Moses and Elijah who were to appear with Jesus to some of his disciples (Mark 9:2–13).

(iii)

The geography of this chapter has puzzled many readers. There seem to be unexplained zig-zags from Gilgal near the Jordan to

Bethel, 4000 feet above and some 15 miles away, then back to Jericho near Gilgal before crossing the Jordan. Of course Bethel simply means "House of God" and Gilgal "Circle" (of standing stones), and there may have been several places we do not know about that bore these names. I prefer to see in these marches the continuing drama of a larger-than-life Elijah putting Elisha to the test. They seem also to be retracing in reverse some of Israel's first steps in its land (Josh. 5–8) before the two men re-enact—eastwards—that earlier wonderful crossing of the Jordan (Josh. 3–4).

The parting of master and servant is beyond straightforward interpretation: it is attempting to describe the indescribable. Some elements are manageable. The double share of Elijah's spirit (2:9) is the proper portion for the eldest son or heir: Elisha is simply asking formally to succeed Elijah. This time Elijah, who has previously seemed to dissuade Elisha, sets as a condition close attention to what will happen. Elisha should "see" as he is "taken" (v.10). And of course to "see" is not simply to spectate—it is also to perceive, to understand.

The scene ends with 'confession' by Elisha (v.12), in both senses of that term. *First* a profession of faith: "My father, my father! the chariots of Israel and its horsemen!" Then *second*, a demonstration of his own unworthiness: the ritual tearing of his clothes. Elisha has "seen"; and he does inherit. With the tangible symbol of that inheritance he recrosses the Jordan as he had first crossed it with his master. And that too is "seen" and understood by the band of prophets from the Jericho area: "The spirit of Elijah rests on Elisha" (v.15). And yet, as so often with our religious understanding, their perception is also a lack of perception. For just as Ahab and Obadiah had once scoured many lands for an Elijah who had disappeared, so the prophets now demand search parties. However, their misunderstanding highlights the understanding of Elisha who realised the pointlessness of the exercise. As we turn now to consider the Elisha stories in the next chapters of 2 Kings, we shall have more to say both about the chariot of fire and the horses of fire, and about the power of Elisha as demonstrated in the stories of cleansing

Jericho's water and punishing impertinent boys that conclude the present chapter (vv.19-25).

CAMPAIGNING IN MOAB

2 Kings 3: 1-27

¹In the eighteenth year of Jehoshaphat king of Judah, Jehoram the son of Ahab became king over Israel in Samaria, and he reigned twelve years. ²He did what was evil in the sight of the Lord, though not like his father and mother, for he put away the pillar of Baal which his father had made. ³Nevertheless he clung to the sin of Jeroboam the son of Nebat, which he made Israel to sin; he did not depart from it.

⁴Now Mesha king of Moab was a sheep breeder; and he had to deliver annually to the king of Israel a hundred thousand lambs, and the wool of a hundred thousand rams. ⁵But when Ahab died, the king of Moab rebelled against the king of Israel. ⁶So King Jehoram marched out of Samaria at that time and mustered all Israel. ⁷And he went and sent word to Jehoshaphat king of Judah, "The king of Moab has rebelled against me; will you go with me to battle against Moab?" And he said, "I will go; I am as you are, my people as your people, my horses as your horses." ⁸Then he said, "By which way shall we march?" Jehoram answered, "By the way of the wilderness of Edom."

⁹So the king of Israel went with the king of Judah and the king of Edom. And when they had made a circuitous march of seven days, there was no water for the army or for the beasts which followed them. ¹⁰Then the king of Israel said, "Alas! The Lord has called these three kings to give them into the hand of Moab." ¹¹And Jehoshaphat said, "Is there no prophet of the Lord here, through whom we may inquire of the Lord?" Then one of the king of Israel's servants answered, "Elisha the son of Shaphat is here, who poured water on the hands of Elijah." ¹²And Jehoshaphat said, "The word of the Lord is with him." So the king of Israel and Jehoshaphat and the king of Edom went down to him.

¹³And Elisha said to the king of Israel, "What have I to do with you? Go to the prophets of your father and the prophets of your mother." But the king of Israel said to him, "No; it is the Lord who has called these three kings to give them into the hand of Moab."

[14]And Elisha said, "As the Lord of hosts lives, whom I serve, were it not that I have regard for Jehoshaphat the king of Judah, I would neither look at you, nor see you. [15]But now bring me a minstrel." And when the minstrel played, the power of the Lord came upon him. [16]And he said, "Thus says the Lord, 'I will make this dry stream-bed full of pools.' [17]For thus says the Lord, 'You shall not see wind or rain, but that stream-bed shall be filled with water, so that you shall drink, you, your cattle, and your beasts.' [18]This is a light thing in the sight of the Lord; he will also give the Moabites into your hand, [19]and you shall conquer every fortified city, and every choice city, and shall fell every good tree, and stop up all springs of water, and ruin every good piece of land with stones." [20]The next morning, about the time of offering the sacrifice, behold, water came from the direction of Edom, till the country was filled with water.

[21]When all the Moabites heard that the kings had come up to fight against them, all who were able to put on armour, from the youngest to the oldest, were called out, and were drawn up at the frontier. [22]And when they rose early in the morning, and the sun shone upon the water, the Moabites saw the water opposite them as red as blood. [23]And they said, "This is blood; the kings have surely fought together, and slain one another. Now then, Moab, to the spoil!" [24]But when they came to the camp of Israel, the Israelites rose and attacked the Moabites, till they fled before them; and they went forward, slaughtering the Moabites as they went. [25]And they overthrew the cities, and on every good piece of land every man threw a stone, until it was covered; they stopped every spring of water, and felled all the good trees; till only its stones were left in Kir-Nareseth, and the slingers surrounded and conquered it. [26]When the king of Moab saw that the battle was going against him, he took with him seven hundred swordsmen to break through, opposite the king of Edom; but they could not. [27]Then he took his eldest son who was to reign in his stead, and offered him for a burnt offering upon the wall. And there came great wrath upon Israel; and they withdrew from him and returned to their own land.

(i)

This is a tantalizing chapter which at several points tells us less than we would like to know. We have to resist the temptation to make good these gaps, and limit ourselves to interpreting the text before us. It opens simply enough (vv.1–3), with the standard note introducing a new reign, and the quite mechanical condemnation of any king of Israel. Jehoram's name may mean "Yahweh is exalted", and he may have bettered the religious situation he inherited from his parents. But as long as the consequences of Jeroboam's "revolt" from the house of David and Temple of Solomon were not unpicked, he was damned for clinging to the sin of the son of Nebat. All straightforward—except for the conflict with 1:17 which places his accession in the reign of Jehoshaphat's son.

King Mesha's revolt from Israel was not just signalled at the beginning of the book (2 Kings 1:1)—we have the rare privilege of being able to read about it in a contemporary document. The so-called Moabite Stone is the longest inscription we possess from the earlier part of the monarchies of Judah and Israel. It demonstrates that the people of Moab also spoke Hebrew, although they worshipped Chemosh and not Yahweh as their great god. It describes how Mesha threw off 40 years of rule by Israel, inaugurated by Omri, by fortifying the northern border towns. It makes no mention of the awful measures the end of this chapter mentions, by which a final Israelite withdrawal was effected. But it is possible that Mesha's triumphal celebratory inscribed stone was set up after his success in the north, but before the rigours of the southern campaign. Yet we may want to pause again before reading 2 Kings 3 as simple historical record.

(ii)

We have already noted tension over dating between 1:17 and 3:1. This may be exacerbated by the claim of Mesha's stone that it was in the reign of Omri's son that he asserted his independence—although "son" could mean "descendant". And the presence of a "king of Edom" as a third colleague (v.9) appears to conflict with 1 Kings 22:47 and 2 Kings 8:20, which talk of Judean control of its south-eastern neighbour. Again, this story repeats significant features of 1 Kings 22: Jehoshaphat and a king of Israel campaigning together in Transjordan, and making their pact in identical terms (v.7 and 1 Kings 22:4); and pious Jehoshaphat requesting "a prophet of the Lord" (v.11 and 1 Kings 22:7). It is also the case that the Chronicler, who in other respects expands considerably the information from Kings about Jehoshaphat, breathes no hint of this campaign. I suspect that, unlike 1 Kings 22, this chapter was not yet in the version of the Book of Kings that the Chronicler knew—he would certainly have approved of verse 14: "were it not that I have regard for Jehoshaphat the king of Judah". It was probably a story told within later biblical tradition to enhance both the authority of Elisha and the reputation of the kings of Judah over against the kings of Israel.

(iii)

Elisha in this chapter is not just reminiscent of Micaiah; he is again ranked alongside his master Elijah (v.11). Jehoshaphat has only to hear that Elisha had served Elijah to be sure that "the word of the Lord is with him" (v.12)! Elisha's first formal words to the king of Israel (v.14—in the previous verse he is attempting to evade a serious response) introduce himself just as Elijah had done (1 Kings 17:1). And the story that follows portrays him assisting a god with power over the rain, as in the contest at Mount Carmel (1 Kings 18); and as in that chapter (1 Kings 18:36) so here too (v.20) the divine intervention occurs at "the time of offering the sacrifice".

The story also takes an interest in the *means* of inspiration. The Lord's power—the Hebrew talks more concretely of his "hand"—comes on him as a minstrel plays (v.15). Many commentators remind us at this point of 1 Samuel 10:5–13 with its group of prophets preceded by a musical band—but that is a story which is critical of Saul and the prophets. I am reminded rather of the lone David playing as Saul's minstrel to invoke the return of Yahweh's good spirit and the removal of the evil spirit afflicting his master (1 Sam. 16:14–23).

(iv)

What does come as a surprise after the exalted scriptural

company in which Elisha has been portrayed is the military advice he has to offer (v.19). Economic warfare or reprisals through rendering the land unfit for agriculture is excluded under Israel's rules for war. And Deuteronomy 20:19-20 specifically prohibits using fruit trees as timber for siege works:

> When you besiege a city for a long time . . . you shall not destroy its trees by wielding an axe against them; for you may eat of them, but you shall not cut them down. Are the trees in the field men that they should be besieged by you?

Having acted as the medium of divine instruction, Elisha recedes from sight at the end of the story. The Moabites are tricked out of their impregnable strongholds by the withdrawal of their enemies and their own misunderstanding of a natural phenomenon. There lurks a double word-play in the telling of this part of the tale (v.22). "Red" in Hebrew (*adom*) is very like "Edom" (*edom*); and both pun on "blood" (*dam*)—the red damp ground towards Edom looked like blood!

Elisha had undertaken that God would give Moab into the hands of the allies; but matters did not turn out that way. We are given no hint that Elisha had overstepped his authority or that the Lord had changed his mind. But Mesha did take a step that biblical tradition found quite appalling—we should recall God's interposition when Abraham was about to do the same (Gen. 22), and the horror with which we read both that story and the awful outcome of Jephthah's vow (Judg. 11). In the face of this public drama of desperation on the walls, Israel simply withdrew.

VARIOUS POWERFUL DEEDS

2 Kings 4:1-44

[1]Now the wife of one of the sons of the prophets cried to Elisha, "Your servant my husband is dead; and you know that your servant feared the Lord, but the creditor has come to take my two children to be his slaves." [2]And Elisha said to her, "What shall I do for you?

Tell me; what have you in the house?" And she said, "Your maidservant has nothing in the house, except a jar of oil." [3]Then he said, "Go outside, borrow vessels of all your neighbours, empty vessels and not too few. [4]Then go in, and shut the door upon yourself and your sons, and pour into all these vessels; and when one is full, set it aside." [5]So she went from him and shut the door upon herself and her sons; and as she poured they brought the vessels to her. [6]When the vessels were full, she said to her son, "Bring me another vessel." And he said to her, "There is not another." Then the oil stopped flowing. [7]She came and told the man of God, and he said, "Go, sell the oil and pay your debts, and you and your sons can live on the rest."

[8]One day Elisha went on to Shunem, where a wealthy woman lived, who urged him to eat some food. So whenever he passed that way, he would turn in there to eat food. [9]And she said to her husband, "Behold now, I perceive that this is a holy man of God, who is continually passing our way. [10]Let us make a small roof chamber with walls, and put there for him a bed, a table, a chair, and a lamp, so that whenever he comes to us, he can go in there."

[11]One day he came there, and he turned into the chamber and rested there. [12]And he said to Gehazi his servant, "Call this Shunammite." When he had called her, she stood before him. [13]And he said to him, "Say now to her, See, you have taken all this trouble for us; what is to be done for you? Would you have a word spoken on your behalf to the king or to the commander of the army?" She answered, "I dwell among my own people." [14]And he said, "What then is to be done for her?" Gehazi answered, "Well, she has no son, and her husband is old." [15]He said, "Call her." And when he had called her, she stood in the doorway. [16]And he said, "At this season, when the time comes round, you shall embrace a son." And she said, "No, my lord, O man of God; do not lie to your maidservant." [17]But the woman conceived, and she bore a son about that time the following spring, as Elisha had said to her.

[18]When the child had grown, he went out one day to his father among the reapers. [19]And he said to his father, "Oh, my head, my head!" The father said to his servant, "Carry him to his mother." [20]And when he had lifted him, and brought him to his mother, the child sat on her lap till noon, and then he died. [21]And she went up and laid him on the bed of the man of God, and shut the door upon him, and went out. [22]Then she called to her husband, and said, "Send me one of the servants and one of the asses, that I may

quickly go to the man of God, and come back again." ²³And he said, "Why will you go to him today? It is neither new moon nor sabbath." She said, "It will be well." ²⁴Then she saddled the ass, and she said to her servant, "Urge the beast on; do not slacken the pace for me unless I tell you." ²⁵So she set out, and came to the man of God at Mount Carmel.

When the man of God saw her coming, he said to Gehazi his servant, "Look, yonder is the Shunammite; ²⁶run at once to meet her, and say to her, Is it well with you? Is it well with your husband? Is it well with the child?" And she answered, "It is well." ²⁷And when she came to the mountain to the man of God, she caught hold of his feet. And Gehazi came to thrust her away. But the man of God said, "Let her alone, for she is in bitter distress; and the Lord has hidden it from me, and has not told me." ²⁸Then she said, "Did I ask my lord for a son? Did I not say, Do not deceive me?" ²⁹He said to Gehazi, "Gird up your loins, and take my staff in your hand, and go. If you meet any one, do not salute him; and if any one salutes you, do not reply; and lay my staff upon the face of the child." ³⁰Then the mother of the child said, "As the Lord lives, and as you yourself live, I will not leave you." So he arose and followed her. ³¹Gehazi went on ahead and laid the staff upon the face of the child, but there was no sound or sign of life. Therefore he returned to meet him, and told him, "The child has not awaked."

³²When Elisha came into the house, he saw the child lying dead on his bed. ³³So he went in and shut the door upon the two of them, and prayed to the Lord. ³⁴Then he went up and lay upon the child, putting his mouth upon his mouth, his eyes upon his eyes, and his hands upon his hands; and as he stretched himself upon him, the flesh of the child became warm. ³⁵Then he got up again, and walked once to and fro in the house, and went up, and stretched himself upon him; the child sneezed seven times, and the child opened his eyes. ³⁶Then he summoned Gehazi and said, "Call this Shunammite." So he called her. And when she came to him, he said, "Take up your son." ³⁷She came and fell at his feet, bowing to the ground; then she took up her son and went out.

³⁸And Elisha came again to Gilgal when there was a famine in the land. And as the sons of the prophets were sitting before him, he said to his servant, "Set on the great pot, and boil pottage for the sons of the prophets." ³⁹One of them went out into the field to gather herbs, and found a wild vine and gathered from it his lap full of wild gourds, and came and cut them up into the pot of pottage,

not knowing what they were. [40]And they poured out for the men to eat. But while they were eating of the pottage, they cried out, "O man of God, there is death in the pot!" And they could not eat it. [41]He said, "Then bring meal." And he threw it into the pot, and said, "Pour out for the men, that they may eat." And there was no harm in the pot.

[42]A man came from Baal-shalishah, bringing the man of God bread of the first fruits, twenty loaves of barley, and fresh ears of grain in his sack. And Elisha said, "Give to the men, that they may eat." [43]But his servant said, "How am I to set this before a hundred men?" So he repeated, "Give them to the men, that they may eat, for thus says the Lord. 'They shall eat and have some left.'" [44]So he set it before them. And they ate, and had some left, according to the word of the Lord.

(i)

In this chapter we find further examples of Elisha stories very reminiscent of tales told of Elijah. Miracles in fact bulk much larger in the traditions concerning Elisha than in the Elijah material. They are a common enough element in religious story-telling. And I have already suggested that part of their purpose is to heighten the importance of Elisha, and claim for him a stature like that of Elijah. Many may share my suspicion that the more claims are made, the less they are to be heeded, and that Elijah continues to shine through as the more important and significant figure of the two. Yet it may be that he is too remote and uncompromising to enjoy popular appeal.

Another aspect of the relationship between the two groups of stories deserves to be aired. In as far as the traditions about Elisha repeat and adapt elements of the Elijah traditions, they also give us a clue as to how these came to be read and understood. We noticed as we dealt with them that several were open to a miraculous reading although they did not require it. Yet, where Elijah's actions were more ambiguous, Elisha's are quite manifestly those of a wonder-worker. And this influences in retrospect our reading of the Elijah stories: when we are puzzled by them, we are *naturally* guided by the more explicit and detailed tales that follow—naturally, but perhaps falsely.

The first story in chapter 4 is a good case in point (vv.1–7). It reminds us of Elijah's assurance to the widow from Zarephath that her stock of meal and oil would feed him too through the drought (1 Kings 17:8–16). Here again we have a widow with a family to support, a family threatened with slavery on account of debt; and the family of a god-fearing prophet for good measure! Elisha works a miracle for her relief, without invoking the Lord's name as Elijah had done; and the resulting oil is used to pay off her debts and provide continuing income.

(ii)

Of the two short episodes that conclude this chapter (vv.38–41,42–44), the story about neutralizing the harm in his provision for the prophets reminds us of Elisha's cleansing of Jericho's water supply in 2:19–22. It is possible that both reflect the sort of superior nature lore that is often the preserve of priests and holy men in so-called 'pre-scientific' societies. Yet, after all we have just noted above, it is more than likely that they are simply two further anecdotes about Elisha's wonderful power. God is mentioned in 2:21, yet as a source of power at Elisha's disposal rather than the authority to whom he too is subject. God is not mentioned in 4:38–41 except (v.40) in the title of his "man".

The story of the pot prepared for the prophets leads on naturally to the feeding of a large company from a gift of first fruits to Elisha. It is striking that he should have received such a dedication at all; for first fruits belonged to God, and were presented more immediately to his priests. But of even greater interest to those familiar with the Gospels is the similarity between this short anecdote and the accounts there of the feeding by Jesus of much larger groups of people on the basis of much lesser supplies. Common to both is the surplus after all have been satisfied.

(iii)

The much more extended centrepiece of this long chapter brings us back to the issue of comparison with Elijah—this time

with the second episode in his dealing with the widow from
Zarephath (1 Kings 17:17–24). Again the context is provided by
a woman's hospitality. Again we are dealing with the subsequent death of her son, which results in blame for the man of
God. Again the recovery of the boy follows the man of God
stretching himself out on the lad.

Yet the differences are quite as interesting. Instead of a poor
foreign widow, the Shunammite is a rich married lady of Israel
(v.8). And this helps to underscore the universal popular appeal
of a figure like Elisha. He is at ease in all sectors of society. He is
not exclusively aligned with the downtrodden and unfortunate
in the community. And he is not waging a high-profile religious
campaign. He is not only happy to accept rich hospitality, but
even suggests—whether seriously or ironically we do not know—
that he can use influence on the lady's behalf with king or
commander-in-chief (v.13). Incidentally, the Shunammite's
reply at this point is a beautifully terse statement of rural or
provincial independence: "I dwell among my own people".

Gehazi may have known from the exchange of gossip in the
servants' quarters what Elisha had not learned from his more
restrained dealings with his hostess: that she was without son,
and with little prospect of one. Her reaction to his offer (v.16)
reminds us of Sarah's laughter (Gen. 18:10–15) and Zechariah's
disbelief (Luke 1:18–20) at similar divine announcements. We
have every sympathy with her angry reaction to the boy's illness
and death, that she was better without a son than to have had
one briefly and lose him. But all this is again conveyed in
splendid brevity: "Did I ask my lord for a son?" (v.28).

Elisha's reaction is immediate, if a little ponderous: but he is
content to deal with the crisis through Gehazi. But in the face of
the mother's crisp obstinacy he has to acquiesce in a more active
role—and the failure of Gehazi and his master's rod proves her
right to have insisted. The end of the story is particularly
reminiscent of the end of 1 Kings 17, but more detailed in its
description of the healer's technique. By contrast, once her son
is restored to her, this mistress of economic communication is
speechless at Elisha's feet in her gratitude.

NAAMAN THE SYRIAN LEPER

2 Kings 5:1–27

¹Naaman, commander of the army of the king of Syria, was a great man with his master and in high favour, because by him the Lord had given victory to Syria. He was a mighty man of valour, but he was a leper. ²Now the Syrians on one of their raids had carried off a little maid from the land of Israel, and she waited on Naaman's wife. ³She said to her mistress, "Would that my lord were with the prophet who is in Samaria! He would cure him of his leprosy." ⁴So Naaman went in and told his lord, "Thus and so spoke the maiden from the land of Israel." ⁵And the king of Syria said, "Go now, and I will send a letter to the king of Israel."

So he went, taking with him ten talents of silver, six thousand shekels of gold, and ten festal garments. ⁶And he brought the letter to the king of Israel, which read, "When this letter reaches you, know that I have sent to you Naaman my servant, that you may cure him of his leprosy." ⁷And when the king of Israel read the letter, he rent his clothes and said, "Am I God, to kill and to make alive, that this man sends word to me to cure a man of his leprosy? Only consider, and see how he is seeking a quarrel with me."

⁸But when Elisha the man of God heard that the king of Israel had rent his clothes, he sent to the king, saying, "Why have you rent your clothes? Let him come now to me, that he may know that there is a prophet in Israel." ⁹So Naaman came with his horses and chariots, and halted at the door of Elisha's house. ¹⁰And Elisha sent a messenger to him, saying, "Go and wash in the Jordan seven times, and your flesh shall be restored, and you shall be clean." ¹¹But Naaman was angry, and went away, saying, "Behold, I thought that he would surely come out to me, and stand, and call on the name of the Lord his God, and wave his hand over the place, and cure the leper. ¹²Are not Abana and Pharpar, the rivers of Damascus, better than all the waters of Israel? Could I not wash in them, and be clean?" So he turned and went away in a rage. ¹³But his servants came near and said to him, "My father, if the prophet had commanded you to do some great thing, would you not have done it? How much rather, then, when he says to you, 'Wash and be clean'?" ¹⁴So he went down and dipped himself seven times in the Jordan, according to the word of the man of God; and his flesh was restored like the flesh of a little child, and he was clean.

¹⁵Then he returned to the man of God, he and all his company, and he came and stood before him; and he said, "Behold, I know that there is no God in all the earth but in Israel; so accept now a present from your servant." ¹⁶But he said, "As the Lord lives, whom I serve, I will receive none." And he urged him to take it, but he refused. ¹⁷Then Naaman said, "If not, I pray you, let there be given to your servant two mules' burden of earth; for henceforth your servant will not offer burnt offering or sacrifice to any god but the Lord. ¹⁸In this matter may the Lord pardon your servant: when my master goes into the house of Rimmon to worship there, leaning on my arm, and I bow myself in the house of Rimmon, when I bow myself in the house of Rimmon, the Lord pardon your servant in this matter." ¹⁹He said to him, "Go in peace."

But when Naaman had gone from him a short distance, ²⁰Gehazi, the servant of Elisha the man of God, said, "See, my master has spared this Naaman the Syrian, in not accepting from his hand what he brought. As the Lord lives, I will run after him, and get something from him." ²¹So Gehazi followed Naaman. And when Naaman saw some one running after him, he alighted from the chariot to meet him, and said, "Is all well?" ²²And he said, "All is well. My master has sent me to say, 'There have just now come to me from the hill country of Ephraim two young men of the sons of the prophets; pray, give them a talent of silver and two festal garments.'" ²³And Naaman said, "Be pleased to accept two talents." And he urged him, and tied up two talents of silver in two bags, with two festal garments, and laid them upon two of his servants; and they carried them before Gehazi. ²⁴And when he came to the hill, he took them from their hand, and put them in the house; and he sent the men away, and they departed. ²⁵He went in, and stood before his master, and Elisha said to him, "Where have you been, Gehazi?" And he said, "Your servant went nowhere." ²⁶But he said to him, "Did I not go with you in spirit when the man turned from his chariot to meet you? Was it a time to accept money and garments, olive orchards and vineyards, sheep and oxen, menservants and maidservants? ²⁷Therefore the leprosy of Naaman shall cleave to you, and to your descendants for ever." So he went out from his presence a leper, as white as snow.

(i)

In any setting where the stories of the Old Testament are read or told this is surely one of the best known. It is certainly one of the best told. A remarkable amount about the character of the main participants is communicated in very few words. And mostly, as is common in Hebrew narrative, this happens through their own speeches.

It is noteworthy in the opening verse that it is the Lord who is credited with using Naaman as his agent to secure Syrian success—even success in a campaign that has involved raids on the land of Israel. Syria, like Philistia, may have been one of Israel's age-old enemies; but it was still subject to, and potentially useful to, the God Israel worshipped. And the three-fold mission given to Elijah at Horeb had had as its first stage the anointing of Hazael king over Syria (1 Kings 19:15). However, the strategic significance within this story of so early a mention of Yahweh in connection with a "foreigner" will become even plainer to us shortly.

Naaman's "leprosy" was not what is clinically known as leprosy today, a disease probably unknown in the Near East until Alexander the Great's troops brought it back from India. It is likely to have been psoriasis, a less serious but still disfiguring skin ailment. Within Israel it would normally have led to exclusion from the community. In that he still had access to his king (v.4), Naaman's disease may not (yet) have been very advanced.

Since the ailment could lead to excommunication from the people at worship, it had even greater 'religious' significance than disease in general. And so it was probably not just because his Israelite maid thought Elisha could do anything, but particularly because of his religious status, that she made her recommendation. And this also gives special point to the king of Israel's horrified "Am I God . . . ?" (v.7).

(ii)

In Hebrew the play on words that leads the king so easily from reading to rending is even more striking, for the original words both look and sound alike. At this national discomfiture Elisha intervenes. He again preserves his status (as in 4:29) by acting through an intermediary—it is particularly important here where he has a great man to impress. However, the initial impression made on Naaman is far from favourable. It is not the sort of diplomacy which normally wins hearts, nor the kind of bedside manner that generally cultivates rich private patients with any success!

Deprived of the expected personal reception and appropriate religious ritual, Naaman stalks off (v.11). Even the specified washing place, pleasant though the Jordan is in many of its upper reaches, is taken as a national insult. His staff are rather more pragmatic (v.13). They both know him and perhaps care for him—he had after all inspired loyalty and concern even in a captured Israelite slavegirl. They have also more experience than their master of being at the receiving end of official high-handedness.

(iii)

The success of Naaman's seven dips in the Jordan transforms his attitude towards Elisha (who also clearly receives him personally on his return) and to Elisha's God (v.15). Because he is merely a servant of that God, Elisha will accept no gift. Naaman takes the hint and proceeds to talk of offerings to Elisha's Master. He pledges himself to offer sacrifice to no other God than Yahweh—but two things he requires for this new service of his in Damascus: a token amount of the land of Israel (v.17), and a dispensation that will allow him to fulfil his ceremonial duties with his king in the temple of Rimmon (v.18). Both are implicitly conceded in Elisha's formula that can cover both absolution and farewell: "Go in peace" (v.19). At the very least, Elisha must have been satisfied with the enthusiasm of the new worshipper.

We cannot resist a rather superior smile at Naaman's request for two loads of *soil* on the basis of his new conviction "that there is no God in all the *earth* but in Israel" (v.15). And we are surely intended to be amused. The absurdity ranks with the folly of Jonah escaping "from the presence of the Lord" (1:2–3), yet saying under interrogation by his shipmates: "I am a

Hebrew; and I fear the Lord, the God of heaven, who made the sea and the dry land" (1:9). His fellows immediately (v.10) get the point that has escaped him: "'What is this that you have done!' For the men knew that he was fleeing from the presence of the Lord, because he had told them."

And yet it is not Naaman's conclusion, but his basic premise that we are invited to question. "There is no God in all the earth but the one whom Israel recognizes" might be an improvement, or might simply protect the absurdity by stating it in a more refined way. Who is being invited to laugh at whom? Often when the Bible wins our assent with a smile, its purpose is to turn and challenge us. Are this story and the story of Jonah concerned with foreign, pagan Syrians and Assyrians, and the possibility or the terms of their conversion to worship of Yahweh? Or are they intended to confront entrenched attitudes within the community of Israel? To ask the question is to answer it. And the clue, as we suggested above, is given emphatically right at the beginning of the story: by Naaman, *Yahweh* had given victory to Syria.

(iv)

The sad humour in the closing episode of Gehazi's greedy fraud underlines some of the lessons already suggested. Even he knows that a servant should not accept what his master does not. What does irk him is that Naaman should receive grace so freely (v.20). And even if this is only his excuse for his own gainful ploy, we may usefully ask ourselves if we are similarly accused.

INVASIONS FROM SYRIA I—TEXT

2 Kings 6:1–7:20

[1]Now the sons of the prophets said to Elisha, "See, the place where we dwell under your charge is too small for us. [2]Let us go to the Jordan and each of us get there a log, and let us make a place for us to dwell there." And he answered, "Go." [3]Then one of them said, "Be pleased to go with your servants." And he answered, "I will go," [4]So

he went with them. And when they came to the Jordan, they cut down trees. ⁵But as one was felling a log, his axe head fell into the water; and he cried out, "Alas, my master! It was borrowed." ⁶Then the man of God said, "Where did it fall?" When he showed him the place, he cut off a stick, and threw it in there, and made the iron float. ⁷And he said, "Take it up." So he reached out his hand and took it.

⁸Once when the king of Syria was warring against Israel, he took counsel with his servants, saying, "At such and such a place shall be my camp." ⁹But the man of God sent word to the king of Israel, "Beware that you do not pass this place, for the Syrians are going down there." ¹⁰And the king of Israel sent to the place of which the man of God told him. Thus he used to warn him, so that he saved himself there more than once or twice.

¹¹And the mind of the king of Syria was greatly troubled because of this thing; and he called his servants and said to them, "Will you not show me who of us is for the king of Israel?" ¹²And one of his servants said, "None, my lord, O king; but Elisha, the prophet who is in Israel, tells the king of Israel the words that you speak in your bedchamber." ¹³And he said, "Go and see where he is, that I may send and seize him." It was told him, "Behold, he is in Dothan." ¹⁴So he sent there horses and chariots and a great army; and they came by night, and surrounded the city.

¹⁵When the servant of the man of God rose early in the morning and went out, behold, an army with horses and chariots was round about the city. And the servant said, "Alas, my master! What shall we do?" ¹⁶He said, "Fear not, for those who are with us are more than those who are with them." ¹⁷Then Elisha prayed, and said, "O Lord, I pray thee, open his eyes that he may see." So the Lord opened the eyes of the young man, and he saw; and behold, the mountain was full of horses and chariots of fire round about Elisha. ¹⁸And when the Syrians came down against him, Elisha prayed to the Lord, and said, "Strike this people, I pray thee, with blindness." So he struck them with blindness in accordance with the prayer of Elisha. ¹⁹And Elisha said to them, "This is not the way, and this is not the city; follow me, and I will bring you to the man whom you seek." And he led them to Samaria.

²⁰As soon as they entered Samaria, Elisha said, "O Lord, open the eyes of these men, that they may see." So the Lord opened their eyes, and they saw; and lo, they were in the midst of Samaria. ²¹When the king of Israel saw them he said to Elisha, "My father,

shall I slay them? Shall I slay them?" ²²He answered, "You shall not slay them. Would you slay those whom you have taken captive with your sword and with your bow? Set bread and water before them, that they may eat and drink and go to their master." ²³So he prepared for them a great feast; and when they had eaten and drunk, he sent them away, and they went to their master. And the Syrians came no more on raids into the land of Israel.

²⁴Afterward Ben-hadad king of Syria mustered his entire army, and went up, and besieged Samaria. ²⁵And there was a great famine in Samaria, as they besieged it, until an ass's head was sold for eighty shekels of silver, and the fourth part of a kab of dove's dung for five shekels of silver. ²⁶Now as the king of Israel was passing by upon the wall, a woman cried out to him, saying, "Help, my lord, O king!" ²⁷And he said, "If the Lord will not help you, whence shall I help you? From the threshing floor, or from the wine press?" ²⁸And the king asked her, "What is your trouble?" She answered, "This woman said to me, 'Give your son, that we may eat him today, and we will eat my son tomorrow.' ²⁹So we boiled my son, and ate him. And on the next day I said to her, 'Give your son, that we may eat him'; but she has hidden her son." ³⁰When the king heard the words of the woman he rent his clothes—now he was passing by upon the wall—and the people looked, and behold, he had sackcloth beneath upon his body— ³¹and he said, "May God do so to me, and more also, if the head of Elisha the son of Shaphat remains on his shoulders today."

³²Elisha was sitting in his house, and the elders were sitting with him. Now the king had despatched a man from his presence; but before the messenger arrived Elisha said to the elders, "Do you see how this murderer has sent to take off my head? Look, when the messenger comes, shut the door, and hold the door fast against him. Is not the sound of his master's feet behind him?" ³³And while he was still speaking with them, the king came down to him and said, "This trouble is from the Lord! Why should I wait for the Lord any longer?" ¹But Elisha said, "Hear the word of the Lord: thus says the Lord, Tomorrow about this time a measure of fine meal shall be sold for a shekel, and two measures of barley for a shekel, at the gate of Samaria." ²Then the captain on whose hand the king leaned said to the man of God, "If the Lord himself should make windows in heaven, could this thing be?" But he said, "You shall see it with your own eyes, but you shall not eat of it."

³Now there were four men who were lepers at the entrance to the

gate; and they said to one another, "Why do we sit here till we die? ⁴If we say, 'Let us enter the city,' the famine is in the city, and we shall die there; and if we sit here, we die also. So now come, let us go over to the camp of the Syrians; if they spare our lives we shall live, and if they kill us we shall but die." ⁵So they arose at twilight to go to the camp of the Syrians; but when they came to the edge of the camp of the Syrians, behold, there was no one there. ⁶For the Lord had made the army of the Syrians hear the sound of chariots, and of horses, the sound of a great army, so that they said to one another, "Behold, the king of Israel has hired against us the kings of the Hittites and the kings of Egypt to come upon us." ⁷So they fled away in the twilight and forsook their tents, their horses, and their asses, leaving the camp as it was, and fled for their lives. ⁸And when these lepers came to the edge of the camp, they went into a tent, and ate and drank, and they carried off silver and gold and clothing, and went and hid them; then they came back, and entered another tent, and carried off things from it, and went and hid them.

⁹Then they said to one another, "We are not doing right. This day is a day of good news; if we are silent and wait until the morning light, punishment will overtake us; now therefore come, let us go and tell the king's household." ¹⁰So they came and called to the gatekeepers of the city, and told them, "We came to the camp of the Syrians, and behold, there was no one to be seen or heard there, nothing but the horses tied, and the asses tied, and the tents as they were." ¹¹Then the gatekeepers called out, and it was told within the king's household. ¹²And the king rose in the night, and said to his servants, "I will tell you what the Syrians have prepared against us. They know that we are hungry; therefore they have gone out of the camp to hide themselves in the open country, thinking, 'When they come out of the city, we shall take them alive and get into the city.'" ¹³And one of his servants said, "Let some men take five of the remaining horses, seeing that those who are left here will fare like the whole multitude of Israel that have already perished; let us send and see." ¹⁴So they took two mounted men, and the king sent them after the army of the Syrians, saying, "Go and see." ¹⁵So they went after them as far as the Jordan; and, lo, all the way was littered with garments and equipment which the Syrians had thrown away in their haste. And the messengers returned, and told the king.

¹⁶Then the people went out, and plundered the camp of the Syrians. So a measure of fine meal was sold for a shekel, and two measures of barley for a shekel, according to the word of the Lord.

¹⁷Now the king had appointed the captain on whose hand he leaned to have charge of the gate; and the people trod upon him in the gate, so that he died, as the man of God had said when the king came down to him. ¹⁸For when the man of God had said to the king, "Two measures of barley shall be sold for a shekel, and a measure of fine meal for a shekel, about this time tomorrow in the gate of Samaria," ¹⁹the captain had answered the man of God, "If the Lord himself should make windows in heaven, could such a thing be?" And he had said, "You shall see it with your own eyes, but you shall not eat of it." ²⁰And so it happened to him, for the people trod upon him in the gate and he died.

INVASIONS FROM SYRIA II—COMMENTARY

2 Kings 6:1-7:20 (*cont'd*)

(i)

As in the case of chapter 4, we are given a further brief reminder of Elisha's miraculous powers (6:1-7) before the main stories begin. The prophets of whom this and so many other of the Elijah and Elisha narratives talk are always spoken of as a group. They are entertained together (4:38-41) from a common pot; and we learn here that they live together too. They did not—or did not all—live a celibate life as in a monastery (4:1 talks of the widow of one of them). Yet they did congregate in that area by the lower Jordan where we know monastic communities have thrived in many historical periods since—from the Qumran community to whom we are indebted for the Dead Sea Scrolls onwards.

Elisha himself, although like Elijah occasionally and exceptionally termed "prophet" in our texts, is not one of them. They acknowledge his authority and value his support; but he is most often referred to as "man of God". Here he is consulted about new quarters and invited to be part of the expedition. And, as so often before, his divine power is invoked to right a relatively minor mishap (although, if this story does come from early in Israel's history, iron was then a rare and specially useful metal).

(ii)

It is hardly a surprise that a man of God of such varied powers can also 'divine' not only the military strategy of the king of Syria (vv. 8–10) but even his most private and intimate confidences (v. 12). As Israel's most valuable asset in military intelligence, he was worth mounting a special expedition for. The story seems to assume that Syria already controlled much of northern Israel, for Dothan lies to the south of the valley of Jezreel, in the northern foothills of the Ephraimite hill-country.

As Elisha's servant was to discover, his master's military potential was not limited to the sphere of intelligence. Elisha asks God to reassure the young man in a vision, which takes a form similar to his own vision at Elijah's departure (2:12). He then asks God to blind his opponents, leads them to the capital, and has their eyes opened to perceive their predicament. Even the king of Israel defers to Elisha (v.21) no less than the prophets had done earlier (v.5); but the king is told that he has to entertain his enemies rather than kill those he has not himself taken. This episode reminds us of the prophetic story at the end of 1 Kings 20—but with the vital difference that the Lord has not devoted this king of Syria to destruction. His purpose is sufficiently served by the cessation of raids once the Syrian army has reported on its latest campaign (v.23).

(iii)

The natural chapter-break belongs after this verse. "Afterward" (v.24) must either denote quite a long time or represent a rather loose link between originally quite separate stories. Despite verse 23 it talks of a new invasion from Syria; and it now names the king in question as one of the many Ben-hadads.

Prices like those quoted for an ass's head or dove's dung are the province of the story-teller rather than the economic historian—if only because records are never kept of such enterprising transactions. They prepare us for the grimmest reversal of proper roles that could occur in siege and famine: when the mother does business over the butchering of the child she has borne and raised (vv.26ff.). Properly appalled at a case much more terrible than the one immortalized in Solomon's verdict (1 Kings 3), the king of Israel loses all deference for Elisha ben-Shaphat.

The text does not make clear to us why Elisha is held responsible. Certainly he does not demur at the king's claim (v.33) that Yahweh is to blame. And so the situation, although not fully explained, reminds us of Ahab's search for Elijah during an earlier famine (1 Kings 18). Equally no royal reaction to Elisha's divine oracle (7:1) is reported. Elisha simply promises a dramatic turn within a day, with prices tumbling on the Samaria exchange back to normal—or perhaps to absurdly low levels. The king's right-hand man is promised an appropriate penalty for disbelief of the divine word (7:2).

(iv)

The kaleidoscope of already used story-elements is shaken yet again, and a new episode is before our eyes linking Syria and leprosy (7:3–10). Four lepers decide they have no more to lose by going over to the Syrian camp, than by remaining as unfed beggars at the edge of their own community. They happen on a beggar's paradise, and enjoy its riches as if they had scooped the pools. They awaken from their dream to a familiar mixture of guilt and fear: what they are doing is not right, and it will be taken out of them if they are found to have suppressed the good news. After they make their report we learn no more of them.

It is presumably the Lord's thunder which the Syrians misinterpret as a vast army of chariotry (7:6). They almost detect what Elisha and then his servant had seen in separate visions. But they attribute the vast forces they hear not to Yahweh but to fabled armies of Egyptians and Hittites of ancient story. In any case they respond as intended—and flee.

Of Elisha too we learn no more. But the fulfilment of the divine word that promised punishment for doubting the divine word is expressly detailed (7:17–20).

VARIOUS STORIES CONTINUED

2 Kings 8:1–29

¹Now Elisha had said to the woman whose son he had restored to life, "Arise, and depart with your household, and sojourn wherever you can; for the Lord has called for a famine, and it will come upon the land for seven years." ²So the woman arose, and did according to the word of the man of God; she went with her household and sojourned in the land of the Philistines seven years. ³And at the end of the seven years, when the woman returned from the land of the Philistines, she went forth to appeal to the king for her house and her land. ⁴Now the king was talking with Gehazi the servant of the man of God, saying "Tell me all the great things that Elisha has done." ⁵And while he was telling the king how Elisha had restored the dead to life, behold, the woman whose son he had restored to life appealed to the king for her house and her land. And Gehazi said, "My lord, O king, here is the woman, and here is her son whom Elisha restored to life." ⁶And when the king asked the woman, she told him. So the king appointed an official for her, saying, "Restore all that was hers, together with all the produce of the fields from the day that she left the land until now."

⁷Now Elisha came to Damascus. Ben-hadad the king of Syria was sick; and when it was told him, "The man of God has come here," ⁸the king said to Hazael, "Take a present with you and go to meet the man of God, and inquire of the Lord through him, saying, 'Shall I recover from this sickness?'" ⁹So Hazael went to meet him, and took a present with him, all kinds of goods of Damascus, forty camel loads. When he came and stood before him, he said, "Your son Ben-hadad king of Syria has sent me to you, saying, 'Shall I recover from this sickness?'" ¹⁰And Elisha said to him, "Go, say to him, 'You shall certainly recover'; but the Lord has shown me that he shall certainly die." ¹¹And he fixed his gaze and stared at him, until he was ashamed. And the man of God wept. ¹²And Hazael said, "Why does my lord weep?" He answered, "Because I know the evil that you will do to the people of Israel; you will set on fire their fortresses, and you will slay their young men with the sword, and dash in pieces their little ones, and rip up their women with child." ¹³And Hazael said, "What is your servant, who is but a dog, that he should do this great thing?" Elisha answered, "The Lord has shown me that you are to be king over Syria." ¹⁴Then he departed from

Elisha, and came to his master, who said to him, "What did Elisha say to you?" And he answered, "He told me that you would certainly recover." [15]But on the morrow he took the coverlet and dipped it in water and spread it over his face, till he died. And Hazael became king in his stead.

[16]In the fifth year of Joram the son of Ahab, king of Israel, Jehoram the son of Jehoshaphat, king of Judah, began to reign. [17]He was thirty-two years old when he became king, and he reigned eight years in Jerusalem. [18]And he walked in the way of the kings of Israel, as the house of Ahab had done, for the daughter of Ahab was his wife. And he did what was evil in the sight of the Lord. [19]Yet the Lord would not destroy Judah, for the sake of David his servant, since he promised to give a lamp to him and to his sons for ever.

[20]In his days Edom revolted from the rule of Judah, and set up a king of their own. [21]Then Joram passed over to Zair with all his chariots, and rose by night, and he and his chariot commanders smote the Edomites who had surrounded him; but his army fled home. [22]So Edom revolted from the rule of Judah to this day. Then Libnah revolted at the same time. [23]Now the rest of the acts of Joram, and all that he did, are they not written in the Book of the Chronicles of the Kings of Judah? [24]So Joram slept with his fathers and was buried with his fathers in the city of David: and Ahaziah his son reigned in his stead.

[25]In the twelfth year of Joram the son of Ahab, king of Israel, Ahaziah the son of Jehoram, king of Judah, began to reign. [26]Ahaziah was twenty-two years old when he began to reign, and he reigned one year in Jerusalem. His mother's name was Athaliah; she was a granddaughter of Omri king of Israel. [27]He also walked in the way of the house of Ahab, and did what was evil in the sight of the Lord, as the house of Ahab had done, for he was son-in-law to the house of Ahab.

[28]He went with Joram the son of Ahab to make war against Hazael king of Syria at Ramoth-gilead, where the Syrians wounded Joram. [29]And King Joram returned to be healed in Jezreel of the wounds which the Syrians had given him at Ramah, when he fought against Hazael king of Syria. And Ahaziah the son of Jehoram king of Judah went down to see Joram the son of Ahab in Jezreel, because he was sick.

Preceding chapters have already elicited our interest in Elisha

and his wonderful doings, in relationships with the major local
power of Damascus, and in the linked fortunes of the royal
houses of Judah and Israel. As if an episode in an ongoing
serial, today's chapter advances each of these stories a little.

(i)

It may come as a surprise to see the territory of the Philistines,
the famous arch-enemy of many Biblical stories, serving as a
place of refuge (vv.2–3). If so, it can usefully jolt us into
remembering over how many centuries the Old Testament story
unravels. Indeed, many political relationships have changed in
much shorter periods of more recent history. In Scottish terms,
both the 'Auld Alliance' (with France) and the 'Auld Enemy'
(England) are now more nostalgic than real. Similarly, at this
time Israel and the Philistines had long since ceased to be active
foes. In any case, the situation in our chapter is one of famine:
and, as we say, 'any port in a storm'.

This opening to the story reminds us of others, like the trek
across the Jordan to Moab by Elimelech and Naomi from
Bethlehem (Ruth 1:1–5), and the import of food from Egypt by
the patriarch Jacob and his final migration there (Gen. chs.
42–47). Israel/Palestine is not a naturally rich country, especially in its central hilly areas, and its economy is very suscepti-
ble to fluctuations in rainfall.

It surprises us too that Gehazi, who paid such a price for his
mischief with Naaman (5:19–27), is still (or again?) on the
scene—and eulogizing his master for the entertainment of his
king (vv.4–5). In fact the various episodes in these chapters are
probably not reported in strict timetable order: the opening
words of this story do not tie it to the one before.

However, it comes as less surprise that, after seven years, the
woman's title to her house and land was no longer secure. We
can only suppose how the refugee's case might have fared at
court on its merits alone. But happily for her she was spotted by
Gehazi just as he reached her part in his story. With a friend at
court she became an instant celebrity and her case was won. The

king even back-dated her restitution of income, in hollow or
absent-minded magnanimity—the produce of seven famine-
torn years had been small enough!

(ii)

The fame of Elisha was quite as well known in the court of
Damascus. That is hardly surprising if the next episode reported (vv.7-15) did actually follow the healing of Naaman (ch. 5)
and the military plight of the Syrians in Samaria (chs. 6-7).
However, the RSV fails to catch the surprise in the original
Hebrew at the end of verse 7: it should be, "The man of God has
come *as far as* here".

Two themes from much earlier in Kings now reappear and
criss-cross. One is Elijah's commission at Horeb to anoint
Hazael king over Syria (1 Kings 19:15), and the other is the
deliberate use of lies to further the Lord's purposes (1 Kings
22:22-23). The orders given to Elijah are now carried out, but
with two modifications. Elisha has become the divine agent, not
his master. And the explicit, public act of anointing (even if
only a figure of speech for appointing) has become a private,
politic nudge. As for the Lord's deceit, it is mouthed not by the
massed ranks of the court prophetic establishment, but by
Elisha himself (v.10).

The ruthlessness of Elisha's advice to Hazael reminds me of
David's final counsel to Solomon (1 Kings 2:1-9). There too the
fatal instructions are never explicitly pronounced. Yet there too
we can have no doubt over what is intended. It is not easy to
decide how—or indeed whether—the story-teller wants us to
evaluate this sort of behaviour. Even if we had to deduce that
the author supported it, a Christian reader *could* decide to look
instead to the New Testament for controlling ethical principles.
And yet the Old Testament has very much more to say about
the world of national life and statesmanship and politics than
the New. Perhaps the Christian too has to be reminded by it
that, in *that* world, moral squeamishness is not a virtue.
Perhaps. I myself am far from sure.

In any case, it is not over his own false answer to a sick man who has approached him as a known healer that Elisha weeps, but over what he knows this Hazael will do to his own people Israel (v.12). Such cruelty to pregnant women and infants is both a fact of war (still), and a theme of prophetic criticism (*eg* Amos 1:13). Hazael's immediate actions mirror Elisha's words: he 'honourably' transmits to Ben-hadad the good news from the healing man of God, before contriving 'accidental' suffocation for him the next day (vv.14–15).

(iii)

The brief accounts of Jehoram (vv.16–24) and Ahaziah his son (vv.25–29), kings of Judah, have much in common. Both are tarred with the awful brush of the house of Omri. The opening of 1 Kings 22 has not told us of Jehoshaphat's marriage alliance with Ahab, although the almost identical 2 Chronicles 18:1 does. The resulting (religious) wickedness tests the strength of God's commitment to the house of David (vv.18–19). It survives the test; yet Edom is lost to Judah and becomes independent again under Jehoram; while Ahaziah sees his Israelite cousin Joram (an alternative spelling of his own father's name) wounded when on a joint expedition against Hazael, now king of Syria. His visit to his ailing fellow monarch in Jezreel (v.29) sets the scene for the famous incident in our next chapter.

THE DRIVING OF JEHU

2 Kings 9:1–37

¹Then Elisha the prophet called one of the sons of the prophets and said to him, "Gird up your loins, and take this flask of oil in your hand, and go to Ramoth-gilead. ²And when you arrive, look there for Jehu the son of Jehoshaphat, son of Nimshi; and go in and bid him rise from among his fellows, and lead him to an inner chamber. ³Then take the flask of oil, and pour it on his head, and say, 'Thus

says the Lord, I anoint you king over Israel.' Then open the door and flee; do not tarry."

⁴So the young man, the prophet, went to Ramoth-gilead. ⁵And when he came, behold, the commanders of the army were in council; and he said, "I have an errand to you, O commander." And Jehu said, "To which of us all?" And he said, "To you, O commander." ⁶So he arose, and went into the house; and the young man poured the oil on his head, saying to him, "Thus says the Lord the God of Israel, I anoint you king over the people of the Lord, over Israel. ⁷And you shall strike down the house of Ahab your master, that I may avenge on Jezebel the blood of my servants the prophets, and the blood of all the servants of the Lord. ⁸For the whole house of Ahab shall perish; and I will cut off from Ahab every male, bond or free, in Israel. ⁹And I will make the house of Ahab like the house of Jeroboam the son of Nebat, and like the house of Baasha the son of Ahijah. ¹⁰And the dogs shall eat Jezebel in the territory of Jezreel, and none shall bury her." Then he opened the door, and fled.

¹¹When Jehu came out to the servants of his master, they said to him, "Is all well? Why did this mad fellow come to you?" And he said to them, "You know the fellow and his talk." ¹²And they said, "That is not true; tell us now." And he said, "Thus and so he spoke to me, saying, 'Thus says the Lord, I anoint you king over Israel.' " ¹³Then in haste every man of them took his garment, and put it under him on the bare steps, and they blew the trumpet, and proclaimed, "Jehu is king."

¹⁴Thus Jehu the son of Jehoshaphat the son of Nimshi conspired against Joram. (Now Joram with all Israel had been on guard at Ramoth-gilead against Hazael king of Syria; ¹⁵but King Joram had returned to be healed in Jezreel of the wounds which the Syrians had given him, when he fought with Hazael king of Syria.) So Jehu said, "If this is your mind, then let no one slip out of the city to go and tell the news in Jezreel." ¹⁶Then Jehu mounted his chariot, and went to Jezreel, for Joram lay there. And Ahaziah king of Judah had come down to visit Joram.

¹⁷Now the watchman was standing on the tower in Jezreel, and he spied the company of Jehu as he came, and said, "I see a company." And Joram said, "Take a horseman, and send to meet them, and let him say, 'Is it peace?' " ¹⁸So a man on horseback went to meet him, and said, "Thus says the king, 'Is it peace?' " And Jehu said, "What have you to do with peace? Turn round and ride behind me." And

the watchman reported, saying, "The messenger reached them, but he is not coming back." ¹⁹Then he sent out a second horseman, who came to them, and said, "Thus the king has said, 'Is it peace?' " And Jehu answered, "What have you to do with peace? Turn round and ride behind me." ²⁰Again the watchman reported, "He reached them, but he is not coming back. And the driving is like the driving of Jehu the son of Nimshi; for he drives furiously."

²¹Joram said, "Make ready." And they made ready his chariot. Then Joram king of Israel and Ahaziah king of Judah set out, each in his chariot, and went to meet Jehu, and met him at the property of Naboth the Jezreelite. ²²And when Joram saw Jehu, he said, "Is it peace, Jehu?" He answered, "What peace can there be, so long as the harlotries and the sorceries of your mother Jezebel are so many?" ²³Then Joram reined about and fled, saying to Ahaziah, "Treachery, O Ahaziah!" ²⁴And Jehu drew his bow with his full strength, and shot Joram between the shoulders, so that the arrow pierced his heart, and he sank in his chariot. ²⁵Jehu said to Bidkar his aide, "Take him up, and cast him on the plot of ground belonging to Naboth the Jezreelite; for remember, when you and I rode side by side behind Ahab his father, how the Lord uttered this oracle against him: ²⁶'As surely as I saw yesterday the blood of Naboth and the blood of his sons—says the Lord—I will requite you on this plot of ground.' Now therefore take him up and cast him on the plot of ground, in accordance with the word of the Lord."

²⁷When Ahaziah the king of Judah saw this, he fled in the direction of Beth-haggan. And Jehu pursued him, and said, "Shoot him also"; and they shot him in the chariot at the ascent of Gur, which is by Ible-am. And he fled to Megiddo, and died there. ²⁸His servants carried him in a chariot to Jerusalem, and buried him in his tomb with his fathers in the city of David.

²⁹In the eleventh year of Joram the son of Ahab, Ahaziah began to reign over Judah.

³⁰When Jehu came to Jezreel, Jezebel heard of it; and she painted her eyes, and adorned her head, and looked out of the window. ³¹And as Jehu entered the gate, she said, "Is it peace, you Zimri, murderer of your master?" ³²And he lifted up his face to the window, and said, "Who is on my side? Who?" Two or three eunuchs looked out at him. ³³He said, "Throw her down." So they threw her down; and some of her blood spattered on the wall and on the horses, and they trampled on her. ³⁴Then he went in and ate and drank; and he said, "See now to this cursed woman, and bury her;

for she is a king's daughter." ³⁵But when they went to bury her, they found no more of her than the skull and the feet and the palms of her hands. ³⁶When they came back and told him, he said, "This is the word of the Lord, which he spoke by his servant Elijah the Tishbite, 'In the territory of Jezreel the dogs shall eat the flesh of Jezebel; ³⁷and the corpse of Jezebel shall be as dung upon the face of the field in the territory of Jezreel, so that no one can say, This is Jezebel.' "

The uncompleted element in Elijah's Horeb commission (1 Kings 19:16) is now undertaken by his follower; yet Elisha does not act by his own hand.

(i)

The opening scene (vv.1–13) sets a nice puzzle for the enquiring reader. It jumps out from the text that Elisha's young man speaks at much greater length (vv.6–10) than either he is instructed by Elisha (v.3) or reported by Jehu (v.12). I have no wish to impose an explanation—only to make three observations that tend in rather different directions.

(a) There are many messenger scenes in the Bible; and it is in fact very common in the telling of them for the message presented to appear to diverge at least slightly from the instructions given. This is often said to be an artistic convention to save the boredom of verbatim repetition. The total message may then be reconstructed by adding together all the details from the instructions and from the delivery.

(b) Such an approach to story-*telling* may well have saved tedium in many cases. But as a *reading* method it could make us blind to other possibilities in the text. The brevity of Elisha and prolixity of the young man may have been deliberately contrasted—and could be explained in different ways. Many seniors do not require to give full instructions on every occasion to their juniors: they are left to fill out the details for themselves. Equally, some inexperienced juniors take pains—and indeed pleasure—over 'correcting' the 'inadequacies' of their superiors, who have in fact said all that is necessary. Have we in our text clues to the characters involved, which should not be swept under a carpet of story-telling convention?

(c) Another possibility is simply that the original briefer story has been amplified (within vv.6–10) by a later editor who wanted to make a link with texts like 1 Kings 16:11–13 and 21:21–24.

At least we can observe that the character of Jehu himself is lightly and nicely sketched in these verses. When the "young man" (v.4) arrives at headquarters and addresses Jehu as the commander, he modestly parries (v.5), suggesting he is but one of several equals. Yet when he reports to his fellow-officers what has passed in the inner room, their immediate and positive reaction hails a pre-eminence all the greater for his modesty.

My final comment on this opening section concerns the title "prophet". I have suggested before that this is often a late editorial addition to the text of Kings. It seems to have been added three times in these verses: *first* in the opening mention of Elisha (v.1); *second* in verse 4, where the clumsy Hebrew should be rendered, "So the young man [the young man, *ie* the prophet] went ... "; and *third* and finally in verse 7, which originally spoke only of "the blood of all the servants of the Lord", the addition of "the blood of my servants the prophets" will reflect a late tradition about prophetic martyrdom.

(ii)

The first word of verse 14 reads oddly, and has in fact no support in the Hebrew text: "Then" would be better than "Thus". Jehu's "conspiracy" is no more than our administrators practise much of the time: the management of the release of information.

A much harder problem faces the translator of the repeated question in verses 18, 19 and 22, and its answers. *Shalom* does mean "peace" and the question could be asking the great commander whether his presence so far from the front meant good news or bad for the nation in its struggle with its northern neighbour—so fast an approach on the person of the king was bound to be unsettling. Yet *shalom* can also refer more widely to general well-being, and the word is frequently used as a simple greeting. With the two envoys, Jehu parries the question quite curtly; and the effect of his command is both to clear his own passage forward and to add to the company over which he has authority.

When we learn that Naboth's piece of land is the meeting place of Jehu and the kings, we know in our bones what the outcome will be. And when we hear Jehu speaking as Elijah might have, denying the possibility of peace or any sort of well-being as long as Jezebel was influential (v.22), we are not surprised that the king takes to flight. Jehu actually recalls Elijah's words to his lieutenant (v.25), acknowledging them as coming from Yahweh himself.

Up to this point Ahaziah of Judah, who had merely come north to visit his sick royal cousin (v.16), has been only a spectator at a drama in Israel. When he draws attention to himself by taking to flight like Joram, a similar fate is ordered for him too. He has never been properly introduced to us: the narrator—rather inconsequentially—only reports his accession to the throne in Jerusalem (v.29) *after* the record of his burial!

However, the last words of this chapter (vv.30–37) belong to Jezebel who has overshadowed the whole narrative ever since 1 Kings 16:31. She had dared threaten the great man from Tishbe (1 Kings 19:1–2); and her death appropriately occurs now just as predicted by Elijah (1 Kings 21:23–24).

JEHU, SLAUGHTER AND SACRIFICE

2 Kings 10:1–36

[1]Now Ahab had seventy sons in Samaria. So Jehu wrote letters, and sent them to Samaria, to the rulers of the city, to the elders, and to the guardians of the sons of Ahab, saying, [2]"Now then, as soon as this letter comes to you, seeing your master's sons are with you, and there are with you chariots and horses, fortified cities also, and weapons, [3]select the best and fittest of your master's sons and set him on his father's throne, and fight for your master's house." [4]But

they were exceedingly afraid, and said, "Behold, the two kings could not stand before him; how then can we stand?" ⁵So he who was over the palace, and he who was over the city, together with the elders and the guardians, sent to Jehu, saying, "We are your servants, and we will do all that you bid us. We will not make any one king; do whatever is good in your eyes." ⁶ Then he wrote to them a second letter, saying, "If you are on my side, and if you are ready to obey me, take the heads of your master's sons, and come to me at Jezreel tomorrow at this time." Now the king's sons, seventy persons, were with the great men of the city, who were bringing them up. ⁷And when the letter came to them, they took the king's sons, and slew them, seventy persons, and put their heads in baskets, and sent them to him at Jezreel. ⁸When the messenger came and told him, "They have brought the heads of the king's sons," he said, "Lay them in two heaps at the entrance of the gate until the morning." ⁹Then in the morning, when he went out, he stood, and said to all the people, "You are innocent. It was I who conspired against my master, and slew him; but who struck down all these? ¹⁰Know then that there shall fall to the earth nothing of the word of the Lord, which the Lord spoke concerning the house of Ahab; for the Lord has done what he said by his servant Elijah." ¹¹So Jehu slew all that remained of the house of Ahab in Jezreel, all his great men, and his familiar friends, and his priests, until he left him none remaining.

¹²Then he set out and went to Samaria. On the way, when he was at Beth-eked of the Shepherds, ¹³Jehu met the kinsmen of Ahaziah king of Judah, and he said, "Who are you?" And they answered, "We are the kinsmen of Ahaziah, and we came down to visit the royal princes and the sons of the queen mother." ¹⁴He said, "Take them alive." And they took them alive, and slew them at the pit of Beth-eked, forty-two persons, and he spared none of them.

¹⁵And when he departed from there, he met Jehonadab the son of Rechab coming to meet him; and he greeted him, and said to him, "Is your heart true to my heart as mine is to yours?" And Jehonadab answered, "It is." Jehu said, "If it is, give me your hand." So he gave him his hand. And Jehu took him up with him into the chariot. ¹⁶And he said, "Come with me, and see my zeal for the Lord." So he had him ride in his chariot. ¹⁷And when he came to Samaria, he slew all that remained to Ahab in Samaria, till he had wiped them out, according to the word of the Lord which he spoke to Elijah.

¹⁸Then Jehu assembled all the people, and said to them, "Ahab

served Baal a little; but Jehu will serve him much. ¹⁹Now therefore call to me all the prophets of Baal, all his worshippers and all his priests; let none be missing, for I have a great sacrifice to offer to Baal; whoever is missing shall not live." But Jehu did it with cunning in order to destroy the worshippers of Baal. ²⁰And Jehu ordered, "Sanctify a solemn assembly for Baal." So they proclaimed it. ²¹And Jehu sent throughout all Israel; and all the worshippers of Baal came, so that there was not a man left who did not come. And they entered the house of Baal, and the house of Baal was filled from one end to the other. ²²He said to him who was in charge of the wardrobe, "Bring out the vestments for all the worshippers of Baal." So he brought out the vestments for them. ²³Then Jehu went into the house of Baal with Jehonadab the son of Rechab; and he said to the worshippers of Baal, "Search, and see that there is no servant of the Lord here among you, but only the worshippers of Baal." ²⁴Then he went in to offer sacrifices and burnt offerings.

Now Jehu had stationed eighty men outside, and said, "The man who allows any of those whom I give into your hands to escape shall forfeit his life." ²⁵So as soon as he had made an end of offering the burnt offering, Jehu said to the guard and to the officers, "Go in and slay them; let not a man escape." So when they put them to the sword, the guard and the officers cast them out and went into the inner room of the house of Baal ²⁶and they brought out the pillar that was in the house of Baal, and burned it. ²⁷And they demolished the pillar of Baal, and demolished the house of Baal, and made it a latrine to this day.

²⁸Thus Jehu wiped out Baal from Israel. ²⁹But Jehu did not turn aside from the sins of Jeroboam the son of Nebat, which he made Israel to sin, the golden calves that were in Bethel, and in Dan. ³⁰And the Lord said to Jehu, "Because you have done well in carrying out what is right in my eyes, and have done to the house of Ahab according to all that was in my heart, your sons of the fourth generation shall sit on the throne of Israel." ³¹But Jehu was not careful to walk in the law of the Lord the God of Israel with all his heart; he did not turn from the sins of Jeroboam, which he made Israel to sin.

³²In those days the Lord began to cut off parts of Israel. Hazael defeated them throughout the territory of Israel: ³³from the Jordan eastward, all the land of Gilead, the Gadites, and the Reubenites, and the Manassites, from Aroer, which is by the valley of the

Arnon, that is, Gilead and Bashan. 34Now the rest of the acts of
Jehu, and all that he did, and all his might, are they not written in
the Book of the Chronicles of the Kings of Israel? 35So Jehu slept
with his fathers, and they buried him in Samaria. And Jehoahaz his
son reigned in his stead. 36The time that Jehu reigned over Israel in
Samaria was twenty-eight years.

Jehu jumps out of these chapters as a ruthless and quite brilliant
politician. The narrative is crisp and economical, and the 'smell'
of the effrontery of real-life leadership clings to it!

(i)

He first throws down the gauntlet before the feet of the
'establishment' in Israel's capital city with an impudent challenge that they should rally round one of Ahab's 70 sons, and
stand up for their master's cause. In the face of the fate of Kings
Joram and Ahaziah, they undertake not to elect an alternative
king, and to come over and serve Jehu without preconditions.
Only then does he specify their first task: to harvest the heads of
those for whom they had been responsible. As so often in life,
an offer they dared not refuse became a trap they could not
escape.

The people at large were less brutally, yet quite as effectively,
'fixed'. Before them, Jehu admitted his own conspiracy against
his "master" (10:9), while clearing them of any guilt. The
relieved multitude was then invited to play jury in the case of the
heads looking out of the baskets with varied imprints of Ahab's
face. The whole Samaria establishment was found guilty in this
'trial', and 'lawfully' executed.

Within the Bible, the seizure of power in Israel at the cost of
the elimination of the 70 sons of the former leader is most
closely paralleled in Judges chapter 9, where Abimelech similarly removes any possibility of counter-claim from the family
of Gideon (or Jerubbaal). It may be that that story reflects in
some way this account of Jehu's usurpation (see my book
Joshua, Judges and Ruth in this series, pp. 182ff.).

As a bloody 'bonus', Jehu eliminates the family of Ahaziah,
cousins to Ahab's sons. They provide him with the opportunity

by 'visiting' their relatives in the north. The Hebrew talks literally of their coming "for the *shalom* of the sons of the king". Of course, this could simply have been a paying of family respects on the death of their brother Joram: Yet Jehu may well have suspected them of having interests of a more active sort in the welfare of their royal relatives!

(ii)

Sandwiched between the two main episodes of this chapter is a significant little report of an encounter between Jehu and Jehonadab. Like many Biblical figures who have fascinated groups in more recent times, the Rechabites are barely known to us. Jeremiah respectfully contrasts their abstemious devotion to this Jehonadab's principles with general Israelite neglect of the traditions of their forefathers. Jehonadab's very name is an amalgam of the divine name and *nadab*, which has associations with words for nobility, generosity, and volunteering offerings or sacrifices beyond the minimum prescribed. And Jehu the usurper is clearly keen to have his own zeal endorsed by this zealot.

(iii)

It will surprise any reader of the last 16 chapters of the Books of Kings that the husband of Jezebel, just deceased and of unlamented memory, should be described as having served Baal only "a little' (v.18) without the people suspecting Jehu of (further) perfidy. Yet what we have read and studied in these many pages is a very loaded account. We have to remember that Ahab's chief minister was a loyal servant of Yahweh—Obadiah; and that the king who succeeded him had a name built from Yahweh—Jeho-ram. Enthusiasts for Baal could have wished for several 'improvements' in their own direction in Ahab's policies. And it was precisely to such enthusiasts that Jehu directed his appeal. They seem to have had no inkling of the price the state would exact for its 'support' of their worship. Indeed, enough seems to have been known of Jehu's single-mindedness—but not his words to Joram about his mother

(9:22)—that the exclusion of any known servants of Yahweh passed without exciting suspicion.

I have fault to find with several of the standard modern translations in verses 18–27 of chapter 10. The Hebrew uses the same common word for the "servants" of Baal and those of the Lord—the word *ebed* which is part of Obadiah's name. There is no cause to distinguish between "worshippers" (RSV) or "ministers" (NEB) of Baal, and "servants" (RSV and NEB) of Yahweh. Nor indeed is there cause to call both groups "devotees" (JB). It is quite unnecessary in this case for the translator to make distinctions which the author has not, although he could have. And, moreover, such differentiation might well have been counter-productive for Jehu's ploy.

The gory outcome (v.25) might have been scripted by the man of God from Judah (1 Kings 13:2) with his vision of the sacrifice on the Bethel altar of its own priests. However, in keeping with the principles of these Books of Kings, even praise of Jehu for extirpating both Ahab's house and Baal's worship is muted *just because* Jeroboam's altars to Yahweh remained in service (vv.29–31). Indeed Israel itself began to be dismembered (vv.32–33).

REFORM OF A KIND I—TEXT

2 Kings 11:1–12:21

¹Now when Athaliah the mother of Ahaziah saw that her son was dead, she arose and destroyed all the royal family. ²But Jehosheba, the daughter of King Joram, sister of Ahaziah, took Joash the son of Ahaziah, and stole him away from among the king's sons who were about to be slain, and she put him and his nurse in a bedchamber. Thus she hid him from Athaliah, so that he was not slain; ³and he remained with her six years, hid in the house of the Lord, while Athaliah reigned over the land.

⁴But in the seventh year Jehoiada sent and brought the captains of the Carites and of the guards, and had them come to him in the house of the Lord; and he made a covenant with them and put them under oath in the house of the Lord, and he showed them the king's

son. 5And he commanded them, "This is the thing that you shall do: one third of you, those who come off duty on the sabbath and guard the king's house 6(another third being at the gate Sur and a third at the gate behind the guards), shall guard the palace; 7 and the two divisions of you, which come on duty in force on the sabbath and guard the house of the Lord, 8shall surround the king, each with his weapons in his hand; and whoever approaches the ranks is to be slain. Be with the king when he goes out and when he comes in."

9The captains did according to all that Jehoiada the priest commanded, and each brought his men who were to go off duty on the sabbath, with those who were to come on duty on the sabbath, and came to Jehoiada the priest. 10And the priest delivered to the captains the spears and shields that had been King David's, which were in the house of the Lord; 11and the guards stood, every man with his weapons in his hand, from the south side of the house to the north side of the house, around the altar and the house. 12Then he brought out the king's son, and put the crown upon him, and gave him the testimony; and they proclaimed him king, and anointed him; and they clapped their hands, and said, "Long live the king!"

13When Athaliah heard the noise of the guard and of the people, she went into the house of the Lord to the people; 14and when she looked, there was the king standing by the pillar, according to the custom, and the captains and the trumpeters beside the king, and all the people of the land rejoicing and blowing trumpets. And Athaliah rent her clothes, and cried, "Treason! Treason!" 15Then Jehoiada the priest commanded the captains who were set over the army, "Bring her out between the ranks; and slay with the sword any one who follows her." For the priest said, "Let her not be slain in the house of the Lord." 16So they laid hands on her; and she went through the horses' entrance to the king's house, and there she was slain.

17And Jehoiada made a covenant between the Lord and the king and people, that they should be the Lord's people; and also between the king and the people. 18Then all the people of the land went to the house of Baal, and tore it down; his altars and his images they broke in pieces, and they slew Mattan the priest of Baal before the altars. And the priest posted watchmen over the house of the Lord. 19And he took the captains, the Carites, the guards, and all the people of the land; and they brought the king down from the house of the Lord, marching through the gate of the guards to the king's house. And he took his seat on the throne of the kings. 20So all the people of the land rejoiced; and the city was quiet after Athaliah had been slain with the sword at the king's house.

21Jehoash was seven years old when he began to reign.

1In the seventh year of Jehu Jehoash began to reign, and he reigned forty years in Jerusalem. His mother's name was Zibiah of Beer-sheba. 2And Jehoash did what was right in the eyes of the Lord all his days, because Jehoiada the priest instructed him. 3Nevertheless the high places were not taken away; the people continued to sacrifice and burn incense on the high places.

4Jehoash said to the priests, "All the money of the holy things which is brought into the house of the Lord, the money for which each man is assessed—the money from the assessment of persons—and the money which a man's heart prompts him to bring into the house of the Lord, 5let the priests take, each from his acquaintance; and let them repair the house wherever any need of repairs is discovered." 6But by the twenty-third year of King Jehoash the priests had made no repairs on the house. 7Therefore King Jehoash summoned Jehoiada the priest and the other priests and said to them, "Why are you not repairing the house? Now therefore take no more money from your acquaintances, but hand it over for the repair of the house." 8So the priests agreed that they should take no more money from the people, and that they should not repair the house.

9Then Jehoiada the priest took a chest, and bored a hole in the lid of it, and set it beside the altar on the right side as one entered the house of the Lord; and the priests who guarded the threshold put in it all the money that was brought into the house of the Lord. 10And whenever they saw that there was much money in the chest, the king's secretary and the high priest came up and they counted and tied up in bags the money that was found in the house of the Lord. 11Then they would give the money that was weighed out into the hands of the workmen who had the oversight of the house of the Lord; and they paid it out to the carpenters and the builders who worked upon the house of the Lord, 12and to the masons and the stonecutters, as well as to buy timber and quarried stone for making repairs on the house of the Lord, and for any outlay upon the repairs of the house. 13But there were not made for the house of the Lord basins of silver, snuffers, bowls, trumpets, or any vessels of gold, or of silver, from the money that was brought into the house of the Lord, 14for that was given to the workmen who were repairing the house of the Lord with it. 15And they did not ask an accounting from the men into whose hand they delivered the money to pay out to the workmen, for they dealt honestly. [16]The money from the guilt offerings and the money from the sin offerings was not brought into the house of the Lord; it belonged to the priests.

[17]At that time Hazael king of Syria went up and fought against Gath, and took it. But when Hazael set his face to go up against Jerusalem, [18]Jehoash king of Judah took all the votive gifts that Jehoshaphat and Jehoram and Ahaziah, his fathers, the kings of Judah, had dedicated, and his own votive gifts, and all the gold that was found in the treasuries of the house of the Lord and of the king's house, and sent these to Hazael king of Syria. Then Hazael went away from Jerusalem.

[19]Now the rest of the acts of Joash, and all that he did, are they not written in the Book of the Chronicles of the Kings of Judah? [20]His servants arose and made a conspiracy, and slew Joash in the house of Millo, on the way that goes down to Silla. [21]It was Jozacar the son of Shimeath and Jehozabad the son of Shomer, his servants, who struck him down, so that he died. And they buried him with his fathers in the city of David, and Amaziah his son reigned in his stead.

REFORM OF A KIND II—COMMENTARY

2 Kings 11:1–12:21 (*cont'd*)

(i)

Violence now spreads southwards from Israel to Judah. A substantial part of the Jerusalem royal house had already been eliminated by Jehu (10:12–14). Athaliah seeks to complete the task. RSV's "all the royal family" is not quite precise: Gray's "all the seed royal" is both more accurate a rendering and more attractive.

The effect of her butchery of members of the family of which she was a part may have been the culmination of Jehu's assault on the Judean royal line. But was her purpose the same? Jehu was bent on eliminating the house of Omri, and with it the service of Baal which it had at least permitted if not fostered. Chapter 11 does not spell out Athaliah's motives; but it does leave some clues which make me think that her aims were the very opposite.

Her principal antagonists were Jehoiada, the leading priest in the Lord's Temple, and her kinswoman Jehosheba (whom, 2 Chron. 22:11 tells us, was also wife to Jehoiada, whether on sound information or not). Both of these had Yahweh-names. And Athaliah's death was immediately followed (v.18) by the sacking of the temple of Baal and murder of its leading priest (Mattan meaning 'Gift'!). We may suppose that this daughter of the house of Omri was in fact seeking desperately to maintain its traditions. She may have had a shrewd suspicion that she would have less influence on the next-in-line than she had enjoyed, as queen mother, over Ahaziah.

To our author, she was not just a bad ruler; she was not even a valid ruler at all. Whereas in Israel the throne could be forcibly usurped, in Judah the ruler had to be a male of the house of David. Accordingly, there is no talk in this chapter of her installation, of the date in Jehu's reign in which she took power, of her burial, or of the succession to her—Jehoash simply "began to reign" (v.21), but not "in her stead".

(ii)

The beginning of Jehoash's reign is properly dated (12:1) to the "seventh year" of the reign of Jehu. And his unhappy demise too is narrated in a manner that includes standard formulae. However, the main content of the chapter presents us with a few puzzles. Some of the issues are brought into rather clearer focus when we compare the material with the largely parallel 2 Chronicles, chapter 24.

RSV may have been too positive in stating that the king did right *all his days* because Jehoiada instructed him (12:2). Certainly the Chronicler's theology would not have permitted him to report that a king who came to a bad end had lived a blameless life. Accordingly it is no surprise that his view is that "Joash did what was right in the eyes of the Lord all the days of Jehoiada the priest" (2 Chron. 24:2). The Hebrew in our chapter is less precise than the English of the RSV. If we substituted "in as much as" for its "because" (2 Kings 12:2), we would make the English reader face the same question as the

Hebrew reader must: did Jehoiada's wise influence last throughout the king's life, or did it terminate with his own death? Was
the priest his youthful teacher, or his ongoing counsellor and
even prop?

There was clearly some tension between monarch and priestly establishment over the financial arrangements for temple
repairs and maintenance. Yet again the precise area of dispute is
hard to pinpoint. Talk in RSV of the priests taking money from
their "acquaintance" (vv.5,7) could be taken as suggesting some
sort of racket such as 'insider dealing'. Yet this actual word is
found nowhere else in the Bible; and, although the extension of
blame in 2 Chronicles 24 to the Levites might reflect a similar
interpretation, attempts have been made to explain this rare
word quite differently. Similar words in related languages have
suggested translations more appropriate to the context, such as
"benefactors", or "assessors' , or "treasurers". The simplest
thing to say is that the debate is far from closed!

A concession was apparently won by which the collection
point at the temple door would be managed by the priests for a
joint commission of 'church and state' (vv.9,10)—but without
compromising the rights of the priests to certain defined dues
(v.16). We all know this sort of compromise well! Its paper
results are hailed as an advance and a victory; yet not very much
of substance is changed.

The chief question for many commentators is how far this
story corresponds to reality in Jehoash's time. There is a lot of
evidence to suggest that responsibility for temple fabric and
finance throughout the period of Judah's monarchy was the
king's alone. Certainly, like others before and since, Jehoash
felt free to use its treasures to buy off Hazael of Syria
(vv.17–19).

KINGS OF ISRAEL AND JUDAH I—TEXT

2 Kings 13:1–14:29

¹In the twenty-third year of Joash the son of Ahaziah, king of

Judah, Jehoahaz the son of Jehu began to reign over Israel in Samaria, and he reigned seventeen years. ²He did what was evil in the sight of the Lord, and followed the sins of Jeroboam the son of Nebat, which he made Israel to sin; he did not depart from them. ³And the anger of the Lord was kindled against Israel, and he gave them continually into the hand of Hazael king of Syria and into the hand of Ben-hadad the son of Hazael. ⁴Then Jehoahaz besought the Lord, and the Lord hearkened to him; for he saw the oppression of Israel, how the king of Syria oppressed them. ⁵(Therefore the Lord gave Israel a saviour, so that they escaped from the hand of the Syrians; and the people of Israel dwelt in their homes as formerly. ⁶Nevertheless they did not depart from the sins of the house of Jeroboam, which he made Israel to sin, but walked in them; and the Asherah also remained in Samaria.) ⁷For there was not left to Jehoahaz an army of more than fifty horsemen and ten chariots and ten thousand footmen; for the king of Syria had destroyed them and made them like the dust at threshing. ⁸Now the rest of the acts of Jehoahaz and all that he did, and his might, are they not written in the Book of the Chronicles of the Kings of Israel? ⁹So Jehoahaz slept with his fathers, and they buried him in Samaria; and Joash his son reigned in his stead.

¹⁰In the thirty-seventh year of Joash king of Judah Jehoash the son of Jehoahaz began to reign over Israel in Samaria, and he reigned sixteen years. ¹¹He also did what was evil in the sight of the Lord; he did not depart from all the sins of Jeroboam the son of Nebat, which he made Israel to sin, but he walked in them. ¹²Now the rest of the acts of Joash, and all that he did, and the might with which he fought against Amaziah king of Judah, are they not written in the Book of the Chronicles of the Kings of Israel? ¹³So Joash slept with his fathers, and Jeroboam sat upon his throne; and Joash was buried in Samaria with the kings of Israel.

¹⁴Now when Elisha had fallen sick with the illness of which he was to die, Joash king of Israel went down to him, and wept before him, crying, "My father, my father! The chariots of Israel and its horsemen!" ¹⁵And Elisha said to him, "Take a bow and arrows"; so he took a bow and arrows. ¹⁶Then he said to the king of Israel, "Draw the bow"; and he drew it. And Elisha laid his hands upon the king's hands. ¹⁷And he said, "Open the window eastward"; and he opened it. Then Elisha said, "Shoot"; and he shot. And he said, "The Lord's arrow of victory, the arrow of victory over Syria! For you shall fight the Syrians in Aphek until you have made an end of

them." ¹⁸And he said, "Take the arrows"; and he took them. And he said to the king of Israel, "Strike the ground with them"; and he struck three times, and stopped. ¹⁹Then the man of God was angry with him, and said, "You should have struck five or six times; then you would have struck down Syria until you had made an end of it, but now you will strike down Syria only three times."

²⁰So Elisha died, and they buried him. Now bands of Moabites used to invade the land in the spring of the year. ²¹And as a man was being buried, lo, a marauding band was seen and the man was cast into the grave of Elisha; and as soon as the man touched the bones of Elisha, he revived, and stood on his feet.

²²Now Hazael king of Syria oppressed Israel all the days of Jehoahaz. ²³But the Lord was gracious to them and had compassion on them, and he turned toward them, because of his covenant with Abraham, Isaac, and Jacob, and would not destroy them; nor has he cast them from his presence until now.

²⁴When Hazael king of Syria died, Ben-hadad his son became king in his stead. ²⁵Then Jehoash the son of Jehoahaz took again from Ben-hadad the son of Hazael the cities which he had taken from Jehoahaz his father in war. Three times Joash defeated him and recovered the cities of Israel.

¹In the second year of Joash the son of Joahaz, king of Israel, Amaziah the son of Joash, king of Judah, began to reign. ²He was twenty-five years old when he began to reign, and he reigned twenty-nine years in Jerusalem. His mother's name was Jeho-addin of Jerusalem. ³And he did what was right in the eyes of the Lord, yet not like David his father; he did in all things as Joash his father had done. ⁴But the high places were not removed; the people still sacrificed and burned incense on the high places. ⁵And as soon as the royal power was firmly in his hand he killed his servants who had slain the king his father. ⁶But he did not put to death the children of the murderers; according to what is written in the book of the law of Moses, where the Lord commanded, "The fathers shall not be put to death for the children, or the children be put to death for the fathers; but every man shall die for his own sin."

⁷He killed ten thousand Edomites in the Valley of Salt and took Sela by storm, and called it Joktheel, which is its name to this day.

⁸Then Amaziah sent messengers to Jehoash the son of Jehoahaz, son of Jehu, king of Israel, saying, "Come, let us look one another in the face." ⁹And Jehoash king of Israel sent word to Amaziah king of Judah, "A thistle on Lebanon sent to a cedar on Lebanon,

saying, 'Give your daughter to my son for a wife'; and a wild beast of Lebanon passed by and trampled down the thistle. ¹⁰You have indeed smitten Edom, and your heart has lifted you up. Be content with your glory, and stay at home; for why should you provoke trouble so that you fall, you and Judah with you?"

¹¹But Amaziah would not listen. So Jehoash king of Israel went up, and he and Amaziah king of Judah faced one another in battle at Beth-shemesh, which belongs to Judah. ¹²And Judah was defeated by Israel, and every man fled to his home. ¹³And Jehoash king of Israel captured Amaziah king of Judah, the son of Jehoash, son of Ahaziah, at Beth-shemesh, and came to Jerusalem, and broke down the wall of Jerusalem for four hundred cubits, from the Ephraim Gate to the Corner Gate. ¹⁴And he seized all the gold and silver, and all the vessels that were found in the house of the Lord and in the treasuries of the king's house, also hostages, and he returned to Samaria.

¹⁵Now the rest of the acts of Jehoash which he did, and his might, and how he fought with Amaziah king of Judah, are they not written in the Book of the Chronicles of the Kings of Israel? ¹⁶And Jehoash slept with his fathers, and was buried in Samaria with the kings of Israel; and Jeroboam his son reigned in his stead.

¹⁷Amaziah the son of Joash, king of Judah, lived fifteen years after the death of Jehoash son of Jehoahaz, king of Israel. ¹⁸Now the rest of the deeds of Amaziah, are they not written in the Book of the Chronicles of the Kings of Judah? ¹⁹And they made a conspiracy against him in Jerusalem, and he fled to Lachish. But they sent after him to Lachish, and slew him there. ²⁰And they brought him upon horses; and he was buried in Jerusalem with his fathers in the city of David. ²¹And all the people of Judah took Azariah, who was sixteen years old, and made him king instead of his father Amaziah. ²²He built Elath and restored it to Judah, after the king slept with his fathers.

²³In the fifteenth year of Amaziah the son of Joash, king of Judah, Jeroboam the son of Joash, king of Israel, began to reign in Samaria, and he reigned forty-one years. ²⁴And he did what was evil in the sight of the Lord; he did not depart from all the sins of Jeroboam the son of Nebat, which he made Israel to sin. ²⁵He restored the border of Israel from the entrance of Hamath as far as the Sea of the Arabah, according to the word of the Lord, the God of Israel, which he spoke by his servant Jonah the son of Amittai, the prophet, who was from Gath-hepher. ²⁶For the Lord saw that

the affliction of Israel was very bitter, for there was none left, bond or free, and there was none to help Israel. 27But the Lord had not said that he would blot out the name of Israel from under heaven, so he saved them by the hand of Jeroboam the son of Joash.

28Now the rest of the acts of Jeroboam, and all that he did, and his might, how he fought, and how he recovered for Israel Damascus and Hamath, which had belonged to Judah, are they not written in the Book of the Chronicles of the Kings of Israel? 29And Jeroboam slept with his fathers, the kings of Israel, and Zechariah his son reigned in his stead.

KINGS OF ISRAEL AND JUDAH II—COMMENTARY

2 Kings 13:1–14:29 (*cont'd*)

(i)

These chapters of Kings offer a miscellany of short notes about several kings of Israel and Judah, together with a farewell to Elisha. Keeping different kings of the same name separate in our minds is made no easier when we are told so little about some of them—yet the problem is no worse than sorting out lesser Jameses, Edwards and Henrys of Scottish and English royalty.

Jehoahaz enjoyed a peaceful succession from his violent father Jehu (10:35; 13:1–9). His difficulties with Syrian pressure are attributed in stock fashion to Jeroboam's revolt (vv.2–3,6). Yet, at the same time (vv.4–5), a divine alleviation is reported in response to royal intercession—rather in the style familiar from the Book of Judges. Some commentators are surprised that the Asherah was still standing in Samaria despite Jehu's purge (10:26–27). Yet that operation was against Baal and his cult. Asherah, like the shrines at Bethel and Dan, even although it was held to be illicit, was in fact part of Yahweh-worship. This has been made clear by an inscription found recently on the southern edges of Judah, which talks provocatively of "Yahweh and his Asherah".

The record of his son Jehoash or Joash (these are simply

alternative spellings of the same name) springs a few minor surprises. There seems something amiss in its arithmetic (contrast 13:10 with 13:1 and 14:1). And a formal conclusion is offered twice (13:12–13 and 14:15–16). Certainly most of what we do learn about this Joash of Israel is gleaned from reports about others; about Elisha (13:14–21) and about Amaziah of Judah (14:8–14).

(ii)

The king of Israel addresses the dying Elisha (13:14) with the very words Elisha had uttered as he gazed at the departing Elijah (2:12). We cannot penetrate with assurance the significance of the two symbolic actions that follow. The successful shooting of an arrow suggests, and might even contribute towards victory. The entry into heavenly space by an arrow suggests penetration of its secrets. And of course death-bed words and actions, especially of a great man, have enhanced significance. The symbol of striking the ground is more clearly explained in the text (vv.18–19); and the king is blamed for his half-heartedness.

Mention of Aphek (v.17) at the foot of the Golan Heights reminds us of 1 Kings 20:26–30, and the role of an unnamed man of God in a victory of Israel over Syria. These were ancestral enemies; their battles had been mostly over the same few towns and routes and passes; and the Syrian rulers were almost always called Hazael or Ben-hadad. It must have been hard for much later Judean historians not to confuse the details.

We do not take our leave of Elisha without a further miracle! Just as no death is reported for his master, who instead is caught up by a whirlwind, so Elisha remains potent even in the grave. One supposes that his tomb was a focus of later pilgrimage, which was in turn fostered by such stories.

(iii)

Amaziah of Judah is given the same sort of qualified approval (14:3–4) as his father Joash (12:2–3); and like his father

(12:20–21), he too met a violent end (14:19–20). Yet the dynasty of David itself was not called into question by these palace revolutions. His adherence to the "book of the law of Moses" is remarked upon (14:5–6) as if unusual, which is interesting in itself. I wonder if the hint is not intended that, had he been less scrupulous, he might not himself have been struck down—by the families he left alive.

The response by Jehoash of Israel to Amaziah's challenge to a face-to-face encounter (vv.9–10) is a fine, terse sample of the use of 'proverbs' or 'parables' in diplomacy. The most detailed example in the Bible is the speech of Jotham (Judg. 9:7–20). We have referred to the matter already in connection with Solomon's fame in proverbs (p. 32). Preserving the stock of such wise sayings is an important part of education in many more traditional societies—we often joke about (and even manufacture) 'ancient Chinese proverbs' to cover any situation. Jehoash's military prowess seems to have been no less than his skill with words!

Jeroboam II was his son; and his long reign saw renewed security for Israel to the east and north (14:23–29). The very brevity of this report is tantalizing, for the title verses of the Books of Hosea and Amos date both these careers to his reign. Some commentators have detected a quiet rebuke to Amos's doom and gloom in verse 27. Yet the prophet Jonah ben-Amittai is the only one named by our author (v.25)—and in a role very different to the one he plays in the book associated with his name. Although we are about to meet in chapters 18–20 the exception that proves the rule, it is generally the case that the prophetic books have remarkably few connections with the Book of Kings.

ISRAEL'S END NEARS I—TEXT

2 Kings 15:1–16:20

¹In the twenty-seventh year of Jeroboam king of Israel Azariah the son of Amaziah, king of Judah, began to reign. ²He was sixteen

years old when he began to reign, and he reigned fifty-two years in Jerusalem. His mother's name was Jecoliah of Jerusalem. ³And he did what was right in the eyes of the Lord, according to all that his father Amaziah had done. ⁴Nevertheless the high places were not taken away; the people still sacrificed and burned incense on the high places. ⁵And the Lord smote the king, so that he was a leper to the day of his death, and he dwelt in a separate house. And Jotham the king's son was over the household, governing the people of the land. ⁶Now the rest of the acts of Azariah, and all that he did, are they not written in the Book of the Chronicles of the Kings of Judah? ⁷And Azariah slept with his fathers, and they buried him with his fathers in the city of David, and Jotham his son reigned in his stead.

⁸In the thirty-eighth year of Azariah king of Judah Zechariah the son of Jeroboam reigned over Israel in Samaria six months. ⁹And he did what was evil in the sight of the Lord, as his fathers had done. He did not depart from the sins of Jeroboam the son of Nebat, which he made Israel to sin. ¹⁰Shallum the son of Jabesh conspired against him, and struck him down at Ible-am, and killed him, and reigned in his stead. ¹¹Now the rest of the deeds of Zechariah, behold, they are written in the Book of the Chronicles of the Kings of Israel. ¹²(This was the promise of the Lord which he gave to Jehu, "Your sons shall sit upon the throne of Israel to the fourth generation." And so it came to pass.)

¹³Shallum the son of Jabesh began to reign in the thirty-ninth year of Uzziah king of Judah, and he reigned one month in Samaria. ¹⁴Then Menahem the son of Gadi came up from Tirzah and came to Samaria, and he struck down Shallum the son of Jabesh in Samaria and slew him, and reigned in his stead. ¹⁵Now the rest of the deeds of Shallum, and the conspiracy which he made, behold, they are written in the Book of the Chronicles of the Kings of Israel. ¹⁶At that time Menahem sacked Tappu-ah and all who were in it and its territory from Tirzah on; because they did not open it to him, therefore he sacked it, and he ripped up all the women in it who were with child.

¹⁷In the thirty-ninth year of Azariah king of Judah Menahem the son of Gadi began to reign over Israel, and he reigned ten years in Samaria. ¹⁸And he did what was evil in the sight of the Lord; he did not depart all his days from all the sins of Jeroboam the son of Nebat, which he made Israel to sin. ¹⁹Pul the king of Assyria came against the land; and Menahem gave Pul a thousand talents of

silver, that he might help him to confirm his hold of the royal power. ²⁰Menahem exacted the money from Israel, that is, from all the wealthy men, fifty shekels of silver from every man, to give to the king of Assyria. So the king of Assyria turned back, and did not stay there in the land. ²¹Now the rest of the deeds of Menahem, and all that he did, are they not written in the Book of the Chronicles of the Kings of Israel? ²²And Menahem slept with his fathers, and Pekahiah his son reigned in his stead.

²³In the fiftieth year of Azariah king of Judah Pekahiah the son of Menahem began to reign over Israel in Samaria, and he reigned two years. ²⁴And he did what was evil in the sight of the Lord; he did not turn away from the sins of Jeroboam the son of Nebat, which he made Israel to sin. ²⁵And Pekah the son of Remaliah, his captain, conspired against him with fifty men of the Gileadites, and slew him in Samaria, in the citadel of the king's house; he slew him, and reigned in his stead. ²⁶Now the rest of the deeds of Pekahiah, and all that he did, behold, they are written in the Book of the Chronicles of the Kings of Israel.

²⁷In the fifty-second year of Azariah king of Judah Pekah the son of Remaliah began to reign over Israel in Samaria, and reigned twenty years. ²⁸And he did what was evil in the sight of the Lord; he did not depart from the sins of Jeroboam the son of Nebat, which he made Israel to sin.

²⁹In the days of Pekah king of Israel Tiglath-pileser king of Assyria came and captured Ijon, Abel-beth-maacah, Janoah, Kedesh, Hazor, Gilead, and Galilee, all the land of Naphtali; and he carried the people captive to Assyria. ³⁰Then Hoshea the son of Elah made a conspiracy against Pekah the son of Remaliah, and struck him down, and slew him, and reigned in his stead, in the twentieth year of Jotham the son of Uzziah. ³¹Now the rest of the acts of Pekah, and all that he did, behold, they are written in the Book of the Chronicles of the Kings of Israel.

³²In the second year of Pekah the son of Remaliah, king of Israel, Jotham the son of Uzziah, king of Judah, began to reign. ³³He was twenty-five years old when he began to reign, and he reigned sixteen years in Jerusalem. His mother's name was Jerusha the daughter of Zadok. ³⁴And he did what was right in the eyes of the Lord, according to all that his father Uzziah had done. ³⁵Nevertheless the high places were not removed; the people still sacrificed and burned incense on the high places. He built the upper gate of the house of the Lord. ³⁶Now the rest of the acts of Jotham, and all that he did,

are they not written in the Book of the Chronicles of the Kings of Judah? ³⁷In those days the Lord began to send Rezin the king of Syria and Pekah the son of Remaliah against Judah. ³⁸Jotham slept with his fathers, and was buried with his fathers in the city of David his father; and Ahaz his son reigned in his stead.

¹In the seventeenth year of Pekah the son of Remaliah, Ahaz the son of Jotham, king of Judah, began to reign. ²Ahaz was twenty years old when he began to reign, and he reigned sixteen years in Jerusalem. And he did not do what was right in the eyes of the Lord his God, as his father David had done, ³but he walked in the way of the kings of Israel. He even burned his son as an offering, according to the abominable practices of the nations whom the Lord drove out before the people of Israel. ⁴And he sacrificed and burned incense on the high places, and on the hills, and under every green tree.

⁵Then Rezin king of Syria and Pekah the son of Remaliah, king of Israel, came up to wage war on Jerusalem, and they besieged Ahaz but could not conquer him. ⁶At that time the king of Edom recovered Elath for Edom, and drove the men of Judah from Elath; and the Edomites came to Elath, where they dwell to this day. ⁷So Ahaz sent messengers to Tiglath-pileser king of Assyria, saying, "I am your servant and your son. Come up, and rescue me from the hand of the king of Syria and from the hand of the king of Israel, who are attacking me." ⁸Ahaz also took the silver and gold that was found in the house of the Lord and in the treasures of the king's house, and sent a present to the king of Assyria. ⁹And the king of Assyria hearkened to him; the king of Assyria marched up against Damascus, and took it, carrying its people captive to Kir, and he killed Rezin.

¹⁰When King Ahaz went to Damascus to meet Tiglath-pileser king of Assyria, he saw the altar that was at Damascus. And King Ahaz sent to Uriah the priest a model of the altar, and its pattern, exact in all its details. ¹¹And Uriah the priest built the altar; in accordance with all that King Ahaz had sent from Damascus, so Uriah the priest made it, before King Ahaz arrived from Damascus. ¹²And when the king came from Damascus, the king viewed the altar. Then the king drew near to the altar, and went up on it, ¹³and burned his burnt offering and his cereal offering, and poured his drink offering, and threw the blood of his peace offerings upon the altar. ¹⁴And the bronze altar which was before the Lord he removed from the front of the house, from the place between his altar and the

house of the Lord, and put it on the north side of his altar. [15]And King Ahaz commanded Uriah the priest, saying, "Upon the great altar burn the morning burnt offering, and the evening cereal offering, and the king's burnt offering, and his cereal offering, with the burnt offering of all the people of the land, and their cereal offering, and their drink offering; and throw upon it all the blood of the burnt offering, and all the blood of the sacrifice; but the bronze altar shall be for me to inquire by." [16]Uriah the priest did all this, as King Ahaz commanded.

[17]And King Áhaz cut off the frames of the stands, and removed the laver from them, and he took down the sea from off the bronze oxen that were under it, and put it upon a pediment of stone. [18]And the covered way for the sabbath which had been built inside the palace, and the outer entrance for the king he removed from the house of the Lord, because of the king of Assyria. [19]Now the rest of the acts of Ahaz which he did, are they not written in the Book of the Chronicles of the Kings of Judah? [20]And Ahaz slept with his fathers, and was buried with his fathers in the city of David; and Hezekiah his son reigned in his stead.

ISRAEL'S END NEARS II—COMMENTARY

2 Kings 15:1–16:20 (*cont'd*)

(i)

Chapter 15 covers several more years than it contains verses. At first sight it seems to be dominated by King Azariah, also called Uzziah, of Judah. Yet we learn remarkably little about him. The mere fact that his formal reign extended over more than half a century ensured that he was mentioned five times as five kings were installed in neighbouring Israel.

Just why this king had two names is not made clear to us. The Chronicler uses only Uzziah; and of course it is under that name that he has come down to posterity—as the king in the year of whose death Isaiah had his vision (Isa. 6:1). In spelling, although not in meaning, the names are much more alike in Hebrew than they appear in English. Azariah means "the Lord has helped"; and Uzziah, "the power of the Lord". Both names seem rather ironic in the light of the one distinctive piece of information provided by our author: that the king was a leper, and his son Jotham required to attend to the administration in his place (v.5).

Certainly 2 Chronicles 26:1–23 tells a much fuller story about this king, more or less presenting his reign as an illustration of the proverb that 'pride comes before a fall'. It reports considerable military successes. The culmination of this part of the tale (2 Chron. 26:15) declares: "And his fame spread far, for he was marvellously helped, till he was strong". That reads like an explanation of both his names.

A last word needs to be said about the RSV's inadequate "*separate* house" (15:5). The Hebrew word refers to 'independence' or 'liberty', like that of the freed slave, or indeed of the "wild ass" (Job 39:5). Is it being suggested that his infirmity had released Azariah into freedom from the constraints of public duty? Or should we remember that the ancient Canaanite poetry of Ugarit used "the house of freedom in the earth" as a euphemism for the underworld? In fact, in the light of this, we should perhaps translate the phrase containing this same word in Psalm 88:5 as 'like one at liberty among the dead'. In that case our king's 'house of freedom' might picture his condition as a kind of living death.

(ii)

Israel's political life seems to have become more and more precarious as the end of her independence approached. Of the five reigns inaugurated in Uzziah's later years, three lasted less than three years in total. Zechariah, son of Jeroboam II, lasted only six months. His usurper Shallum was himself able to hold power only one month, before falling to Menahem.

Menahem, of all things, means 'Comforter'. One imagines that occasioned some wry comment among those who witnessed his 'pacification' of the region from Tirzah to Tappuah (v.16). His methods included barbarities such as Amos had recently expected his hearers to denounce as intolerable even for foreigners (Amos 1:13)! Our author does not amplify his report. Did he imagine that his few words would be enough to make us shiver with revulsion? Or was he so one-track minded that he was content to brand Menahem simply with the standard crime of continuing in "the sins of Jeroboam the son of Nebat" (15:18).

Menahem, despite—or was it because of?—his brutality, had to pay heavy tribute to Assyria to prop up his position. After his ten-year reign, his son Pekahiah lasted only two years before being usurped by his commander—whose name, Pekah, rather confusingly, was simply a shortened form of his own. Having gained power by the sword, he lost it the same way twenty years later—but not without first losing a very large part of his territory (v.29) to the Assyrian monarch Tiglath-pileser. His assassin, Hoshea, was to be Israel's last king.

(iii)

Uzziah's son Jotham of Judah is passed over in almost uneventful silence (15:32–38), but for the first rumblings of trouble for Judah from an alliance of Israel and Syria (v.37). Much more is said about his son Ahaz (16:1–20), the royal *bête noire* of Isaiah chapter 7.

After centuries of hostility, Israel and Syria were thrust into each other's arms by the common menace of Assyria. They sought to secure their rear by forcing Judah's compliance, but failed doubly. Jerusalem withstood their siege; and Ahaz in fact bought efficient Assyrian protection—he was shortly able to meet Tiglath-pileser in Damascus. Yet his own basic weakness was shown in the loss of southern territory (16:6). And his indebtedness to Assyria had to be paid in religious as well as monetary terms (16:10–18).

ISRAEL'S EPITAPH REWRITTEN I—TEXT

2 Kings 17:1–41

[1]In the twelfth year of Ahaz king of Judah Hoshea the son of Elah

began to reign in Samaria over Israel, and he reigned nine years. ²And he did what was evil in the sight of the Lord, yet not as the kings of Israel who were before him. ³Against him came up Shalmaneser king of Assyria; and Hoshea became his vassal, and paid him tribute. ⁴But the king of Assyria found treachery in Hoshea; for he had sent messengers to So, king of Egypt, and offered no tribute to the king of Assyria, as he had done year by year; therefore the king of Assyria shut him up, and bound him in prison. ⁵Then the king of Assyria invaded all the land and came to Samaria, and for three years he besieged it. ⁶In the ninth year of Hoshea the king of Assyria captured Samaria, and he carried the Israelites away to Assyria, and placed them in Halah, and on the Habor, the river of Gozan, and in the cities of the Medes.

⁷And this was so, because the people of Israel had sinned against the Lord their God, who had brought them up out of the land of Egypt from under the hand of Pharaoh king of Egypt, and had feared other gods ⁸and walked in the customs of the nations whom the Lord drove out before the people of Israel, and in the customs which the kings of Israel had introduced. ⁹And the people of Israel did secretly against the Lord their God things that were not right. They built for themselves high places at all their towns, from watchtower to fortified city; ¹⁰they set up for themselves pillars and Asherim on every high hill and under every green tree; ¹¹and there they burned incense on all the high places, as the nations did whom the Lord carried away before them. And they did wicked things, provoking the Lord to anger, ¹²and they served idols, of which the Lord had said to them, "You shall not do this." ¹³Yet the Lord warned Israel and Judah by every prophet and every seer, saying, "Turn from your evil ways and keep my commandments and my statutes, in accordance with all the law which I commanded your fathers, and which I sent to you by my servants the prophets." ¹⁴But they would not listen, but were stubborn, as their fathers had been, who did not believe in the Lord their God. ¹⁵They despised his statutes, and his covenant that he made with their fathers, and the warnings which he gave them. They went after false idols, and became false, and they followed the nations that were round about them, concerning whom the Lord had commanded them that they should not do like them. ¹⁶And they forsook all the commandments of the Lord their God, and made for themselves molten images of two calves; and they made an Asherah, and worshipped all the host of heaven, and served Baal. ¹⁷And they burned their sons and their

daughters as offerings, and used divination and sorcery, and sold themselves to do evil in the sight of the Lord, provoking him to anger. ¹⁸Therefore the Lord was very angry with Israel, and removed them out of his sight; none was left but the tribe of Judah only.

¹⁹Judah also did not keep the commandments of the Lord their God, but walked in the customs which Israel had introduced. ²⁰And the Lord rejected all the descendants of Israel, and afflicted them, and gave them into the hand of spoilers, until he had cast them out of his sight.

²¹When he had torn Israel from the house of David they made Jeroboam the son of Nebat king. And Jeroboam drove Israel from following the Lord and made them commit great sin. ²²The people of Israel walked in all the sins which Jeroboam did; they did not depart from them, ²³until the Lord removed Israel out of his sight, as he had spoken by all his servants the prophets. So Israel was exiled from their own land to Assyria until this day.

²⁴And the king of Assyria brought people from Babylon, Cuthah, Avva, Hamath, and Sepharvaim, and placed them in the cities of Samaria instead of the people of Israel; and they took possession of Samaria, and dwelt in its cities. ²⁵And at the beginning of their dwelling there, they did not fear the Lord; therefore the Lord sent lions among them, which killed some of them. ²⁶So the king of Assyria was told, "The nations which you have carried away and placed in the cities of Samaria do not know the law of the god of the land; therefore he has sent lions among them, and behold, they are killing them, because they do not know the law of the god of the land." ²⁷Then the king of Assyria commanded, "Send there one of the priests whom you carried away thence; and let him go and dwell there, and teach them the law of the god of the land." ²⁸So one of the priests whom they had carried away from Samaria came and dwelt in Bethel, and taught them how they should fear the Lord.

²⁹But every nation still made gods of its own, and put them in the shrines of the high places which the Samaritans had made, every nation in the cities in which they dwelt; ³⁰the men of Babylon made Succoth-benoth, the men of Cuth made Nergal, the men of Hamath made Ashima, ³¹and the Avvites made Nibhaz and Tartak; and the Sepharvites burned their children in the fire to Adrammelech and Anammelech, the gods of Sepharvaim. ³²They also feared the Lord, and appointed from among themselves all sorts of people as priests

of the high places, who sacrificed for them in the shrines of the high places. ³³So they feared the Lord but also served their own gods, after the manner of the nations from among whom they had been carried away. ³⁴To this day they do according to the former manner.

They do not fear the Lord, and they do not follow the statutes or the ordinances or the law or the commandment which the Lord commanded the children of Jacob, whom he named Israel. ³⁵The Lord made a covenant with them, and commanded them, "You shall not fear the other gods or bow yourselves to them or serve them or sacrifice to them; ³⁶but you shall fear the Lord, who brought you out of the land of Egypt with great power and with an outstretched arm; you shall bow yourselves to him, and to him you shall sacrifice. ³⁷And the statutes and the ordinances and the law and the commandment which he wrote for you, you shall always be careful to do. You shall not fear other gods, ³⁸and you shall not forget the covenant that I have made with you. You shall not fear other gods, ³⁹but you shall fear the Lord your God, and he will deliver you out of the hand of all your enemies." ⁴⁰However they would not listen, but they did according to their former manner.

⁴¹So these nations feared the Lord, and also served their graven images; their children likewise, and their children's children—as their fathers did, so they do to this day.

ISRAEL'S EPITAPH REWRITTEN II—COMMENTARY

2 Kings 17:1–41 (*cont'd*)

This lengthy explanation of the fall of Israel and its significance ties together many loose ends in the Books of Kings. And yet the package is not entirely easy to deal with, for the knots have been retied and also supplemented several times.

(i)

The first part of the chapter recounts in all brevity (vv.1–6) the nine years of Hoshea, Israel's last king. His name, like so many we have noted, sounds like a rather grim joke—for it means 'deliverer'. The prophet of the same Hebrew name we spell differently, Hosea. This royal *deliverer* not only *loses* the heartland of his kingdom; but his name (as Num. 13:8 and 16 make clear) is actually an alternative form of 'Joshua'. What an ironic counterpart to the first Joshua who settled Israel in their new land—and not least because this 'Joshua' had hoped for Egyptian *help* against his Assyrian masters! Even the short report of the Assyrian response appears to be told twice (vv.3-4 and 5-6), with the second version anticipating the Judean report (18:9-12). Is it because of his name, or is it because of his fate, or is it because he tried to end Assyrian domination which had had religious implications in Israel no less than in Judah, that our author says of him that "he did what was evil in the sight of the Lord, *yet not as the kings of Israel who were before him*" (v.2)?

(ii)

The next section (vv.7-23) reviews Israel's religious history from a rather longer perspective, and explains the fall as the result of accumulating divine displeasure. Most of the account makes straightforward reading. The language and style of the complaints are familiar from the Books of Deuteronomy and Joshua. The arch-sin of Jeroboam is reserved for the climax of the list (vv.21ff.).

Some of the accusations seem to be drawn from Jeremiah's scathing rhetoric. At least it was probably he who coined the jibe in verse 15 about following false idols and becoming false. The jibe is partly a pun; for the Hebrew word rendered "false" or "false idols" looks and sounds rather like "Baal". It really means 'empty' or 'insubstantial', rather than "false". Jeremiah's joke that Baal is too much of a lightweight to be worth following (Jer. 2:5) is nicely capped (Jer. 2:13) in his bitter picture of his people's double mistake:

. . . .

for my people have committed two evils:
    they have forsaken me,
the fountain of living waters,
    and hewed out cisterns for themselves,
broken cisterns,
    that can hold no water.

Of course the other side of Jeremiah's analysis is that we
become like those we consort with—in this case that Israel
became as empty as Baal.

All that happened came to pass despite the faithful role of a
series of prophetic "servants" (vv.13,23), who had both stood
for and expounded the best traditions of the past, and had
warned of what would happen if Israel did not change its ways.
The talk of Judah in verses 18 and 19 is rather intrusive. Yet we
must remember that these later historians, like Jeremiah
himself who taught some hundred years after these events, were
less interested in the events as they affected Israel. They
focussed on Israel's fate as a warning which Judah failed to
take. At the time, Judah simply thought she had escaped!

(iii)

Having dealt with the religious causes, our authors turn now to
the religious consequences. And the implications that interest
these (Judean) historians are concerned less with the *people* of
Israel than with the northern part of the *land* of Israel from
which they had been removed. Assyrian policy was to 'divide
and rule'. Israelites were deported to widely separate parts of
the Assyrian empire, and apparently they integrated fully. The
only truth in the many legends about Israel's 'lost tribes' is that
they did disappear!

Distant foreigners were drafted in to take their place; and one
of the purposes of verses 24–41 is to lay at their door the blame
for the 'bastardized' form of Yahwism which later Judah so
abhorred in the neighbouring imperial province of Samaria.
Here too the critique is not quite consistent: there are at least
two minds in the text on whether these northerners feared the
Lord or not.

The main text (vv.24–34*a*) reports that they did not do so at first until rampaging lions (remember the fate of the man of God from Judah in 1 Kings ch. 13) resulted in some religious education from a deported priest. It is a rich idea, after all that we have read about the cult of Jeroboam's Bethel and Dan, that one of their personnel could improve the situation! Following this priest's instruction, they *did* fear the Lord (vv.28, 32–33), *while continuing* in their former practices (vv.29–31).

Such an interpretation is rejected as impossible nonsense in verses 34*b*–40. They insist, as the Ten Commandments do, that worship cannot be shared between the Lord and any other god(s). The closing verse attempts a neat side-stepping compromise by noting that they *feared* the Lord and *served* the others. Thus, it accepts the facts as reported in the first version, and also the religious analysis that undergirds the second— namely that fear of both or service of both was impossible.

Sadly it seems to be consistency of thought that fuels Church conflicts—and fudged compromise that serves to cement biblical and ecumenical theologies!

A NOTE ON 2 KINGS CHAPTERS 18–20

Hezekiah of Judah succeeded Ahaz not many years before the fall of Samaria and lived to see Jerusalem almost, although in the event not quite, going the same way. The bare bones of his record are presented in 2 Kings 18:1–12 and 20:20–21, and we shall say something about his reforms (see 18:4) in our next section. The extended intervening narrative in 18:13–20:19, which tells of Jerusalem's deliverance from the Assyrians and in which the prophet Isaiah plays a prominent role, is, however, also found in Isaiah chapters 36–39. The variants between the two accounts are mostly minor, but an important paragraph right at the beginning of the Kings version (18:14–16) is omitted in Isaiah and Hezekiah's psalm of thanksgiving after his recovery from illness (Isa. 38:9–20) is not recorded in Kings. The story of Hezekiah's illness and Isaiah's part in its cure is also slightly longer in Kings (20:1–11) than in Isaiah (38:1–8, 21–22), and is sufficiently different in its arrangement to be worth noting.

Professor Sawyer has already given an excellent full commentary on this long, shared narrative in his *Isaiah Volume II* (pp. 19–42) in the Daily Study Bible series, including discussion of the variants mentioned above; and it would be superfluous to go over the same ground here, especially as I am in substantial agreement with his conclusion that the narrative is more interested in the religious significance of the events it records than in relating them exactly as they happened. Indeed, it may be fortunate that the volumes on Isaiah preceded this one on Kings, since there are several other passages in Isaiah, notably in chapters 28–33, which bear upon the Assyrian attack on Jerusalem in Hezekiah's reign and the city's 'miraculous' deliverance; and a study of these is essential background to understanding what is going on in 2 Kings chapters 18–20 (see, *eg*, Professor Sawyer's commentary on Isa. 31:1–9 in *Isaiah Volume I*, pp. 257ff.). The narrative is often supposed to have been taken into Isaiah from Kings at some stage in the long history of the composition of that prophetic book; but even if that is true, it must in its turn have reached Kings via Isaianic circles. In any case its contents and interests belong in a real sense to Isaiah more than to Kings. Due to the vagaries of the Daily Study Bible timetable, therefore, it gets its fullest treatment in the most appropriate volume.

A further account of Hezekiah's reign, quite different in its emphasis from 2 Kings chapters 18–20 (and Isaiah chapters 36–39), is given in 2 Chronicles, chapters 29–32. Professor Sawyer also brings this into his discussion; and readers may like to refer as well to Dr McConville's commentary on *Chronicles*, pp. 227ff.

For the convenience of readers of the present volume, Professor Sawyer's commentary on Isaiah chapters 36–39 is (with his kind permission) reproduced in the Appendix. Here it will be enough to print those portions of the Kings text which are not in the Appendix or which give more information than the Isaiah text.

Introductory account of Hezekiah's reign
(2 Kings 18:1–12)
¹In the third year of Hoshea son of Elah, king of Israel, Hezekiah the son of Ahaz, king of Judah, began to reign. ²He was twenty-five years old when he began to reign, and he reigned twenty-nine years in Jerusalem. His mother's name was Abi the daughter of Zechariah. ³And he did what was right in the eyes of the Lord, according to all that David his father had done. ⁴He removed the high places,

and broke the pillars, and cut down the Asherah. And he broke in pieces the bronze serpent that Moses had made, for until those days the people of Israel had burned incense to it; it was called Nehushtan. ⁵He trusted in the Lord the God of Israel; so that there was none like him among all the kings of Judah after him, nor among those who were before him. ⁶For he held fast to the Lord; he did not depart from following him, but kept the commandments which the Lord commanded Moses. ⁷And the Lord was with him; wherever he went forth, he prospered. He rebelled against the king of Assyria, and would not serve him. ⁸He smote the Philistines as far as Gaza and its territory, from watchtower to fortified city.

⁹In the fourth year of King Hezekiah, which was the seventh year of Hoshea son of Elah, king of Israel, Shalmaneser king of Assyria came up against Samaria and besieged it ¹⁰and at the end of three years he took it. In the sixth year of Hezekiah, which was the ninth year of Hoshea king of Israel, Samaria was taken. ¹¹The king of Assyria carried the Israelites away to Assyria, and put them in Halah, and on the Habor, the river of Gozan, and in the cities of the Medes, ¹²because they did not obey the voice of the Lord their God but transgressed his covenant, even all that Moses the servant of the Lord commanded; they neither listened nor obeyed.

Hezekiah pays tribute to Sennacherib, king of Assyria
(2 Kings 18:14–16)
¹⁴And Hezekiah king of Judah sent to the king of Assyria at Lachish, saying, "I have done wrong; withdraw from me; whatever you impose on me I will bear." And the king of Assyria required of Hezekiah king of Judah three hundred talents of silver and thirty talents of gold. ¹⁵And Hezekiah gave him all the silver that was found in the house of the Lord, and in the treasuries of the king's house. ¹⁶At the time Hezekiah stripped the gold from the doors of the temple of the Lord, and from the doorposts which Hezekiah king of Judah had overlaid and gave it to the king of Assyria.

Hezekiah's illness and recovery
(2 Kings 20:1–11; cf. Isaiah 38:1–8, 21–22)
¹In those days Hezekiah became sick and was at the point of death. And Isaiah the prophet the son of Amoz came to him, and said to him, "Thus says the Lord, 'Set your house in order; for you shall die, you shall not recover.'" ²Then Hezekiah turned his face to the wall, and prayed to the Lord, saying, ³"Remember now, O Lord, I

beseech thee, how I have walked before thee in faithfulness and with a whole heart, and have done what is good in thy sight." And Hezekiah wept bitterly. ⁴And before Isaiah had gone out of the middle court, the word of the Lord came to him: ⁵"Turn back, and say to Hezekiah the prince of my people, Thus says the Lord, the God of David your father: I have heard your prayer, I have seen your tears; behold, I will heal you; on the third day you shall go up to the house of the Lord. ⁶And I will add fifteen years to your life. I will deliver you and this city out of the hand of the king of Assyria, and I will defend this city for my own sake and for my servant David's sake." ⁷And Isaiah said, "Bring a cake of figs. And let them take and lay it on the boil, that he may recover."

⁸And Hezekiah said to Isaiah, "What shall be the sign that the Lord will heal me, and that I shall go up to the house of the Lord on the third day?" ⁹And Isaiah said, "This is the sign to you from the Lord, that the Lord will do the thing that he has promised: shall the shadow go forward ten steps, or go back ten steps?" ¹⁰And Hezekiah answered, "It is an easy thing for the shadow to lengthen ten steps; rather let the shadow go back ten steps." ¹¹And Isaiah the prophet cried to the Lord; and he brought the shadow back ten steps, by which the sun had declined on the dial of Ahaz.

Final notice of Hezekiah's reign
(2 Kings 20:20–21)
²⁰The rest of the deeds of Hezekiah, and all his might, and how he made the pool and the conduit and brought water into the city, are they not written in the Book of the Chronicles of the Kings of Judah? ²¹And Hezekiah slept with his fathers; and Manasseh his son reigned in his stead.

ROYAL HEIGHTS AND DEPTHS I—TEXT

2 Kings 21:1–22:20

¹Manasseh was twelve years old when he began to reign, and he reigned fifty-five years in Jerusalem. His mother's name was Hephzibah. ²And he did what was evil in the sight of the Lord, according to the abominable practices of the nations whom the Lord drove out before the people of Israel. ³For he rebuilt the high places which Hezekiah his father had destroyed; and he erected

altars for Baal, and made an Asherah, as Ahab king of Israel had done, and worshipped all the host of heaven, and served them. ⁴And he built altars in the house of the Lord, of which the Lord had said, "In Jerusalem will I put my name." ⁵And he built altars for all the host of heaven in the two courts of the house of the Lord. ⁶And he burned his son as an offering, and practised soothsaying and augury, and dealt with mediums and with wizards. He did much evil in the sight of the Lord, provoking him to anger. ⁷And the graven image of Asherah that he had made he set in the house of which the Lord said to David and to Solomon his son, "In this house, and in Jerusalem, which I have chosen out of all the tribes of Israel, I will put my name for ever; ⁸and I will not cause the feet of Israel to wander any more out of the land which I gave to their fathers, if only they will be careful to do according to all that I have commanded them, and according to all the law that my servant Moses commanded them." ⁹But they did not listen, and Manasseh seduced them to do more evil than the nations had done whom the Lord destroyed before the people of Israel.

¹⁰And the Lord said by his servants the prophets, ¹¹"Because Manasseh king of Judah has committed these abominations, and has done things more wicked than all that the Amorites did, who were before him, and has made Judah also to sin with his idols; ¹²therefore thus says the Lord, the God of Israel, Behold, I am bringing upon Jerusalem and Judah such evil that the ears of every one who hears of it will tingle. ¹³And I will stretch over Jerusalem the measuring line of Samaria, and the plummet of the house of Ahab; and I will wipe Jerusalem as one wipes a dish, wiping it and turning it upside down. ¹⁴And I will cast off the remnant of my heritage, and give them into the hand of their enemies, and they shall become a prey and a spoil to all their enemies, ¹⁵because they have done what is evil in my sight and have provoked me to anger, since the day their fathers came out of Egypt, even to this day."

¹⁶Moreover Manasseh shed very much innocent blood, till he had filled Jerusalem from one end to another, besides the sin which he made Judah to sin so that they did what was evil in the sight of the Lord.

¹⁷Now the rest of the acts of Manasseh, and all that he did, and the sin that he committed, are they not written in the Book of the Chronicles of the Kings of Judah? ¹⁸And Manasseh slept with his fathers, and was buried in the garden of his house, in the garden of Uzza; and Amon his son reigned in his stead.

¹⁹Amon was twenty-two years old when he began to reign, and he reigned two years in Jerusalem. His mother's name was Meshullemeth the daughter of Haruz of Jotbah. ²⁰And he did what was evil in the sight of the Lord, as Manasseh his father had done. ²¹He walked in all the way in which his father walked, and served the idols that his father served, and worshipped them; ²²he forsook the Lord, the God of his fathers, and did not walk in the way of the Lord. ²³And the servants of Amon conspired against him, and killed the king in his house. ²⁴But the people of the land slew all those who had conspired against King Amon, and the people of the land made Josiah his son king in his stead. ²⁵Now the rest of the acts of Amon which he did, are they not written in the Book of the Chronicles of the Kings of Judah? ²⁶And he was buried in his tomb in the garden of Uzza; and Josiah his son reigned in his stead.

¹Josiah was eight years old when he began to reign, and he reigned thirty-one years in Jerusalem. His mother's name was Jedidah the daughter of Adaiah of Bozkath. ²And he did what was right in the eyes of the Lord, and walked in all the way of David his father, and he did not turn aside to the right hand or to the left.

³In the eighteenth year of King Josiah, the king sent Shaphan the son of Azaliah, son of Meshullam, the secretary, to the house of the Lord, saying, ⁴"Go up to Hilkiah the high priest, that he may reckon the amount of the money which has been brought into the house of the Lord, which the keepers of the threshold have collected from the people; ⁵and let it be given into the hand of the workmen who have the oversight of the house of the Lord; and let them give it to the workmen who are at the house of the Lord, repairing the house, ⁶that is, to the carpenters, and to the builders, and to the masons, as well as for buying timber and quarried stone to repair the house. ⁷But no accounting shall be asked from them for the money which is delivered into their hand, for they deal honestly."

⁸And Hilkiah the high priest said to Shaphan the secretary, "I have found the book of the law in the house of the Lord." And Hilkiah gave the book to Shaphan, and he read it. ⁹And Shaphan the secretary came to the king, and reported to the king, "Your servants have emptied out the money that was found in the house, and have delivered it into the hand of the workmen who have the oversight of the house of the Lord." ¹⁰Then Shaphan the secretary told the king, "Hilkiah the priest has given me a book." And Shaphan read it before the king.

¹¹And when the king heard the words of the book of the law, he

rent his clothes. [12]And the king commanded Hilkiah the priest, and Ahikam the son of Shaphan, and Achbor the son of Micaiah, and Shaphan the secretary, and Asaiah the king's servant, saying, [13]"Go, inquire of the Lord for me, and for the people, and for all Judah, concerning the words of this book that has been found; for great is the wrath of the Lord that is kindled against us, because our fathers have not obeyed the words of this book, to do according to all that is written concerning us."

[14]So Hilkiah the priest, and Ahikam, and Achbor, and Shaphan, and Asaiah went to Huldah the prophetess, the wife of Shallum the son of Tikvah, son of Harhas, keeper of the wardrobe (now she dwelt in Jerusalem in the Second Quarter); and they talked with her. [15]And she said to them, "Thus says the Lord, the God of Israel: 'Tell the man who sent you to me, [16]Thus says the Lord, Behold, I will bring evil upon this place and upon its inhabitants, all the words of the book which the king of Judah has read. [17]Because they have forsaken me and have burned incense to other gods, that they might provoke me to anger with all the work of their hands, therefore my wrath will be kindled against this place, and it will not be quenched. [18]But as to the king of Judah, who sent you to inquire of the Lord, thus shall you say to him, Thus says the Lord, the God of Israel: Regarding the words which you have heard, [19]because your heart was penitent, and you humbled yourself before the Lord, when you heard how I spoke against this place, and against its inhabitants, that they should become a desolation and a curse, and you have rent your clothes and wept before me, I also have heard you, says the Lord. [20]Therefore, behold, I will gather you to your fathers, and you shall be gathered to your grave in peace, and your eyes shall not see all the evil which I will bring upon this place.'" And they brought back word to the king.

ROYAL HEIGHTS AND DEPTHS II—COMMENTARY

2 Kings 21:1–22:20 (*cont'd*)

(i)

The Books of Kings present the later rulers of Judah in the full century before her own collapse as her best and her worst. After Ahaz who "even burned his son as an offering" (16:3), came

Hezekiah who "did what was right in the eyes of the Lord,
according to all that David his father had done" (18:3). In fact
Hezekiah is measured not just by the standards of David, but
also by those of Moses: "he held fast to the Lord; he did not
depart from following him, but kept the commandments which
the Lord commanded Moses" (18:6). The evidence for such
high praise we glimpse briefly in 18:4—his removal of forms
and places of worship which the historians found as detestable
as he did. It is interesting that these included an ancient snake
image associated with Moses himself. Numbers 21:4–9 tells
how Moses was instructed to make it as an aid to healing.
However, as time had passed, it had actually become a *focus* of
worship, and required destruction no less than alien religious
imports. Doubtless it was easier for a king whose fidelity to
Moses' teachings and principles was not in doubt to dispense
with one of his 'sacred' relics. (We might note in passing that the
Chronicler, although devoting three chapters, 2 Chron. chs.
29–31, to Hezekiah's reforms, makes no mention of this one.)

(ii)

Having ascended the throne at 12 years old, Manasseh, Hezekiah's son, was to outdo even Azariah/Uzziah and his reign of
52 years (21:1). Yet in no sense were his long life and reign
a prize for righteousness! In terse fury our historians document
a reign that plumbed the depths of official iniquity (21:2–7) and
set Judah on course for a fate like that of her sister Israel
(21:11–15).

We can detect a 'progression' in the list of Manasseh's
retrogressive misdemeanours. We start with a general charge
made against many before him, that he returned to the practices
of pre-Israelite Canaan (v.2). This was all the more blameworthy because it was a deliberate undoing of the achievements of
his father—it had not happened gradually or through ignorance (v.3a). He is next aligned with Ahab of Israel (v.3b), of
whom we were told earlier that "there was none who sold
himself to do what was evil in the sight of the Lord like Ahab"

(1 Kings 21:25). The catalogue continues with charges concerning altars for additional deities in and near the Temple of Yahweh (vv.4–5), despite the fact that Yahweh's name was on the property and he claimed sole rights to it. He also sacrificed his son (v.6), as Ahaz had done.

Yet, clearly worst of all, he erected the Asherah symbol *within* the very shrine itself (v.7). Whatever the precise significance of Asherah—was she regarded as Yahweh's consort?— the placing of this image was manifestly more heinous than its mere existence somewhere in Jerusalem. The opening prohibition of the Ten Commandments forbids other gods *"before* me", which we might render as *"obtruding* on me". Whatever that might or might not mean, it obviously excluded confronting the Lord with the statue of another god in his own house. Such behaviour is no less than the religious equivalent of a man setting up his mistress alongside his wife in his family house.

Though all this is detailed in 2 Chronicles 33:1–10 as well, the Chronicler also reports Assyrian pressure on Manasseh and a subsequent conversion to Yahweh and religious reform. This is part of the evidence that has led many scholars to suppose that the portrait of unrelieved blackness in Kings has been deliberately exaggerated, and that Manasseh has been cast as a foil to the righteous Hezekiah before him and Josiah shortly after. The short reign of Amon his son (21:19–26) apparently continued his worst excesses.

(iii)

King Josiah outshines even Hezekiah as the hero of the Books of Kings. He did not just walk "in all the way of David his father" (22:2, cf. 18:3); but even more precisely, "he did not turn aside to the right hand or to the left". And that tribute means that only he of all the kings of Israel and Judah was held to fulfill Moses' brief instructions for future kingship in Deuteronomy 17:14–20.

This is no accident. The evaluation of Josiah and the authority of Deuteronomy are closely intertwined. It is widely believed that the document found by the high priest during work on the Temple was the Book of Deuteronomy itself, or at least the core of the present book—something like the familiar chapters 12–26, or even 5–30. Be that as it may in terms of historical fact, there is no doubt at all that both Deuteronomy and Kings seek to cultivate that impression. Hezekiah may be the brighter star in the Chronicler's firmament; but Josiah in Kings is the Deuteronomic ideal.

The tension and tragedy of his situation in national terms is nicely caught in the response of Huldah when consulted about the threats (although perhaps unrighteous) in the book just read against the people. She affirmed sentence of death on the nation—but declared a stay of execution to permit a peaceful end for the just king (22:15–20).

COVENANTED REFORM AND ARMAGEDDON I
—TEXT

2 Kings 23:1–30

¹Then the king sent, and all the elders of Judah and Jerusalem were gathered to him. ²And the king went up to the house of the Lord, and with him all the men of Judah and all the inhabitants of Jerusalem, and the priests and the prophets, all the people, both small and great; and he read in their hearing all the words of the book of the covenant which had been found in the house of the Lord. ³And the king stood by the pillar and made a covenant before the Lord, to walk after the Lord and to keep his commandments and his testimonies and his statutes, with all his heart and all his soul, to perform the words of this covenant that were written in this book; and all the people joined in the covenant.

⁴And the king commanded Hilkiah, the high priest, and the priests of the second order, and the keepers of the threshold, to bring out of the temple of the Lord all the vessels made for Baal, for Asherah, and for all the host of heaven; he burned them outside Jerusalem in the fields of the Kidron, and carried their ashes to Bethel. ⁵And he deposed the idolatrous priests whom the kings of

Judah had ordained to burn incense in the high places at the cities of Judah and round about Jerusalem; those also who burned incense to Baal, to the sun, and the moon, and the constellations, and all the host of the heavens. ⁶And he brought out the Asherah from the house of the Lord, outside Jerusalem, to the brook Kidron, and burned it at the brook Kidron, and beat it to dust and cast the dust of it upon the graves of the common people. ⁷And he broke down the houses of the male cult prostitutes which were in the house of the Lord, where the women wove hangings for the Asherah. ⁸And he brought all the priests out of the cities of Judah, and defiled the high places where the priests had burned incense, from Geba to Beer-sheba; and he broke down the high places of the gates that were at the entrance of the gate of Joshua the governor of the city, which were on one's left at the gate of the city. ⁹However, the priests of the high places did not come up to the altar of the Lord in Jerusalem, but they ate unleavened bread among their brethren. ¹⁰And he defiled Topheth, which is in the valley of the sons of Hinnom, that no one might burn his son or his daughter as an offering to Molech. ¹¹And he removed the horses that the kings of Judah had dedicated to the sun, at the entrance to the house of the Lord, by the chamber of Nathan-melech the chamberlain, which was in the precincts; and he burned the chariots of the sun with fire. ¹²And the altars on the roof of the upper chamber of Ahaz, which the kings of Judah had made, and the altars which Manasseh had made in the two courts of the house of the Lord, he pulled down and broke in pieces, and cast the dust of them into the brook Kidron. ¹³And the king defiled the high places that were east of Jerusalem, to the south of the mount of corruption, which Solomon the king of Israel had built for Ashtoreth the abomination of the Sidonians, and for Chemosh the abomination of Moab, and for Milcom the abomination of the Ammonites. ¹⁴And he broke in pieces the pillars, and cut down the Asherim, and filled their places with the bones of men.

¹⁵Moreover the altar at Bethel, the high place erected by Jeroboam the son of Nebat, who made Israel to sin, that altar with the high place he pulled down and he broke in pieces its stones, crushing them to dust; also he burned the Asherah. ¹⁶And as Josiah turned, he saw the tombs there on the mount; and he sent and took the bones out of the tombs, and burned them upon the altar, and defiled it, according to the word of the Lord which the man of God proclaimed, who had predicted these things. ¹⁷Then he said, "What

is yonder monument that I see?" And the men of the city told him, "It is the tomb of the man of God who came from Judah and predicted these things which you have done against the altar at Bethel." [18]And he said, "Let him be; let no man move his bones." So they let his bones alone, with the bones of the prophet who came out of Samaria. [19]And all the shrines also of the high places that were in the cities of Samaria, which kings of Israel had made, provoking the Lord to anger, Josiah removed; he did to them according to all that he had done at Bethel. [20]And he slew all the priests of the high places who were there, upon the altars, and burned the bones of men upon them. Then he returned to Jerusalem.

[21]And the king commanded all the people, "Keep the passover to the Lord your God, as it is written in this book of the covenant." [22]For no such passover had been kept since the days of the judges who judged Israel, or during all the days of the kings of Israel or of the kings of Judah; [23]but in the eighteenth year of King Josiah this passover was kept to the Lord in Jerusalem.

[24]Moreover Josiah put away the mediums and the wizards and the teraphim and the idols and all the abominations that were seen in the land of Judah and in Jerusalem, that he might establish the words of the law which were written in the book that Hilkiah the priest found in the house of the Lord. [25]Before him there was no king like him, who turned to the Lord with all his heart and with all his soul and with all his might, according to all the law of Moses; nor did any like him arise after him.

[26]Still the Lord did not turn from the fierceness of his great wrath, by which his anger was kindled against Judah, because of all the provocations with which Manasseh had provoked him. [27]And the Lord said, "I will remove Judah also out of my sight, as I have removed Israel, and I will cast off this city which I have chosen, Jerusalem, and the house of which I said, My name shall be there."

[28]Now the rest of the acts of Josiah, and all that he did, are they not written in the Book of the Chronicles of the Kings of Judah? [29]In his days Pharaoh Neco king of Egypt went up to the king of Assyria to the river Eu-phrates. King Josiah went to meet him; and Pharaoh Neco slew him at Megiddo, when he saw him. [30]And his servants carried him dead in a chariot from Megiddo, and brought him to Jerusalem, and buried him in his own tomb. And the people of the land took Jehoahaz the son of Josiah, and anointed him, and made him king in his father's stead.

COVENANTED REFORM AND ARMAGEDDON II
— COMMENTARY

2 Kings 23:1–30 (*cont'd*)

(i)

Having been given clearance by Huldah the prophetess that the book presented to him was what it purported to be, King Josiah called a comprehensively representative assembly to hear a public reading of the document (vv.1–2). His position by the pillar (v.3) reminds us of the installation of Joash after Athaliah's usurpation (2 Kings 11:14), but also surely of Joshua's stone of witness (Josh. 24:27), which "heard" the proceedings at an earlier and no less fateful national assembly.

The description of Josiah's solemn pledge is a rather suggestive summary of the main highlights of the Book of Deuteronomy. "His commandments and his testimonies and his statutes" remind us of the introduction to Deuteronomy's central legislation in Deuteronomy 12:1 (although this phrase, often slightly modified, is anticipated many times in the earlier chapters). "With all his heart and all his soul" recalls the "Hear, O Israel" of Deuteronomy 6:4–9, and its "you shall love the Lord your God with all your heart, and with all your soul, and with all your might". Then "the words of this covenant" are Deuteronomic language for the Ten Commandments (Deut. 5:6–21); Deuteronomy distinguishes between God's *covenant*, spoken directly to Israel at Horeb (Deut. 5:2–4) and written on stone (Deut. 9:9), and his *law/teaching*, mediated through Moses. The first phrase also neatly mirrors the advice we heard David give Solomon at the beginning of this volume (1 Kings 2:3), and reminds us how few echoes we have heard of such concerns from the intervening kings.

(ii)

The account that follows of Josiah's actual reform measures (vv.4–20) makes this same point rather more positively and specifically. With one odd exception, every single new cultic measure we have read of in the Books of Kings is detailed again here; every false innovation is reported as having been purged. Some of them are recapitulated more summarily, as in verses 4–5, 10–12*a*, and 19. In other cases the guilty names are blamed—Ahaz and Manasseh (v.12*b*), Solomon (v.13), and Jeroboam I (v.15). Josiah thus offers a comprehensive solution to the accumulated perversion of the religion of Israel and Judah over four centuries. The surprising exception is the 'reform' of Ahaz as reported in 2 Kings 16:10–18, although that monarch is one of his named villains. Perhaps the account of his Damascus-inspired altar was not an original part of the work of the main historian responsible for these books.

It comes as no surprise that the greatest space is reserved for the righting of the wrongs of Jeroboam at Bethel (vv.15–20). Our historian had portrayed the whole history of separate Israel as languishing under their shadow; and had also tended to blame on Israel's perverted traditions some of Judah's more recent wrongs. Yet this climax is anticipated in the naming and blaming of Solomon, whose excesses had helped trigger Jeroboam's revolt, and who had worshipped a Sidonian goddess in Jerusalem long before Jezebel encouraged Phoenician religion in Samaria. No finger is pointed at the founder of the dynasty— David after all barely figures in these books, and in any case had been prevented from any religious innovation other than bringing the ark to his new capital. But these Books of Kings make a largely negative judgment on the religious role of the kings they review.

(iii)

The superficial silence of the greater part of the Books of Kings on the issues that really concern our historian is nicely, and this time explicitly, illustrated in the matter of the festival of passover (vv.21–23). Although it is well known in post-exilic times as one of the most important of the annual Jewish feasts, it is barely mentioned before Josiah. In fact the Bible reports only a first Israelite passover (at the time of the departure from Egypt—Exod. ch. 12), a second (when leaving Sinai—Num. ch. 9), and then the feast held by Joshua immediately after crossing the Jordan and entering the promised land (Josh. ch. 5). Our author concedes that this celebration had not been so vital as it was to become.

As it was to become. The story of Josiah written 'on the lines' may seem a backward-looking righting of old—some very old!—wrongs. But 'between the lines' it in fact lays down the ground-rules for the people's religious life as it should be in the future. A good history, like a good funeral, is not for the dead but for the living. Hilkiah the priest plays a remarkably prominent role 'behind' 2 Kings chapters 22–23: one that is not fully described, but merely noted again and again. And that too is pregnant with a future in which Judah would no longer be a state led by another in the line of discredited kings, but would be a province distinctive for its religion and with a prominent chief priest.

(iv)

Josiah's own end comes as a surprise. His death in battle with the Egyptian Pharaoh (vv.29–30) fails to fulfil the latter part of Huldah's oracle (22:18–20); and this is not explained in the text. Indeed it must be said that even the part of her oracle that does come to pass (the collapse of Judah) is no less surprising in its way. For, if the divine decision was in fact provoked by Manasseh (vv.26–27), one might have expected Josiah's point by point unravelling of his—and all his predecessors'—tangled wrongs to tip the scales the other way.

The tension between an ideally righteous career and an unsatisfactory end in battle at Megiddo was to cause considerable religious speculation in later centuries. (The expanded account in 2 Chron. 35:20–25 adds to the aura around Josiah, and credits Jeremiah with uttering a lament for him.) This puzzle may even have supplied the original 'irritant' which produced in time the 'pearl' of Armageddon ("Mount Megiddo") in Revelation 16:16, where the final decisive battle would be fought between the forces of good and evil.

JUDAH'S LAST KINGS I—TEXT

2 Kings 23:31–25:30

31Jehoahaz was twenty-three years old when he began to reign, and he reigned three months in Jerusalem. His mother's name was Hamutal the daughter of Jeremiah of Libnah. 32And he did what was evil in the sight of the Lord, according to all that his fathers had done. 33And Pharaoh Neco put him in bonds at Riblah in the land of Hamath, that he might not reign in Jerusalem, and laid upon the land a tribute of a hundred talents of silver and a talent of gold. 34And Pharaoh Neco made Eliakim the son of Josiah king in the place of Josiah his father, and changed his name to Jehoiakim. But he took Jehoahaz away; and he came to Egypt, and died there. 35And Jehoiakim gave the silver and the gold to Pharaoh, but he taxed the land to give the money according to the command of Pharaoh. He exacted the silver and the gold of the people of the land, from every one according to his assessment, to give it to Pharaoh Neco.

36Jehoiakim was twenty-five years old when he began to reign, and he reigned eleven years in Jerusalem. His mother's name was Zebidah the daughter of Pedaiah of Rumah. 37And he did what was evil in the sight of the Lord, according to all that his fathers had done.

1In his days Nebuchadnezzar king of Babylon came up, and Jehoiakim became his servant three years; then he turned and rebelled against him. 2And the Lord sent against him bands of the Chaldeans, and bands of the Syrians, and bands of the Moabites, and bands of the Ammonites, and sent them against Judah to destroy it, according to the word of the Lord which he spoke by his servants the prophets. 3Surely this came upon Judah at the command of the Lord, to remove them out of his sight, for the sins of Manasseh, according to all that he had done. 4and also for the innocent blood that he had shed; for he filled Jerusalem with innocent blood, and the Lord would not pardon. 5Now the rest of the deeds of Jehoiakim, and all that he did, are they not written in the Book of the Chronicles of the Kings of Judah? 6So Jehoiakim slept with his fathers, and Jehoiachin his son reigned in his stead. 7And the king of Egypt did not come again out of his land, for the king of Babylon had taken all that belonged to the king of Egypt from the Brook of Egypt to the river Eu-phrates.

8Jehoiachin was eighteen years old when he became king, and he reigned three months in Jerusalem. His mother's name was Ne-hushta the daughter of Elnathan of Jerusalem. ⁹And he did what was evil in the sight of the Lord, according to all that his father had done.

¹⁰At that time the servants of Nebuchadnezzar king of Babylon came up to Jerusalem, and the city was besieged. ¹¹And Nebuchad-nezzar king of Babylon came to the city, while his servants were besieging it; ¹²and Jehoiachin the king of Judah gave himself up to the king of Babylon, himself, and his mother, and his servants, and his princes, and his palace officials. The king of Babylon took him prisoner in the eighth year of his reign, ¹³and carried off all the treasures of the house of the Lord, and the treasures of the king's house, and cut in pieces all the vessels of gold in the temple of the Lord, which Solomon king of Israel had made, as the Lord had foretold. ¹⁴He carried away all Jerusalem, and all the princes, and all the mighty men of valour, ten thousand captives, and all the craftsmen and the smiths; none remained, except the poorest people of the land. ¹⁵And he carried away Jehoiachin to Babylon; the king's mother, the king's wives, his officials, and the chief men of the land, he took into captivity from Jerusalem to Babylon. ¹⁶And the king of Babylon brought captive to Babylon all the men of valour, seven thousand, and the craftsmen and the smiths, one thousand, all of them strong and fit for war. ¹⁷And the king of Babylon made Mattaniah, Jehoiachin's uncle, king in his stead, and changed his name to Zedekiah.

¹⁸Zedekiah was twenty-one years old when he became king, and he reigned eleven years in Jerusalem. His mother's name was Hamutal the daughter of Jeremiah of Libnah. ¹⁹And he did what was evil in the sight of the Lord, according to all that Jehoiakim had done. ²⁰For because of the anger of the Lord it came to the point in Jerusalem and Judah that he cast them out from his presence.

And Zedekiah rebelled against the king of Babylon. ¹And in the ninth year of his reign, in the tenth month, on the tenth day of the month, Nebuchadnezzar king of Babylon came with all his army against Jerusalem, and laid siege to it; and they built siegeworks against it round about. ²So the city was besieged till the eleventh year of King Zedekiah. ³On the ninth day of the fourth month the famine was so severe in the city that there was no food for the people of the land. ⁴Then a breach was made in the city; the king with all the men of war fled by night by the way of the gate between the two walls, by the king's garden, though the Chaldeans were around the city. And they went in the direction of the Arabah. ⁵But the army of the Chaldeans pursued the king, and overtook him in the plains of Jericho; and all his army was scattered from him. ⁶Then they captured the king, and brought him up to the king of Babylon at Riblah, who passed sentence upon him. ⁷They slew the sons of Zedekiah before his eyes, and put out the eyes of Zedekiah, and bound him in fetters, and took him to Babylon.

⁸In the fifth month, on the seventh day of the month—which was the nineteenth year of King Nebuchadnezzar, king of Babylon— Nebuzaradan, the captain of the bodyguard, a servant of the king of Babylon, came to Jerusalem. ⁹And he burned the house of the Lord, and the king's house and all the houses of Jerusalem; every great house he burned down. ¹⁰And all the army of the Chaldeans, who were with the captain of the guard, broke down the walls around Jerusalem. ¹¹And the rest of the people who were left in the city and the deserters who had deserted to the king of Babylon, together with the rest of the multitude, Nebuzaradan the captain of the guard carried into exile. ¹²But the captain of the guard left some of the poorest of the land to be vine-dressers and ploughmen.

¹³And the pillars of bronze that were in the house of the Lord, and the stands and the bronze sea that were in the house of the Lord, the Chaldeans broke in pieces, and carried the bronze to Babylon. ¹⁴And they took away the pots, and the shovels, and the snuffers, and the dishes for incense and all the vessels of bronze used in the temple service, ¹⁵the firepans also, and the bowls. What was of gold the captain of the guard took away as gold, and what was of silver, as silver. ¹⁶As for the two pillars, the one sea, and the stands, which Solomon had made for the house of the Lord, the bronze of all these vessels was beyond weight. ¹⁷The height of the one pillar was eighteen cubits, and upon it was a capital of bronze; the height of the capital was three cubits; a network and pomegranates, all of bronze, were upon the capital round about. And the second pillar had the like, with the network.

¹⁸And the captain of the guard took Seraiah the chief priest, and Zephaniah the second priest, and the three keepers of the threshold; ¹⁹and from the city he took an officer who had been in command of the men of war, and five men of the king's council who were found in the city; and the secretary of the commander of the army who mustered the people of the land; and sixty men of the people of the land who were found in the city. ²⁰And Nebuzaradan the captain of the guard took them, and brought them to the king of Babylon at

Riblah. ²¹And the king of Babylon smote them, and put them to death at Riblah in the land of Hamath. So Judah was taken into exile out of its land.

²²And over the people who remained in the land of Judah, whom Nebuchadnezzar king of Babylon had left, he appointed Gedaliah the son of Ahikam, son of Shaphan, governor. ²³Now when all the captains of the forces in the open country and their men heard that the king of Babylon had appointed Gedaliah governor, they came with their men to Gedaliah at Mizpah, namely, Ishmael the son of Nethaniah, and Johanan the son of Kareah, and Seraiah the son of Tanhumeth the Netophathite, and Ja-azaniah the son of the Maacathite. ²⁴And Gedaliah swore to them and their men, saying, "Do not be afraid because of the Chaldean officials; dwell in the land, and serve the king of Babylon, and it shall be well with you." ²⁵But in the seventh month, Ishmael the son of Nethaniah, son of Elishama, of the royal family, came with ten men, and attacked and killed Gedaliah and the Jews and the Chaldeans who were with him at Mizpah. ²⁶Then all the people, both small and great, and the captains of the forces arose, and went to Egypt; for they were afraid of the Chaldeans.

²⁷And in the thirty-seventh year of the exile of Jehoiachin king of Judah, in the twelfth month, on the twenty-seventh day of the month, Evil-merodach king of Babylon, in the year that he began to reign, graciously freed Jehoiachin king of Judah from prison; ²⁸and he spoke kindly to him, and gave him a seat above the seats of the kings who were with him in Babylon. ²⁹So Jehoiachin put off his prison garments. And every day of his life he dined regularly at the king's table; ³⁰and for his allowance, a regular allowance was given him by the king, every day a portion, as long as he lived.

JUDAH'S LAST KINGS II—COMMENTARY

2 Kings 23:31–25:30 (*cont'd*)

(i)

The 22 years after the death of Josiah, recounted in this final portion of Kings, saw four kings on Judah's throne. The first and third lasted only three months each: Jehoahaz and Jehoiachin were deposed, one by Neco of Egypt in favour of Jehoia-

kim, and the other by Nebuchadnezzar of Babylon in favour of
Zedekiah. Each vassal was to remain in post for 11 years.

As we turn from the extended portraits of Hezekiah, Manasseh and Josiah, with their very clearly stated evaluations, to
these final pages, we seem to be dealing with straightforward
reporting. That may be the very reason I find it difficult to
describe the impression these chapters make on me. They seem
so dispassionate about the disappearance of their state that it is
not true. Perhaps it is because they did believe that Judah
herself was mortally wounded in the fatal blow to Josiah, and
that her subsequent movements were of no greater consequence
than the twitchings of a decapitated corpse. That Jehoiakim
and Zedekiah were puppets simply underscored the unreality of
it all. We have to look elsewhere in the Bible for the appropriate
passion:

> How lonely sits the city
>   that was full of people!
> How like a widow has she become,
>   she that was great among the nations!
> She that was a princess among the cities
>   has become a vassal.
>
> She weeps bitterly in the night,
>   tears on her cheeks;
> among all her lovers
>   she has none to comfort her;
> all her friends have dealt
>   treacherously with her,
> they have become her enemies.
>
> Judah has gone into exile because of affliction
>   and hard servitude;
> she dwells now among the nations,
>   but finds no resting place;
> her pursuers have all overtaken her
>   in the midst of her distress.

(Lam. 1:1–3)

Little Judah in these years, like so many smaller states today, was simply caught up in the turmoil of big-power conflict. This had in fact long been the case; however, now even the pretence to independence is dropped. Much bigger events were happening off the Jerusalem stage. Long-dominant Assyria had fallen to a reborn Babylonian empire. The capital itself fell in 612 B.C. Pharaoh's move northwards in 609 B.C. which was temporarily obstructed by the hapless Josiah at Megiddo, was an attempt to strengthen the remnants of his old rivals against this new menace. This ploy of neutralizing the Mesopotamian rivals by keeping them in balance failed, and Babylon defeated Egypt at Carchemish in Syria in 605 B.C. Judah automatically came under their control, but revolted prematurely when Pharaoh captured Gaza to their south-west in an attempt to push Babylon back (24:1). It was not until 598 B.C. that Nebuchadnezzar could field an army to recover the situation (24:10–11).

(ii)

The precise concerns of this last part of Kings can be glimpsed by contrasting its record with two other largely parallel biblical reports. The final chapter (52) of the Book of Jeremiah is almost identical to 2 Kings 24:18–25:30. But instead of 25:22–26 (a topic dealt with much more fully in Jer. chs. 40–43) it provides (52:28–30) a count of the deportees rather different from what we read in 2 Kings 24:14, 16.

The closing chapter of the Chronicler's history (2 Chron. ch. 36) is briefer (23 verses), actually mentions the prophet Jeremiah (36:12,21), and tells the story from a still later perspective. The Chronicler may well have shortened and rewritten his source; and yet our fuller story in Kings is stamped with some of the distinctive marks of that book. The introduction to Jehoahaz is made standard, that he too "did what was evil in the sight of the Lord" (23:32); and Manasseh comes in for special blame yet again (24:3). Kings also goes into much greater detail about the objects removed from the sanctuary: in 24:13 (contrast 2 Chron. 36:10) and 25:13–17 (contrast 2 Chron. 36:18–19). This is surprising, given the Chronicler's normally greater concern for matters cultic, and especially the trappings of Jerusalem's Temple.

Both histories end in similar forward-looking spirit, but quite different words. The Chronicler is able to report a proclamation by Cyrus the Persian, just after he had toppled the Babylonian empire in 539 B.C., promising the building of a Temple in Jerusalem. The last verses of Kings (25:27–30) are rather more cryptic. They report how a new king of Babylon (who would have called himself something more like 'Amel–Marduk') promoted Jehoiachin within the ranks of exiled monarchs as part of an amnesty on his accession in 561 B.C. For deportees, caution—if not total silence—about future expectations is wise. And it is a little surprising that this book should seem to invest much hope in a king already blamed as being as evil as his father (24:9). However, these verses may be a covert 'signature' by the authors of the history, who were fellow exiles in Babylon. They claimed to be the true continuing Judah (25:21*b*), as opposed to rival parties left in Judah or moved to Egypt (vv.22–26).

APPENDIX: PROFESSOR SAWYER'S COMMENTARY ON ISAIAH CHAPTERS 36-39 (= 2 KINGS 18:13-20:19)

The following commentary is reproduced by kind permission of Professor Sawyer from his commentary on Isaiah in this series, Volume II, pp. 19-42. It should be read in conjunction with the Note on 2 Kings chapters 18-20 (above pp. 212ff.).

Isaiah 36:1-3 (= 2 Kings 18:13,17-18)

[1]In the fourteenth year of King Hezekiah, Sennacherib king of Assyria came up against all the fortified cities of Judah and took them. [2]And the king of Assyria sent the Rabshakeh from Lachish to King Hezekiah at Jerusalem, with a great army. And he stood by the conduit of the upper pool on the highway to the Fuller's Field. [3]And there came out to him Eliakim the son of Hilkiah, who was over the household, and Shebna the secretary, and Joah the son of Asaph, the recorder.

Chapters 36-39 are composed for the most part of prose narrative, telling the story of Sennacherib's invasion of Judah, Hezekiah's illness and the arrival of ambassadors from Babylon. The narrative re-appears almost word for word in 2 Kings 18:13-20:19, but there are two significant differences in the Isaianic version which indicate that our author was even less concerned with what actually happened than the author of Kings. In the *first* place, three revealing verses have been left out after 36:1. The second Book of Kings (18:14-16) tells how Hezekiah surrendered to the Assyrians:

And Hezekiah king of Judah sent to the king of Assyria at Lachish, saying, "I have done wrong; withdraw from me; whatever you impose on me I will bear." And the king of Assyria required of Hezekiah king of Judah three hundred talents of silver and thirty talents of gold. And Hezekiah gave him all the silver that was found in the house of the Lord, and in the treasuries of the king's house. At that time Hezekiah stripped the gold from the doors of the temple of the Lord, and from the doorposts which Hezekiah king of Judah had overlaid, and gave it to the king of Assyria.

The Isaianic account tells only of victory. The *second* difference is the splendid psalm of thanksgiving in chapter 38 which does not appear in Kings.

It is an important feature of this narrative that it contains three prayers, including the long psalm just mentioned (37:16–20; 38:3; 38:10–26, and four prophecies (37:6–7; 37:21–35; 38:5–8; 39:6–7), so that we can hardly avoid approaching this section of the book as theological discourse rather than historical narrative. There is actually another account (2 Chron. chs. 29–32), in which the story of Hezekiah is rather differently elaborated. Not only is his ignominious surrender omitted altogether, as in the Isaianic account, but so also are his defeatism (Isa. 37:3–4) and the key role of Isaiah who is mentioned only once in passing (2 Chron. 32:20). The exciting events of Isaiah chapters 38–39 are reduced to passing references (2 Chron. 32:24–31), while a brief mention (not in Isa.) in 2 Kings 18:4 is expanded into three long chapters describing far-reaching religious reforms by Hezekiah (2 Chron. 29–31). The Chronicler moreover gives no dates after "the first year of his reign" (2 Chron. 29.3). Our concern, when we approach all three of these versions of events, must therefore be with what the individual authors are saying rather than with what actually happened, with timeless theology rather than ancient history. Especially is this so in the context of the Book of the Prophet Isaiah, where "the fourteenth year of King Hezekiah" (36:1) has to be taken in sequence with dates given in 1:1, 6:1 and 14:28.

All four chapters (36–39) are set in the same year. It was "in those days" that Hezekiah was given another fifteen years to live after his illness (38:1,5), adding up to a total reign of twenty-nine years (2 Kings 18:2). It was also "at that time" that the arrival of the Babylonian ambassadors at Jerusalem prompted, we are meant to think, Isaiah's Babylonian prophecies (39:1, 5–7 and chs. 40–48). Yet the actual date of Sennacherib's invasion, according to the Assyrian records (preserved in the form of clay tablets written at the time), was 701 B.C., corresponding to the twenty-fourth year of Hezekiah's reign, not the fourteenth (v.1). Perhaps the Old Testament preserves a memory of another Assyrian invason in 713–711 B.C. (*ie*, the fourteenth year), referred to in chapter 20. There is, on the historical level, obviously some confusion; but it is not our task in this commentary to unravel it, but rather to take the book as we find it and concentrate on its religious message.

According to 2 Kings 18:7, Hezekiah led a heroic rebellion against the Assyrians and the invasion was therefore not unprovoked. The reign of Sennacherib (704–681 B.C.) is well-known to us both from contemporary Assyrian records such as the horrific portrayal of the capture of Lachish on wall-reliefs from Nineveh (now in the British Museum), and from legends both biblical and apocryphal:

> The Assyrian came down like a wolf on the fold;
> His cohorts were gleaming with purple and gold.

> (Byron, *The Destruction of Sennacherib*)

Isaiah 5:26–30 and 10:27–32 have already given vivid glimpses into the effect his advancing army had on the citizens of Jerusalem.

The omission of any reference to peace negotiations (see 2 Kings 18:14–16) makes the sudden appearance (36:2) of an Assyrian, the "Rabshakeh", with a great army near the city, all the more effective. The precise reference (v.2) to "the conduit of the upper pool on the highway to the Fuller's Field" recalls an earlier crisis when the heart of the king "and the heart of his people shook as the trees of the forest shake before the wind" (7:2–3).

The three Hebrew terms for the officials mentioned in verse 3 match the Assyrian "Rabshakeh". They are clearly arranged in descending order of importance (see 22:15–25) and the proposal that the third should be translated as "herald" rather than "recorder" is very attractive. The scene is being set for a confrontation between the people of God and the enemies of God.

Isaiah 36:4–22 (= 2 Kings 18:19–37)

[4]And the Rabshakeh said to them, "Say to Hezekiah, 'Thus says the great king, the king of Assyria: On what do you rest this confidence of yours? [5]Do you think that mere words are strategy and power for war? On whom do you now rely, that you have rebelled against me? [6]Behold, you are relying on Egypt, that broken reed of a staff, which will pierce the hand of any man who leans on it. Such is Pharaoh king of Egypt to all who rely on him. [7]But if you say to me, "We rely on the Lord our God," is it not he whose high places and altars Hezekiah has removed, saying to Judah and to Jerusalem, "You shall worship before this altar"? [8]Come now, make a wager with my master the king of Assyria: I will give you two thousand horses, if you are able on your part to set riders upon them. [9]How then can you repulse a single captain among the least of my master's servants, when you rely on Egypt for chariots and for horsemen? [10]Moreover, is it without the Lord that I have come up against this land to destroy it? The Lord said to me, Go up against this land, and destroy it.'"

[11]Then Eliakim, Shebna, and Joah said to the Rabshakeh, "Pray, speak to your servants in Aramaic, for we understand it; do not speak to us in the language of Judah within the hearing of the people who are on the wall." [12]But the Rabshakeh said, "Has my master sent me to speak these words to your master and to you, and not to the men sitting on the wall, who are doomed with you to eat their own dung and drink their own urine?"

[13]Then the Rabshakeh stood and called out in a loud voice in the language of Judah: "Hear the words of the great king, the king of Assyria! [14]Thus says the king: 'Do not let Hezekiah deceive you, for he will not be able to deliver you. [15]Do not let Hezekiah make you rely on the Lord by saying, "The Lord will surely deliver us; this city will not be given into the hand of the king of Assyria." [16]Do not listen to Hezekiah; for thus says the king of Assyria: Make your peace with me and come out to me; then every one of you will eat of his own vine, and every one of his own fig tree, and every one of you will drink the water of his own cistern; [17]until I come and take you away to a land like your own land, a land of grain and wine, a land of bread and vineyards. [18]Beware lest Hezekiah mislead you by saying, "The Lord will deliver us." Has any of the gods of the nations delivered his land out of the hand of the king of Assyria? [19]Where are the gods of Hamath and Arpad? Where are the gods of

Sepharvaim? Have they delivered Samaria out of my hand? 20Who among all the gods of these countries have delivered their countries out of my hand, that the Lord should deliver Jerusalem out of my hand?'"

21But they were silent and answered him not a word, for the king's command was, "Do not answer him." 22Then Eliakim the son of Hilkiah, who was over the household, and Shebna the secretary, and Joah the son of Asaph, the recorder, came to Hezekiah with their clothes rent, and told him the words of the Rabshakeh.

The battle of words between Assyria and Jerusalem is skilfully built up of allusive, emotive theological language. The Rabshakeh, who does most of the talking, quotes all kinds of Isaianic statements and claims. All that Eliakim, Shebna and Joah can do is plead with him to speak in a language their fellow citizens will not understand (v.11), and silently rend their garments (vv.21–22).

In his *first* speech, the Rabshakeh introduces the words of the king of Assyria as though they were the very words of God: "Thus says the great king . . . " (v.4). The words for "rely" (v.5) and "confidence" (v.4) are drawn from earlier Isaianic tradition (*eg* 30:15;31:1;32:9–11,17), and parodied by the Assyrian. Reliance on Egypt was condemned by Isaiah himself (30:1;31:1), which makes the Assyrian's comments all the more forceful. The "broken reed" metaphor (v.6), highly appropriate when applied by him to Egypt, is also used in a prophecy against Egypt by Ezekiel (29:6).

The tradition that Hezekiah removed the "high places and altars" (v.7) is not recorded elsewhere in Isaiah, but is well-known from 2 Kings 18:4 and 2 Chronicles 29:3ff. and 31:21. The Assyrian's argument is thus ironically neutralized for the readers because they would be aware that it was just because Hezekiah *relied* on God that he carried out his reforms (2 Kings 18:5). In Isaiah 36:8 the Assyrian mocks Judah's lack of manpower, and in verse 9 the futility of relying on Egypt again. The double irony is once more evident since we know that, according to Isaianic teaching (*eg* 31:1–3), salvation comes neither from manpower nor from Egyptian horses and chariots, but from the Lord.

Finally, verse 10 brilliantly alludes to such passages as 10:5-6 and 7:17-20, in which Assyria is said to be acting under God's instructions. Thus the Rabshakeh's last argument is that he even has Judah's God on his side; but the readers would know differently.

The dramatic irony of the next incident is masterly too (36:11-12). Aramaic was the language of international diplomacy and would have been the normal medium of communication in such a situation. But it might also have had the effect of concealing from some of the bystanders what was actually going on. When the Assyrian insists on speaking Hebrew, the language of Judah, which everyone understands, and moreover speaking it "in a loud voice" (v.13) for everyone to hear, we can enjoy anticipating the spectacle of him being humiliated later in full view of the citizens of Jerusalem. This takes the sting out of his disgusting allusion to the effects of a siege in verse 12.

The Rabshakeh's *second* speech (vv.13ff.) recalls a similar situation thirty years before when Isaiah's task was to convince another king that faith in God is what is needed in times of crisis (ch.7). But this time the threat is not the two little kingdoms on Judah's northern border—Ephraim and Syria—but the Great King, the king of Assyria himself, "the waters of the River, mighty and many" (8:7). The words of the Great King are introduced again as the word of God, as in verse 4. His arguments are simple and convincing; in human terms. Hezekiah is far too weak to withstand the might of Assyria (v.14). The Lord is just one among many local deities who present no challenge whatever to the Assyrians (vv.15,18). Hamath and Arpad in Syria, and Samaria (whose God *was* the Lord), were captured by them within the space of a few years (vv.19-20). Sepharvaim and the other names mentioned in parallel passages (37:13; 2 Kings 18:34) are unknown, but 2 Kings 17 tells us something about the false gods they worshipped (v.31):

> And the Sepharvites burned their children in the fire to Adrammelech and Anammelech, the gods of Sepharvaim.

The term "deliver" used in Isaiah 36:15 by the Rabshakeh, a foreigner, and used elsewhere of idols and false gods (44:17), contrasts with the magisterial term "save" which Hezekiah (37:20) and Isaiah (37:35) use when they refer to what the Lord can do for his people.

In the middle part of his argument, the Assyrian tries to persuade Jerusalem to surrender by depicting how blissful life would be under Assyrian rule (v.16). The word for such a "peace" in verse 16 is the one usually translated "blessing" (*eg* 44:3) and reflects a change of tone from abuse to cajoling. This is, after all, the voice of Satan trying everything to break the faith of God's people. "But they were silent" (37:21) signifies both deep anguish on the part of the three officials—this was how Job's comforters reacted (Job 2:13)—and at the same time an attempt to cling to their faith in God as in 30:15, and elsewhere:

Be still, and know that I am God.

(Ps.46:10)

Isaiah 37:1-20 (=2 Kings 19:1-19)

[1]When King Hezekiah heard it, he rent his clothes, and covered himself with sackcloth, and went into the house of the Lord. [2]And he sent Eliakim, who was over the household, and Shebna the secretary, and the senior priests, clothed with sackcloth, to the prophet Isaiah the son of Amoz. [3]They said to him, "Thus says Hezekiah, 'This day is a day of distress, of rebuke, and of disgrace; children have come to the birth, and there is no strength to bring them forth. [4]It may be that the Lord your God heard the words of the Rabshakeh, whom his master the king of Assyria has sent to mock the living God, and will rebuke the words which the Lord your God has heard; therefore lift up your prayer for the remnant that is left.'"

[5]When the servants of King Hezekiah came to Isaiah, [6]Isaiah said to them, "Say to your master, 'Thus says the Lord: Do not be afraid because of the words that you have heard, with which the servants of the king of Assyria have reviled me. [7]Behold, I will put a spirit in him, so that he shall hear a rumour, and return to his own land; and

I will make him fall by the sword in his own land.'" ⁸The
Rabshakeh returned, and found the king of Assyria fighting against
Libnah; for he had heard that the king had left Lachish. ⁹Now the
king heard concerning Tirhakah king of Ethiopia, "He has set out
to fight against you." And when he heard it, he sent messengers to
Hezekiah, saying, ¹⁰"Thus shall you speak to Hezekiah king of
Judah: 'Do not let your God on whom you rely deceive you by
promising that Jerusalem will not be given into the hand of the king
of Assyria. ¹¹Behold, you have heard what the kings of Assyria have
done to all lands, destroying them utterly. And shall you be
delivered? ¹²Have the gods of the nations delivered them, the
nations which my fathers destroyed, Gozan, Haran, Rezeph, and
the people of Eden who were in Telassar? ¹³Where is the king of
Hamath, the king of Arpad, the king of the city of Sepharvaim, the
king of Hena, or the king of Ivvah?'"

¹⁴Hezekiah received the letter from the hand of the messengers,
and read it; and Hezekiah went up to the house of the Lord, and
spread it before the Lord. ¹⁵And Hezekiah prayed to the Lord: ¹⁶"O
Lord of hosts, God of Israel, who art enthroned above the
cherubim, thou art the God, thou alone, of all the kingdoms of the
earth; thou hast made heaven and earth. ¹⁷Incline thy ear, O Lord,
and hear; open thy eyes, O Lord, and see; and hear all the words of
Sennacherib, which he has sent to mock the living God. ¹⁸Of a
truth, O Lord, the kings of Assyria have laid waste all the nations
and their lands, ¹⁹and have cast their gods into the fire; for they were
no gods, but the work of men's hands, wood and stone; therefore
they were destroyed. ²⁰So now, O Lord our God, save us from his
hand, that all the kingdoms of the earth may know that thou alone
art the Lord."

The king's reaction is in two parts. *First* he immediately
acknowledges his own weakness. This he does through the
usual ritual signs of penitence and self-abasement (v.1). This is
the nearest the present account comes to the story of Hezekiah's
surrender to the Assyrians as recorded in 2 Kings 18:14–16,
where he admits he was wrong. But these are the rituals of
repentance which, as the Jonah story illustrates so graphically
(chs. 3–4), are the prelude to salvation. That Hezekiah visits the
Temple, rather than the "conduit of the upper pool on the
highway to the Fuller's Field" (36:2), or his military head-

quarters, for an emergency meeting of his cabinet, symbolizes his rejection of the way of the flesh, and his acknowledgment of the power of the spirit (31:3, 40:6).

His *second* reaction is to turn to Isaiah the prophet (v.2), and the rest of the story centres on this. The prophet's very name, which means "the Lord saves", reminds us that "salvation" is at hand and points forward to verses 20 and 35 of the present chapter, 38:20, and numerous passages in chapters 40–55, where the terms "save", "saviour" and "salvation" emerge as key words in Isaianic tradition.

Hezekiah's message to the prophet (vv.3–4) begins with a proverb. The situation, he says, is like the critical moment in childbirth, when the baby is at the mouth of the womb but the woman is too weak to deliver it. Skilled obstetricians are urgently needed to save the baby. The word translated "birth" actually means "breaking-point" and perfectly links the two critical situations: the woman in labour and Jerusalem in danger.

Verse 4, beginning "It may be that ... ", gathers up three themes that together will answer the Rabshakeh and hold out hope for the city. It is the "living God" who has been insultingly compared to the false gods of Hamath and Arpad (36:19): the "living God" is Israel's God, and he has heard the Assyrian abuse; and Jerusalem is "the remnant" which embodies Israel's hope in so many contexts, some of them, like 1:9 and the present chapter (vv.4, 31–32) associated with the Assyrian crisis. It will be recalled that "the remnant" was an idea built into the name of Isaiah's first son, *Shear-jashub*; "a remnant will return" (7:3).

The prophet's reply is in the form of a 'salvation oracle' (vv.6–7; see the commentary on 41:8–10). It begins with the formula, "Fear not", goes on to comment upon the present situation (the Assyrian blasphemy), and then concludes with a prophecy foretelling the arrival of a rumour that causes the king of Assyria to withdraw suddenly, and his subsequent assassination. Verses 8–9 begin to unfold immediately how these prophecies were fulfilled—like those of the witches in *Macbeth*—as the story progresses. The invasion was continuing. Lachish had fallen and Sennacherib had moved on to the next city when the *first* part of the prophecy was fulfilled. Sennacherib's fate, like Macbeth's, was sealed. The "rumour" about Tirhakah, king of Ethiopia, and eventually of Egypt too, may reflect the fact that, at about the same time, Sennacherib defeated an Egyptian army at Eltekeh. But it is the dramatic effect of the rumour, coming so soon after Isaiah's prophecy, that is most impressive.

Before the *second* part of the prophecy about Sennacherib is fulfilled (in vv.37–38), another story is told about the Assyrian crisis, comprising the same four elements as the one just finished: a taunting message from the Rabshakeh in almost the same words as he had used before (vv.10–13); Hezekiah's reaction (vv.14–20); a prophecy by Isaiah (vv.21–35); and its fulfilment (v.36). With this section must be taken another of Isaiah's prophecies, recorded in 31:8:

> And the Assyrian shall fall by a sword, not of man;
> and a sword, not of man, shall devour him.

Whether this second story, which adds to the account of Sennacherib's withdrawal (an account of a terrible slaughter among the Assyrians), is based on an alternative tradition of what happened in 701 B.C., or whether, with its strong hint of the miraculous (v.36), it owes more to theological wishful thinking than to accurate historical memories, is a matter for strenuous argument among the scholars. It is not an argument into which we can meaningfully enter in this commentary; and, as so often, we are better advised to concentrate on the aims and interests of the author.

Once again the Rabshakeh's message focusses on a theological issue, categorizing the Lord as one of the false gods who had shown themselves incapable of defending some of the other nations invaded by the Assyrians. A number of other names are added to the earlier list (36:19) to heighten the effect (vv.12–13).

Hezekiah's prayer in the Temple (vv.16–20) recalls the great formal prayers of David (2 Sam. 7) and Solomon (1 Kings 8). *First*, it introduces the theme of *monotheism* (as in 2 Sam.

7:22), a theme which is to be greatly developed later (*eg* 45:5–6, 14, 21–22).

> Thou art the God, thou alone, of all the kingdoms of the earth.
> (Isa. 37:16)

Second, the belief that the Lord of hosts is creator of all things (also v.16) makes nonsense of the comparison between him and the gods of wood and stone ridiculed even by the Rabshakeh here (v.12) and frequently in the later Babylonian chapters (*eg* 44).

Two final theological points are made in verse 20: (1) the contrast between the hollow victories of Assyria over gods of wood and stone, in comparison with the power of "the Lord our God", is summed up in the choice of the loaded word "save", of which we were reminded at the beginning of the chapter (see the comment on v.2); and (2) the ultimate purpose of God's intervention in the history of his people is not their safety or peace or happiness, but his own glory, a point made even more emphatically later in chapter 48 (see v.11):

> For my own sake, for my own sake, I do it . . . My glory I will not give to another.

Isaiah 37:21–38 (=2 Kings 19:20–37)

[21]Then Isaiah the son of Amoz sent to Hezekiah, saying, "Thus says the Lord, the God of Israel: Because you have prayed to me concerning Sennacherib king of Assyria, [22]this is the word that the Lord has spoken concerning him:
  'She despises you, she scorns you—
     the virgin daughter of Zion;
  she wags her head behind you—
     the daughter of Jerusalem.

[23]'Whom have you mocked and reviled?
     Against whom have you raised your voice
  and haughtily lifted your eyes?
     Against the Holy One of Israel!
[24]By your servants you have mocked the Lord,
     and you have said, With my many chariots

I have gone up the heights of the mountains,
  to the far recesses of Lebanon;
I felled its tallest cedars,
  its choicest cypresses;
I came to its remotest height,
  its densest forest.
25I dug wells
  and drank waters,
and I dried up with the sole of my foot
  all the streams of Egypt.

26"Have you not heard
  that I determined it long ago?
I planned from days of old
  what now I bring to pass,
that you should make fortified cities
  crash into heaps of ruins,
27while their inhabitants, shorn of strength,
  are dismayed and confounded,
and have become like plants of the field
  and like tender grass,
like grass on the housetops,
  blighted before it is grown.

28"I know your sitting down
  and your going out and coming in,
  and your raging against me.
29Because you have raged against me
  and your arrogance has come to my ears,
I will put my hook in your nose
  and my bit in your mouth,
and I will turn you back on the way
  by which you came.'"

30"And this shall be the sign for you: this year eat what grows of
itself, and in the second year what springs of the same; then in the
third year sow and reap, and plant vineyards, and eat their fruit.
31And the surviving remnant of the house of Judah shall again take
root downward, and bear fruit upward; 32for out of Jerusalem shall
go forth a remnant, and out of Mount Zion a band of survivors.
The zeal of the Lord of hosts will accomplish this.

³³"Therefore thus says the Lord concerning the king of Assyria: He shall not come into this city, or shoot an arrow there, or come before it with a shield, or cast up a siege mound against it. ³⁴By the way that he came, by the same he shall return, and he shall not come into this city, says the Lord. ³⁵For I will defend this city to save it, for my own sake and the sake of my servant David."

³⁶And the angel of the Lord went forth, and slew a hundred and eighty-five thousand in the camp of the Assyrians; and when men arose early in the morning, behold, these were all dead bodies. ³⁷Then Sennacherib king of Assyria departed, and went home and dwelt at Nineveh. ³⁸And as he was worshipping in the house of Nisroch his god, Adrammelech and Sharezer, his sons, slew him with the sword, and escaped into the land of Ararat. And Esarhaddon his son reigned in his stead.

Most of this section of the narrative consists of Isaiah's long prophecy (vv.21–35); there is then a brief appendix recording the three remaining events through which his prophecies were fulfilled and the Assyrian threat finally removed (vv.36–38). Apart from 38:6 and a passing reference in 52:4, Assyria is not mentioned again. The prophecy is introduced initially by the common formula, "Thus says the Lord . . . ". But in addition it is presented as the answer to a particular prayer "concerning Sennacherib king of Assyria".

The prophecy is in three parts. The *first* (vv.22–29) is in the form of a taunt-song addressed to the king of Assyria, and may be compared to chapters 14 and 47 in which the king of Babylon is taunted in similar terms. It begins with a splendid image; in God's eyes Jerusalem is like a proud, courageous young woman dismissing an unwelcome suitor with a scornful toss of her head (better than "wags her head", RSV). To Sennacherib she appears an easy conquest; while God recognizes fearlessness and invincibility in her, because to have designs on the Holy City (48:2; 52:1) is to have designs on the "Holy One of Israel" himself (v.23). It is not against flesh and blood that Sennacherib is fighting, but against the one true God.

Verses 24–25 contain the Assyrian's boast, corresponding to those of the king of Babylon in 14:13–14; five sentences beginning with "I". He claims to have climbed higher than the highest mountain, like the builders of the Tower of Babel (Gen. 11), and cut down the tallest cedars of Lebanon. Then he claims to have conquered Egypt with one contemptuous gesture (37:25), a reference to Eltekeh (see the comment on v.9). Only the Lord can properly do such things (*eg* 51:10), and all along Assyria has been merely a tool in his hand, with which he chose to punish the nations of the world (10:5). The rise and fall of nations is God's handiwork, not man's (vv.26-28). The similes for fading pomp in verse 27 anticipate a more famous passage in chapter 40: "All flesh is grass . . . " (v.6). Everything is planned and controlled by God; verse 28 is a bitter parody of Psalm 121 and other passages, in which God's loving care for his people is transformed into a terrifying image of God as someone like "Big Brother" in Orwell's *Nineteen Eighty-four*. Job's parody of Psalm 8:4 is another poignant example (Job 7:17-18).

Final judgment is described (v.29) in terms of taming a wild beast, like Leviathan, "king over all the sons of pride" (Job 41:34), in the spectacular climax of the speeches of the Lord in Job (41:1-34):

> Though the sword reaches him, it does not avail;
> nor the spear, the dart, or the javelin.
> He counts iron as straw,
> and bronze as rotten wood.
> The arrow cannot make him flee;
> for him slingstones are turned to stubble.
>
> (Job 41:26-28)

Such is the king of Assyria, and like Leviathan he will be tamed and dragged back to his lair (37:7, 34).

The *second* part of the prophecy addressed to Hezekiah (vv.30-32) has the same form as one or two of those addressed earlier to Ahaz (*eg* 7:10-17; 8:1-8). It begins with a sign, concerned, like the Immanuel sign in 7:14, with the timing of events. Just as "what grows of itself" (a technical agricultural term from Lev. 25:5, 11) is enough to live on for two years, and normal crops will be harvested in the third, so the "remnant of the house of Judah" (v.31) will have the strength and resilience to spring up again after the Assyrian threat is past.

The Zion prophecy beginning, "Out of Jerusalem . . . " (v.32) is an effective variation of the one in 2:3 and Micah 4:2, and alluded to elsewhere (*eg* Amos 1:2; Joel 3:16). "The zeal of the Lord of hosts will accomplish this" occurs only here and in 9:7. With this flurry of "Zionist" fervour, we are in the mainstream of Isaianic tradition.

Curiously the *third* part of the prophecy (vv.33–35) foretells nothing of the imminent bloody slaughter of the Assyrians in verse 36. We have already noted this omission and the problem it sets for historians. Perhaps the words recorded here are trying to put a favourable interpretation on what actually happened in 701 B.C. The real reason for Sennacherib's withdrawal without a blow being struck was that Hezekiah surrendered. This is recorded in 2 Kings 18:14–16, but, as we have seen, the Isaianic account omits any mention of it. Its purpose is to represent what happened as an act of divine intervention; notice especially how the theological key word "save" is reintroduced from 37:20.

Verse 36 then takes this theological line of interpretation still further by describing the divine victory in the most extreme terms, as befits the ultimate annihilation of evil. The "angel of the Lord" here, as in 63:9, is synonymous with the "Saviour": that is, God himself, who "saves" his people in his own way. Intrigued by this story, later tradition ingeniously sought to account for what happened in naturalistic terms: one tradition tells how a plague of field-mice invaded the Assyrian camp and gnawed through their bow-strings and shield-thongs (the two pieces of equipment mentioned in v.33). But our text is more concerned to proclaim that, with God's help, people of faith like Isaiah and the citizens of Jerusalem, can conquer evil. The fate of the wicked, like a battlefield littered with corpses (66:24), is the sad corollary of a salvation such as the one envisaged in verses 30–32.

Finally verses 37–38 tell how the other part of Isaiah's prophecy in 37:7, which concerns the king of Assyria himself, was fulfilled. According to the Assyrian records, Sennacherib was killed twenty years after the invasion of Judah. His successor Esarhaddon is referred to in Ezra 4:2. Ararat (ancient Urartu) was a mountainous region north of Assyria, covering part of what is now Eastern Turkey and Armenia. From both a literary and a theological point of view, the concentration of strange Assyrian names fading away into the distance in these final verses, rounds off the story of Jerusalem's miraculous victory over the powers of evil.

Isaiah 38:1–22 (cf. 2 Kings 20:1–11)

¹In those days Hezekiah became sick and was at the point of death. And Isaiah the prophet the son of Amoz came to him, and said to him, "Thus says the Lord: Set your house in order; for you shall die, you shall not recover." ²Then Hezekiah turned his face to the wall, and prayed to the Lord, ³and said, "Remember now, O Lord, I beseech thee, how I have walked before thee in faithfulness and with a whole heart, and have done what is good in thy sight." And Hezekiah wept bitterly. ⁴Then the word of the Lord came to Isaiah: ⁵"Go and say to Hezekiah, Thus says the Lord, the God of David your father: I have heard your prayer, I have seen your tears; behold, I will add fifteen years to your life. ⁶I will deliver you and this city out of the hand of the king of Assyria, and defend this city.

⁷"This is the sign to you from the Lord, that the Lord will do this thing that he has promised: ⁸Behold, I will make the shadow cast by the declining sun on the dial of Ahaz turn back ten steps." So the sun turned back on the dial the ten steps by which it had declined.

⁹A writing of Hezekiah king of Judah, after he had been sick and had recovered from his sickness:

¹⁰I said, In the noontide of my days
    I must depart;
I am consigned to the gates of Sheol
    for the rest of my years.
¹¹I said, I shall not see the Lord
    in the land of the living;
I shall look upon man no more
    among the inhabitants of the world.

¹²My dwelling is plucked up and removed from me
    like a shepherd's tent;
like a weaver I have rolled up my life;
    he cuts me off from the loom;
from day to night thou dost bring me to an end;
    ¹³I cry for help until morning;
like a lion he breaks all my bones;
    from day to night thou dost bring me to an end.

¹⁴Like a swallow or a crane I clamour,
    I moan like a dove.
My eyes are weary with looking upward.
    O Lord, I am oppressed; be thou my security!
¹⁵But what can I say? For he has spoken to me,
    and he himself has done it.
All my sleep has fled
    because of the bitterness of my soul.

¹⁶O Lord, by these things men live,
    and in all these is the life of my spirit.
    Oh, restore me to health and make me live!
¹⁷Lo, it was for my welfare
    that I had great bitterness;
but thou hast held back my life
    from the pit of destruction,
for thou has cast all my sins
    behind thy back.
¹⁸For Sheol cannot thank thee,
    death cannot praise thee;
those who go down to the pit cannot hope
    for thy faithfulness.

¹⁹The living, the living, he thanks thee,
    as I do this day;
the father makes known to the children
    thy faithfulness.

²⁰The Lord will save me,
    and we will sing to stringed instruments
all the days of our life,
    at the house of the lord.

²¹Now Isaiah had said, "Let them take a cake of figs, and apply it to the boil, that he may recover." ²²Hezekiah also had said, "What is the sign that I shall go up to the house of the Lord?"

This fascinating chapter contains two distinct types of material: a prose account of the words and actions of Isaiah and Hezekiah (vv.1–8 and 21–22), and a beautiful psalm of thanksgiving written by Hezekiah on his recovery from illness (vv.9–20). The scene is set in Jerusalem, during the Assyrian crisis (vv.1,6), and still further elaborates the theme of God's concern for Jerusalem and his servant David (37: 35; 38:5,20).

As in the previous story, we begin with a crisis: the "Lord's anointed" (Pss. 2:2; 89:51;132:10) is going to die, and furthermore the prophet's initial reaction is judgmental. As when in the days of the judges a prophet told suffering and pleading Israel that they deserved all they got (Judg. 6:7–10), so now Isaiah tells the king he is doomed. Hezekiah's prayer in verse 2 contains no explicit repentance: instead he wins God's protection by his faithfulness and piety. He "turned" away from Isaiah and the others standing by his bedside—that is what "to the wall" means (1 Kings 21:4)—and "wept bitterly" as he prayed. But his prayer begins, "Remember now, O Lord": in these words we are to forget his panic of 37:33–4 (and his surrender in 2 Kings 18:14–16), and think instead of his reform in 2 Kings 18:1–8, omitted in Isaiah, but elaborately expanded in 2 Chronicles 29–31. See 2 Kings 18:5–6:

> He trusted in the Lord the God of Israel; so that there was none like him among all the kings of Judah after him, nor among those who were before him. For he held fast to the Lord; he did not depart from following him, but kept the commandments which the Lord commanded Moses.

"Faithfulness" (v.3) is what Isaiah called for in earlier crises (7:9; 30:15). It was a permanent characteristic of the ideal Jerusalem, "the city of righteousness, the faithful city" (1:21–26). "A whole heart" (38:3) meant single-minded devotion to God (1 Kings 8:61;11:4).

So now the prophet foretells, in one breath (vv.5–6), Hezekiah's recovery and the survival of Jerusalem; two of the main themes of this section of the book (37:35). Fifteen years' extension to Hezekiah's life, in the fourteenth year of his reign (36:1), adds up to the total of twenty-nine years given in 2 Kings 18:2. Far from reaching an untimely end "in the noontide of his days" (38:10), more than half of his reign is still to come.

In the Kings version (2 Kings 20:8) the king at this point asks for a sign in words very similar to those in verse 22, and experts have suggested that verse 22 should (with v.21) be moved back to follow verse 6 (see NEB). But this still leaves the question of why verse 22 is placed where it is; and in any case it should be remembered that this would not be the first time that a king had refused to ask for a sign (7:12). However that may be, the sign that Isaiah gives has no parallel and defies natural explanation—as miracles should. The Hebrew of verse 8 is difficult. There is in fact no word for "[sun] dial" (RSV). The word translated "steps" usually refers to steps leading up to the Temple (*eg* Ezek. 40:6) or the altar (Ezek. 43:17) or Jerusalem (Neh. 3:15) or the like, and it is the same word as that translated "dial". But what the "steps of Ahaz" might have been is unknown. They sound like some architectural feature of the palace, visible from Hezekiah's bedroom. Whatever he actually saw the shadows doing, they demonstrated the power of a God who controls the movement of the heavenly bodies (40:26). See also Job 9:7,9:

> Who commands the sun and it does not rise;
>> who seals up the stars...
> who made the Bear and Orion,
>> the Pleiades and the chambers of the south.

The same God who made the sun "stand still" for Joshua (Josh. 10:12–14) made it "turn back" for Isaiah. Hezekiah's recovery follows immediately (v.9).

Hezekiah's thanksgiving is an impressive example of Hebrew religious poetry. Like other psalms it contains few references to any particular situation, let alone that of Hezekiah's illness, but it is not inappropriate. The crisis comes almost exactly at the midpoint—"noontide"—of his reign (v.10). He thought he would never recover (vv.10–13): God had told him this through the prophet Isaiah (v.1). "Save" in verse 20 picks up the theological key-word from an earlier part of the Hezekiah story (37:20,35), and the theme of *miraculous survival* is what the whole book is about. Maybe as we read verse 18 we are to think of the 185 000 Assyrian corpses (37:36) and the king of Babylon in *Sheol* (14:9–11). The psalm was written down (v.9) perhaps to be placed with gratitude in the Temple (v.20).

Like Jonah (2:2) Hezekiah begins by recalling how he felt when he first realized he was dying (vv.10–11). "I thought" (NEB) is better than "I said" (RSV). Verses 12–14 each contain one or two images and an appeal to God. Verse 12 compares death to the sudden loss of one's home, or the irreversible cutting of the threads on a loom when the cloth is finished. Verse 13, as it stands, analyses the courageous effort to get through a night of pain and suffering. Both verses 12 and 13 end with a kind of refrain on the suddenness with which death would come upon Hezekiah. Verse 14 compares his cries of anguish to the incessant twittering and moaning of birds, and ends, like the two previous verses, with an appeal to God: "Be thou my security". In modern idiom this might be rendered, 'Bail me out'.

Verses 15–17 are difficult, but seem to move from reminiscing about the past, to present thanksgiving. *God has spoken . . . God has acted* (v.15) surely refers to Isaiah's prophecy and the miracle of the sun turning back in verses 7–8. "All my sleep has fled" (RSV) is based on an emended text: Hebrew has "I shall walk humbly all my years because of the bitterness of my soul" (cf.AV). "By these things" in verse 16 again refers to the signs of divine intervention mentioned in the previous verse; and the haunting prayer for health and life corresponds to the mournful refrain at the end of verses 12 and 13. Verse 17 appears to tackle, albeit very briefly, the problem of suffering in the world. On the one hand, some good has come out of it insofar as the psalmist now experiences a new "welfare" (*shalom*) beyond his former bitterness. On the other hand, there is a connection between sin and disease since, like Jesus healing the paralytic (Matt. 9:1-8), God has healed the psalmist by first forgiving his sins (see also 33:24).

The psalm of thanksgiving ends, like Psalm 115, by contrasting the fate of the dead who do not know the joy of singing hymns of thanksgiving in the Temple, with that of the living, like Hezekiah, who do (vv.18-20).

Verse 21 adds a couple of medical details to the story: Hezekiah had been suffering from a similar disease to that of Job (not just one "boil" as in the RSV!); and Isaiah, after the manner of Elisha (2 Kings 6:10) and Jesus (John 9:6-7), had prescribed a form of treatment for it.

Verse 22 does not need to be misplaced here (see comment on v.6). Is it not an exclamation: "[What a miracle!] I shall go up to the house of the Lord?"

Isaiah 39:1-8 (=2 Kings 20:12-19)

¹At that time Merodach-baladan the son of Baladan, king of Babylon, sent envoys with letters and a present to Hezekiah, for he heard that he had been sick and had recovered. ²And Hezekiah welcomed them; and he showed them his treasure house, the silver, the gold, the spices, the precious oil, his whole armoury, all that was found in his store-houses. There was nothing in his house or in all his realm that Hezekiah did not show them. ³Then Isaiah the prophet came to King Hezekiah, and said to him, "What did these men say? And whence did they come to you?" Hezekiah said, "They have come to me from a far country, from Babylon." ⁴He said, "What have they seen in your house?" Hezekiah answered, "They have seen all that is in my house; there is nothing in my storehouses that I did not show them."

⁵Then Isaiah said to Hezekiah, "Hear the word of the Lord of hosts: ⁶Behold, the days are coming, when all that is in your house, and that which your fathers have stored up till this day, shall be carried to Babylon; nothing shall be left, says the Lord. ⁷And some of your own sons, who are born to you, shall be taken away; and they shall be eunuchs in the palace of the king of Babylon." ⁸Then said Hezekiah to Isaiah, "The word of the Lord which you have spoken is good." For he thought, "There will be peace and security in my days."

The final story about Hezekiah leads us forward into the Babylonian chapters which follow (40ff.). It reminds us that, although Jerusalem survived the Assyrian invasion, it was to fall to the Babylonians, and that the prophet would then be called to comfort his people in exile (40:1).

"At that time" clearly places this incident in the same year as the preceding stories, "the fourteenth year of King Hezekiah" (36:1), which leaves him with fifteen years of "peace and security" (39:8). The experts tell us that the Babylonian king Merodach-baladan's dates were 721–710 B.C., and that he made various attempts to stir up rebellion against the Assyrians. It is certainly more likely that he was trying to enlist Hezekiah's support for such an enterprise, than that he was merely sending him a letter congratulating him on his recovery. Or had he heard something of the astronomical phenomenon of 38:8?

The arrival of the ambassadors is reminiscent of the encounter between Solomon and the Queen of Sheba (1 Kings 10), and the arrival of the Ethiopians in chapter 18. The dramatic irony is obvious here: Hezekiah's innocent delight as he exposes all the treasures of his city to the Babylonians, is grimly overshadowed by the prophecy in verses 6 and 7, and the all too familiar tale of how Nebuchadnezzar carried off all the treasures of Jerusalem a century later (2 Kings 24:10–17).

Isaiah's appearance on the scene in verses 3–4, ignorant of what has happened, highlights Hezekiah's naïve optimism. It is noteworthy that Hezekiah is not guilty of any sin here: he is represented as totally innocent. The subsequent defeat of Jerusalem was not due to anything he had done, but to the abominations committed by his notorious successor, Manasseh (2 Kings 21:10–15). The fact that Hezekiah himself surrendered three hundred talents of silver and thirty talents of gold to the Assyrians (2 Kings 18:14–16) is not mentioned: God had "cast all [Hezekiah's] sins behind [his] back" (38:17). In Rabbinic tradition, however, Hezekiah's folly is compounded with arrogance and even deceit. When Isaiah asked him "What did these men say?" (v.3), he did not answer directly, presumably ashamed of what he had done. Instead Hezekiah answered the second question ("And whence did they come to you?") with the boast, "They have come *to me* from a far country". Only later did he confess his political error (v.4). For this he was punished by being forced to hear the ominous words of the prophecy in verses 5–7.

The prophecy is introduced by a conventional prophetic formula: "Hear the word of the Lord of hosts" (*eg* 1:10; Jer.7:2; Ezek. 37:4). "Behold, the days are coming" is also a frequent formula, especially in Jeremiah (*eg* 7:32; 9:25; 31:31) and Amos (4:2; 8:11; 9:13).

No mention is made in this prophecy of the fall of Jerusalem or the destruction of the Temple. This may well be due to the fact that it was composed before the final blow fell in 587 B.C. This would agree with the appearance of the Jeremianic expressions in verses 5 and 6. Alternatively the author may have wished to concentrate on the fate of Hezekiah's treasure and his sons, rather than on what happened to the buildings. After all, possessions are a recurring theme in the Hezekiah narratives (2 Kings 18:14–16; 20:13; 2 Chron. 31:2–10).

Hezekiah's "sons" (39:7) include of course descendants of the royal line down to and including Josiah, who was mercifully delivered from the fate here prophesied (2 Kings 22:19–20), Jehoiachin who was taken prisoner by Nebuchadnezzar (2 Kings 24:12), and Zedekiah whose eyes were put out and who was bound in fetters and taken to Babylon (2 Kings 25:7). The humiliating term "eunuchs" (39:7) need not mean literally castrated, but rather stripped of their royal power and dignity and condemned to live, like any other foreign servant, at the court of the king of Babylon.

Verse 8 is in two parts. In the *first*, Hezekiah simply acknowledges that what Isaiah said is right, perhaps also admitting his mistake. This would have been an appropriate place at which to end the story of the Babylonian visit. The *second* part, however, appears to suggest that Hezekiah was rather callous; "thinking to himself that peace and security would last out his lifetime" (NEB). But surely it is more likely that the author is rounding off his account of Hezekiah's glorious reign in phraseology familiar from 30:15; 32:17; 38:3,17 and elsewhere, without the least intention of commenting on his character. The parallel in 2 Kings 20:19 is different, clearly more closely related to the preceding story of political ineptitude, and it is followed by the usual conclusion: "The rest of the deeds of Hezekiah, and all his might . . . " (2 Kings 20:20–21). Isaiah 39:8 has none of this.

Unimaginable "success and faithfulness" were the hall-marks of Hezekiah's reign. Surely "peace and security" (RSV, NEB) miss the miraculous and religious dimensions of the story. Chapter 32, and especially verses 16–20, fill in the details of such a reign—in this world and the next.

FURTHER READING

Aharoni, Yohanon, and Michael Avi-Yonah. *The Macmillan Bible Atlas,* rev. ed. New York: Macmillan Co., 1977.

Gray, John. *I & II Kings,* 2nd ed., rev. Philadelphia: Westminster Press, 1971.

Herrmann, Siegfried. *A History of Israel in Old Testament Times,* 2nd ed. Philadelphia: Fortress Press, 1981.

Jones, G. H. *1 and 2 Kings.* Grand Rapids: Wm. B. Eerdmans Publishing Co., 1984.

May, Herbert G., ed. *Oxford Bible Atlas.* New York: Oxford University Press, 1985.

Mayes, A.D.H. *The Story of Israel Between Settlement and Exile.* London: SCM Press, 1983.

Montgomery, James A. *Kings.* Naperville, Ill.: Alec R. Allenson, 1960.

Noth, Martin. *The Deuteronomistic History.* Winona Lake, Ind.: Eisenbrauns, 1981.

Robinson, J., ed. *The First/The Second Book of Kings.* New York: Cambridge University Press, 1972/1977.

Sandmel, Samuel. *The Enjoyment of Scripture: The Law, the Prophets, and the Writings.* New York: Oxford University Press, 1972.

Soggin, J. Alberto. *A History of Israel.* Philadelphia: Westminster Press, 1985.